O vercome with loneliness and ~~so~~ ~~longing~~, ~~he~~ ~~decided~~ ~~that~~ he couldn't wait any longer to speak with her.

The streets were still ankle-deep in mud, but Marcus picked his way through the puddles to cross Main Street. He hurried to catch Sheridan before she entered the hotel.

He called her name, and she turned. Just at that moment, the sun broke through the clouds, and it seemed to Marcus that her turning had caused it. His heart caught in his throat, she looked so fresh and pretty. Her eyes seemed to shimmer in the light as he moved closer.

"Sheridan," he said again hoarsely. "We need to talk."

Palisades.
Pure Romance.

A · PALISADES · HISTORICAL · ROMANCE

EVERLASTING

AMANDA MacLEAN

PALISADES

EVERLASTING
published by Palisades
a part of the Questar publishing family

© 1996 by Amanda MacLean
International Standard Book Number: 0-88070-929-4

Cover illustration by George Angelini
Cover designed by David Carlson and
Mona Weir-Daly
Edited by Paul Hawley

Printed in the United States of America

For information:
QUESTAR PUBLISHERS, INC.
POST OFFICE BOX 1720
SISTERS, OREGON 97759

96 97 98 99 00 01 02 03 — 10 9 8 7 6 5 4 3 2 1

For Linda

my cousin and beloved friend

Through the years we've shared laughter, tears,

joys, sorrows, and prayers—

the essence of an everlasting friendship.

"I have loved you with an everlasting love."

JEREMIAH 31:3

One

❧

San Francisco Bay
Fall 1855

Raven-haired Sheridan O'Brian caught up her skirts with slender fingers and daintily moved up the ladder from the steam tender to the wharf. The small vessel creaked and groaned against the ropes that held it to the dock. Sheridan swayed with the movement and clutched the railing.

In the bay behind her, the clipper ship *Gypsy* rocked in the choppy, white-capped waters. The graceful and sturdy three-masted Cape Horner had anchored just hours before, and as Sheridan stepped onto the wharf, the solid wooden planks felt welcome after her weeks aboard the schooner.

Letting out a deep breath, Sheridan surveyed the rough and jostling mass of people before her. "Shamus O'Brian," she muttered under her breath, "I'll not soon be forgivin' you for causin' me to be here." Shivering, she glanced down at the murky green Pacific waters slapping against the pilings. "I've never been so far from Ireland. And I'm not likin' it one bit, dear Shamus. Not a bit. Not that you'd care about your poor sister comin' all this way to find you...." Misty-eyed, she gazed again into the crowd, wondering about Aunt Fiona's wisdom in sending her on such a wild-goose chase.

A stiff breeze kicked up from the rough waters of the bay, whipping a strand of Sheridan's hair across her face. Her felt hat threatened to fly from her head. Holding it in place with one hand, she tucked the errant strand of hair behind her ear as she squinted across the sun-dappled, wood-slatted wharf.

Dockhands and sailors, shoving and elbowing their way, moved boisterously among the milling merchants, traders, whalers, and families with children and servants. Wagons and carts clattered along the wharf, moving to and from the small mountains of trunks, satchels, and pieces of furniture being unloaded from nearby ships.

Sheridan squared her shoulders and lifted her chin, determined not to let her fears show. She again caught up her skirt and moved to a mound of baggage to search for her belongings. She would gather them efficiently and calmly. And when her carriage arrived, she would appear ready, unruffled, confident, in control. She swallowed hard and stooped to retrieve a tapestry satchel on the edge of the nearest heap.

Across the wharf, Marcus Jade brushed a shock of unruly hair from his forehead and frowned into the crowd, searching for O'Brian. He smoothed his wrinkled coat and pants and attempted to straighten his tie. It sagged to one side, and he finally gave up and yanked it off, jamming it into his coat pocket. As usual, his clothes looked slept in. And they were. He'd spent the night in his office, preparing for his meeting with O'Brian.

A day's growth of stubble covered his jaw, and he rubbed his hand across it, vaguely conscious of his scruffy appearance. *Well, no matter,* he thought wryly. He certainly wasn't trying to impress O'Brian.

He pulled a crumpled paper from his pocket and again scanned O'Brian's letter.

Editor, Grizzlyclaw Gazette
San Francisco, California

Dear Sir:
In two months I will be boarding the Gypsy in New Orleans for passage to California. I am traveling with the express purpose of finding my brother, one Shamus O'Brian, who disappeared more than a year ago in the vicinity of his gold mine, a claim which he named Rainbow's End. I am posting this letter to be sent on the Flying Cloud, *hoping it will reach San Francisco before the Gypsy.*

Someone told me of your newspaper's interest in the recent disappearances among the miners, and that is why I am appealing to you for help. I fear my brother may be one of those who has met with the mysterious fate about which you have written. This leads me to my question: Will you recommend a detective who can travel with me and help me in my quest? I am prepared to pay a fair daily rate. Please know that you have my permission to engage these services on my behalf sometime before the first week in October, when the Gypsy is scheduled to dock at San Francisco Bay.

I am most anxious to begin the immediate search for my brother and would be grateful if you would have the

detective meet me at the harbor. Thank you for your help.
If you incur any prior expense on behalf of my search, I
am prepared to recompense you.

Yours very respectfully,
M. Sheridan O'Brian

P.S. I have dark hair and a slight build and, for recogni-
tion, will wear a blue felt hat. Please pass this description
to the detective so that he will recognize me at the wharf.

Marcus moved his gaze across the crowded wharf, searching for the letter writer. From the description, particularly
the blue felt hat, he imagined this O'Brian to be a bit of a
dandy. An Irish dandy, no doubt, with a name like Sheridan
O'Brian. If the hat had been green, he'd have imagined a leprechaun, he acknowledged with a grin.

Well, no matter what he thought about O'Brian's looks,
he simply wanted to use the opportunity to solve a mystery
that had kept him working nights, obsessed with finding the
murdering claim jumpers of the California mother lode.

It was ironic — perhaps even providential — that the
name of the claim in question was Rainbow's End. He dusted
off his rumpled coat. Leprechaun or not, O'Brian was about
to lead Marcus to the pot of gold at Rainbow's End. All
because he planned to temporarily assume the role of
Marcus Jade, private detective. The title suited him, he
thought with a grin. And he would play the role with
aplomb.

Marcus again scanned the milling crowd on the dock. He
saw no one wearing a blue hat. He began to pace in front of

the several tenders that had docked at the wharf, examining each one who passed. Ruffians, dandies, and a pickpocket or two jostled past; children scampered and darted; old people moved slowly across the docks. Miners, traders, and merchants argued loudly near piles of cargo being set up for auction. Snatches of words in Chinese and Spanish drifted across the wharf. He squinted through the crowds. Still no one fit O'Brian's description.

An hour passed. Some of the passengers left on tenders for clippers anchored in the bay, clearing the docks somewhat. Others climbed into carriages and wagons. Suddenly, the wharf seemed nearly empty. Only a few dockhands and sailors remained. A pretty woman stood by her baggage, waiting for portage. And a young couple with squirming children talked loudly to each other about a missing trunk. He noticed a dirty-faced, redheaded ruffian scavenging for something to eat, not unusual at the wharf. San Francisco had its share of children begging for handouts.

The late afternoon sun slanted across the water, reflecting a silvery light on the worn wood of the dock. Marcus leaned against a sturdy pole, closing his eyes in weariness and protection against the sun's bright glare.

"Sir?"

The voice was soft, lilting. Irish, perhaps.

His eyes opened; he cocked his head. The small pretty woman he'd noticed earlier now stood directly in front of him. The sun was behind her, creating a halo of light on her raven-wing hair, on her ribbon- and flower-trimmed blue felt hat.

Blue hat? Marcus's eyes opened wider, then immediately narrowed. "Yes," he growled, not wanting to hear her next words.

"Sir, would you be waitin' for a Sheridan O'Brian?" She smiled, and even in the shadow cast by her hat, Marcus could see the dimple in her chin and the color of her eyes — the exact blue of the blasted hat.

"Now, how would you know who I'm waiting for?" He hoped he was wrong, but he inwardly groaned as his gaze again settled on the hat. "You wouldn't be, ah — O'Brian — ah, Sheridan O'Brian, now would you?"

She laughed. He was struck by the music in the sound. It somehow reminded him of northern moors and distant seas — faraway places he'd only read about.

"Aye, sir. That I am," Sheridan replied. Her voice dropped, and she frowned. "But you seem surprised. I thought you were expectin' me. My letter —"

Marcus interrupted. "What are you doing with a name like that — like Sheridan? That's a man's name."

She moved back and coolly assessed him, ignoring his question. Her expression changed. "You're the detective I asked the *Grizzlyclaw* editor to hire, but you're not expectin' me?" She squinted at him, her eyes beginning to glitter. Marcus didn't know whether it was from anger or fear. Or maybe amusement. She stepped backward again, considering him. "Not much of a detective now, are you?"

Marcus grinned slowly. "I reckon not," he said, shaking his head.

But Sheridan didn't smile.

"You surprised me, that's all," he said, combing his fingers through his wheat-colored hair. "When I was...ah...hired to work for you, I...ah...just assumed, that M. Sheridan O'Brian was a man." He'd never stammered so much in his life. He felt himself blush as he considered her. Why hadn't he guessed from something as simple as her penmanship that she was as feminine as any woman he'd ever set eyes on?

"What's the 'M' stand for then?" he muttered.

"Sir?"

"The 'M' before your name in the letter." He reached into his pocket and pulled out the missive. "You signed it, 'M. Sheridan O'Brian.'" He thrust it at her as if she couldn't remember her own signature.

"Mary," she said, ignoring the crumpled paper and wondering if the man was addle-brained. "My name is Mary Elizabeth Sheridan O'Brian."

"It appeared to be 'M' as in 'Master Sheridan O'Brian.'"

"It could just as easily have been 'M' as in 'Mistress O'Brian,'" she said, lifting her chin a bit and gazing at him evenly.

Marcus combed his fingers through his hair and moved his eyes away from hers. When Sheridan didn't speak, he turned to her again and, looking into her wide, clear eyes, was suddenly conscious of his careless appearance. He rubbed the stubble on his jaw. "We should be seeing about getting you settled into a hotel, now, shouldn't we?" he mumbled. "Later we can talk about the journey ahead, about the arrangements I've made for packhorses, gear, and such —"

Sheridan interrupted. "There are a few things I'd first like to discuss."

Marcus raised an eyebrow. "And these are?"

"You've made a ruckus as big as the Bear Flag Revolt out of my name, but you've not had the simple courtesy to give me yours."

Marcus felt himself color. Weeks ago he'd begun his designs to hoodwink this O'Brian. Oh, yes, he'd laid out his

17

plans in detail, down to a toad's toenail, how he'd be in control from the first meeting at the wharf through to finding O'Brian's brother in the mother lode. Now here he stood, as bumbling and illiterate as a shy schoolboy in front of a pretty schoolmarm. And it was clear who was in charge.

"I apologize, Miss O'Brian," he finally said. "I should've known better. The name's Jade. Marcus Jade." He stuck out his hand, then immediately thought better of it: a handshake was no way to greet a lady such as the beauty in front of him. He jammed his hand back into his pocket, swallowing hard. "You said you had a few things to discuss?"

"Aye," Sheridan said. "That I did. Your name was the first. The second is a request. I'd like for you to direct me to the *Grizzlyclaw* office."

"Pardon me?" Marcus lifted an eyebrow. He had figured O'Brian might want to meet the man she wrote to, but he hadn't figured it to be so soon.

Sheridan wondered if he was deaf as well as feeble-minded. "I said I would like to be directed to the *Grizzlyclaw Gazette.* I want to meet the editor."

Marcus swallowed again. "Yes, yes — of course," he said too quickly. The pot of gold he'd imagined O'Brian would bring the *Grizzlyclaw* now faded to something resembling lumps of coal. That was the last place he could take her. He let out a sigh. "And the third item you wanted to discuss?"

Sheridan smiled sweetly, the dimple in her chin turning her face into that of a cherub. "The third," she paused, her blue-eyed gaze never leaving his, "is that you are dismissed, Mr. Jade. I intend to see the editor of the *Grizzlyclaw* about hiring another private detective."

Two

❦

"Hire someone else?" Marcus Jade's voice was low, almost a growl.

Sheridan was surprised by the disappointment on the man's face. She had assumed from Mr. Jade's cavalier attitude that he didn't care about the case one way or another.

"You have no idea the trouble I've gone to on your behalf, Miss O'Brian," he continued. "The endless inquiries about horses, the equipment, and supplies."

"I'm sure that's true, Mr. Jade. And you'll be paid for those services."

"May I ask your reasons?" But before Sheridan could answer, Marcus sighed and shook his head slowly as if he'd already guessed her thinking. "I know we got off to an uncomfortable start," he said quietly. "It's just that I'd been up all night working." He paused, frowning. "When you presented yourself, I was expecting a man. You can't blame me for being surprised at your appearance."

"Nonetheless, I'd like to consult the editor of the

Grizzlyclaw. Too much is at stake for me to take a chance...."
She hesitated, feeling her determination to fire the man waning. There was something disarming about his words, about his hesitant manner. Maybe she'd decided too hastily. But her life and her brother's would be in the hands of the man she hired. And she wasn't sure she could trust this Mr. Marcus Jade.

Marcus suddenly smiled gently. "I understand your concerns, Miss O'Brian. You're worried sick about your brother. He's been missing for how long now?"

"It's been nearly two years since our last letter."

"And he wrote regularly before that?"

Sheridan nodded.

Marcus frowned, looking concerned.

"He wrote to our Aunt Fiona in New York every few months. She then sent the letters on to me at Oberlin College, then later to my home in Natchez."

Marcus took her arm, escorting her across the wharf to the trunks where she'd been standing earlier. As they walked, he asked more questions. "Where was he last? I mean, where was his final letter posted?"

"A place called Everlasting Diggins."

"Some big strikes coming out of there."

Sheridan stopped near her trunk and gazed up at Marcus. "Shamus wrote that he'd struck gold, a lot of gold."

"Then the letters stopped?"

She nodded. "Aye, they did. Though it took months, nearly a year, before Aunt Fiona realized something was wrong. By the time she contacted me, another few months had passed. Then, of course, we lost more time with my weeks aboard the *Gypsy*." She gestured to the American clip-

20

per in the bay. "I'm gettin' a late start with the search. I only hope I'm not too late to find my twin brother." Her voice dropped, and she looked out to sea, feeling a sting behind her eyes.

"Your twin?" His eyes searched hers. "You're very close then." It was a statement, not a question.

"Aye." She appreciated the insight.

"I'd like to help you, Miss O'Brian, if you'd allow me," Marcus's expression was intent. "I've already begun making inquiries."

Sheridan considered the man in front of her. For the first time, she looked beyond the unkempt hair, the day's growth of beard, his rumpled clothing. His eyes were clear and intelligent — perhaps even kindhearted, she thought, though she didn't want to be taken in by her own misguided assumptions. Her years working with the Underground Railroad had taught her that much.

Then Marcus Jade smiled again, and she noticed the contrast of his tanned skin with his light eyes, his sun-streaked hair.

"I'll think about it," she said, suddenly feeling weary. "But for right now, will you please see me to my hotel? After I rest, perhaps we can meet to discuss the search."

Marcus nodded, signaling for help with her bags. "Perhaps over supper?" Noticing her frown, he hurried on. "San Francisco is no place for a lady to dine alone." Beside them, two Chilean dockhands hurried to lift Sheridan's trunk onto a cart. Sheridan nodded toward the floral satchel and two smaller cases, and the dockhands placed them next to the trunk.

"Surely I'll be safe in the hotel dining room," she protested as she walked with him from the wharf to the cabbie he had just signaled.

"You don't know San Francisco," he said as her baggage was loaded into the back of the carriage.

They now stood clear of the wharf, and Sheridan gazed up at the rolling hills of town. In the waning daylight, she could see a maze of dirt, mud, and sometimes cobbled streets rising on a steep incline away from the waterfront. Wood-slatted sidewalks lined the roadways in front of rows of high, narrow wooden buildings leading up to what she supposed was the center of town.

Marcus opened the carriage door, and Sheridan pulled her dark blue cape around her as she settled into the soft leather seat. Light was fading as the sun sank lower into the ocean, and now a chilly fog had begun to drift inland.

The driver flicked a whip over the horse's back, and the vehicle rocked and rattled away from the wharf.

"I thought you might enjoy the California Palace," Marcus said. "It's one of the finer hotels. I made arrangements for you to stay two nights, thinking that we'll need a day or two to buy the rest of our supplies."

Sheridan didn't comment on his assumption that he'd be accompanying her.

Marcus explained about the turbulent, cosmopolitan makeup of San Francisco as they drove to the hotel. She shivered as he told her about Sydney Town, Little Chile, Five Points, and Seven Dials — areas often ravaged by fires set by villainous thugs trying to run out foreigners. These places, Marcus acknowledged, were indeed filled with every kind of ruffian, from pickpockets to murderers.

"Those are the only sections where one finds such

scoundrels — the vigilante thugs and the murdering thieves?" Sheridan asked, remembering the cosmopolitan crowd at the wharf.

"No," he said, understanding her meaning. "No one group is responsible for San Francisco's crime. Americans are as guilty as the Chinese, Germans, Chileans, English, Sicilians, French, and Australians."

"And how about the Irish?" She cast him a sideways glance.

Marcus grinned. "Now, that I wouldn't be knowin'. It seems they're too busy pannin' in the gold fields to bother with thievery."

"The right thing to say, Mr. Jade. Aye, the right thing indeed," she said, smiling at his attempt to sound Irish.

The carriage passed a parade of ox-drawn carts with lacy mantilla-veiled young women seated inside, each flanked by two riders on horseback. The prancing horses' manes had been brushed gleaming and long, and the riders wore dark costumes glittering with silver braids and buttons.

Sheridan looked questioningly at Marcus.

"Señoritas traveling to a party," he explained. "Probably on their way to a hacienda in the hills.

"San Francisco is a town of extremes," he continued. "We've got people drawn here because of the gold rush — from nearly every country you can imagine. Just a few years ago this was a quiet seaside town. Then some forty thousand gold hunters arrived by sea. Suddenly, the place was transformed into a real city. Another thirty thousand folks plodded across the Great Basin — then another nine or ten thousand moved up here from Mexico." He shook his head slowly, grinning. "I came here with my father in '47 — about the

23

time the name changed from Yerba Buena to San Francisco."

Marcus glanced back at the bay. "By '51, we had eight hundred ships riding anchor in the cove. Seems the crews were overcome with the fever. Left them nearly senseless."

She smiled. "Ah — you're meanin' the gold fever. Some say it's worse than cholera." The carriage rocked along a cobbled street, stopped to let a well-dressed family cross, then swayed as the driver again urged the horse forward.

Marcus grinned. "In many cases they're right."

After a moment she spoke again as the vehicle rumbled over a pothole, then another. "You said that San Francisco is a city of extremes. How do you mean?"

"Besides every nationality you can name — we've got those who are very rich living next to those who don't know where they'll find their next hunk of bread. We've got more God-fearing citizens than you can shake a stick at. But the crime —" He frowned, referring back to what he'd said earlier. "Just since '50, there've been some fourteen hundred murders. Only three of the murderers were hanged for their crimes."

Sheridan gazed through the carriage window at the milling crowds on the streets. "'Tis a rougher place than I'd imagined," she murmured.

Nodding, Marcus continued. "The city now boasts some fifty thousand folks. Besides those who still come and go from the mother lode, there are traders, whalers, merchants, seamen —"

The carriage swayed as they rounded a hilly curve. Sheridan fought to keep her balance. "What do you mean, 'those who *still* come and go'? Have many left their strikes?" She thought of Shamus.

"Most give up sooner or later if they don't strike it rich.

The gold rush peaked in the early '50s. In the last few years thousands have left the gold fields." He chuckled. "It seems that everybody except the miners got rich. At the peak of the gold rush, eggs sold for a dollar apiece. More money can be made by selling to the miners than by mining."

"What do they do once they stop mining? What if they have no other trade?"

"The wise ones save some of the gold they've found and use it to buy a ranch, a few head of cattle, a small business in town, or a ticket home. If they don't have any gold, they can at least sell their equipment. Some even sell their claims to enterprising merchants who get someone else to work it in hopes of striking a new vein."

The rig was passing through a dark and rough part of the city now. The streets were packed earth, and taverns lined the wooden walkways.

"Still others can't overcome their disappointment at failure," Marcus continued softly. "They once had big dreams of grandeur and wealth. They write to relatives in the East, telling of striking it rich. When the mines bottom out, they can't face the humiliation."

"And?" Sheridan's voice was shaking. "And what do those men do?"

He nodded to the saloons, the rough-looking men milling in and out of the swinging doors, the tinny sounds of pianos, the shouting and coarse laughter spilling into the cobbled street. "Places like that are filled with broken dreams," he said simply. "Drinking, gambling — and worse. That's how many end up."

"Not Shamus," said Sheridan, turning her head from the sight. "Not my brother. I don't know what happened. But I know he wouldn't end up there."

He fought the urge to take her small hand in his and comfort her. The carriage swayed as the driver turned off the street onto a narrow, rutted road leading up a steep hillside.

"We're nearly there," Marcus explained. "The California Palace is on top of the hill. From your window, you'll have a nice view of the city — all the way to the bay." The carriage tipped sharply as they rounded another curve, then slowed as the hotel came into view.

Sheridan smiled. It was a welcome sight. Surrounded by small cypress trees and leafy oaks, the sprawling two-story edifice nearly covered the hilltop. The structure rose loftily from an open courtyard. Its look was at once inviting and grand. Trailing bougainvillaea hung gracefully from narrow wooden boxes adorning the base of every window and from the latticework arbors at the entrance. Kerosene lamps had been lit around the cobbled driveway, and their light threw a warm glow into the misty night.

Soon they came to a halt in front of the hotel. The driver opened the carriage door and Sheridan lifted her cape and skirt and stepped to the ground.

At once, Marcus Jade alighted from the carriage and moved to her side. "About supper tonight?"

Behind them the driver signaled a young boy at the hotel's entrance for help with the baggage.

She nodded briskly. "Aye, that will be fine."

"I'll hire a carriage and pick you up at eight?"

"That won't be necessary," Sheridan said as he escorted her toward the hotel's entrance. "An elegant place such as this I'm sure has adequate dining on the premises. We'll take our supper here."

Jade grinned. "Ah," he murmured. "A woman with a mind of her own."

"Sir?" she said, looking up quizzically.

He stopped and held her gaze with something akin to admiration in his eyes. "When I first saw that O'Brian wasn't …ah…who I expected, quite aside from my surprise, I wondered at a woman's — especially a woman as delicate and refined as you…." He faltered, obviously searching for words. "That is, I wondered about your ability to make decisions, to travel to one of the roughest and most violent regions of the state."

"So that's what angered you when you first saw me? You didn't think I could do a man's job?"

Marcus swallowed hard. "No, no," he said hurriedly. "I didn't think that at all."

"That's what you just said, Mr. Jade."

Around them hotel guests hurried by. The carriage driver looked impatiently toward the couple, and the young boy who'd helped with Sheridan's baggage hovered, waiting for his service gratuity.

"What I was trying to say," Marcus began, looking intently into her eyes, "is that even in the short time we've been together, I've seen your determination, your deep caring for your brother. If I had any doubts about your capability to see the search through — even in the most difficult of circumstances — they're gone. That's what I so clumsily attempted to tell you."

"You have no idea of my capabilities, Mr. Jade," Sheridan replied, her voice soft. She looked away from him, thinking about her work with the Underground Railroad in Oberlin, her near capture by the slave hunters, her harrowing experiences in the deep South starting a new station on the line. "You really have no idea," she said, lifting her skirts to ascend the stone steps leading to the hotel lobby.

Marcus caught up with her and pulled open the entrance door, then saw to her accommodations at the front desk and the portage of her trunk and other bags to her room.

As he bade her good-bye, he took a deep breath. "You'll still dine with me tonight — here in the hotel, I mean?" Marcus brushed his hair from his forehead, suddenly looking boyishly expectant.

A smile played at her lips. "Aye," she said. "We'll meet at eight."

"Oh, and Mr. Jade?" She called to him as he started to walk away. He turned. "Your vast knowledge of San Francisco strikes me as very curious." She frowned in thought. "I would expect someone of your profession to have a certain understanding of the city and its history, but I find your detailed account of its population statistics and ethnic and social makeup quite remarkable."

For a moment Marcus searched her face. Then he swallowed hard and gave her a curt nod. "Yes," he said. "It is remarkable, isn't it?" Without awaiting her answer, he strode through the door to the still-waiting carriage.

Before his vehicle was out of sight, Sheridan returned to the hotel clerk. "Hire me a carriage," she said briskly.

The clerk nodded and signaled to the boy at the entrance. The young man ran to do the clerk's bidding. Within minutes, a carriage rounded the corner from the stables behind the hotel. A lantern swung from each corner of the vehicle, lighting the way in the gathering dusk.

The rotund driver helped Sheridan into the plush inner

compartment. As she settled comfortably against the seat, she looked into the big man's pleasant face. "Take me to the building that houses the *Grizzlyclaw Gazette*," she said. "And be quick about it. I don't have much time."

"As you wish, Miss." The driver lifted his heavy frame to the driver's seat. "As you wish." He chuckled as he cracked the whip above the horse's back.

Jolting and lurching, the carriage sped down the winding road to the city. Sheridan stared from the carriage window, lost in thought.

She hoped to arrive at the *Gazette* before the doors were locked for the night. She had to speak with the editor to whom she'd written. Obviously, he had believed in this private detective, Marcus Jade, enough to hire him on her behalf.

But now she wanted to meet this editor in person, tell him of her concerns about Marcus Jade. Even though she'd softened toward him somewhat, Sheridan still had some doubts. Visiting the *Grizzlyclaw*, she hoped, would put those misgivings from her mind.

Then tonight at supper, she and Marcus Jade could speak of the business ahead. He said he'd done some preliminary work on her behalf. That was good. And she had more information about Shamus — details from the last letter to Aunt Fiona — that she needed to give to the detective.

She settled back into the seat, feeling that somehow meeting this editor would set everything straight, would tell her she could wholly trust this agent.

Because, she realized as she gazed from the carriage window, there was nothing she'd like better than to hire this fascinating man, Marcus Jade. She remembered the line of his jaw, the light in his eyes. *Aye,* she thought, *this Marcus Jade is cut from fine cloth.* Then she felt herself blush at thinking such things about a man she hardly knew.

The carriage slowed in front of a tall, dingy building. Her eyes widened.

"Here we are," the driver announced, opening her door. "And you're in luck — it appears there's still someone on the premises. Shall I wait?"

Sheridan nodded, almost absently. "Aye," she murmured as she stepped from the carriage and into the muddy street. "Please do."

She stopped and drew in a deep breath. Through the single dirty window, she could see a small printing press and a feeble-looking old man stooped over a table. A single lamp cast a dim light across the room.

Somehow Sheridan had imagined the *Grizzlyclaw Gazette* to be a much larger operation, though she didn't know why. Maybe just wishful thinking, she now realized.

Fighting her disappointment, Sheridan stepped onto the sidewalk.

A moment later she tried the handle and felt the door give way. When she pushed it open, a bell on the other side announced her arrival. The old man glanced up in surprise. The look on his withered face told her that visitors didn't often stop by.

"Can I help you, Miss?" His voice was surprisingly strong for one who looked so frail.

"Are you the editor?"

"Eh?"

"Sir," she enunciated the words. "Are you the *Gazette* editor?"

30

"Who wants to know?"

"Well, sir, I do. My name is Sheridan O'Brian."

"Eh?" The old man put his hand to his ear.

"Ah, my name is Sheridan O'Brian." By now she was nearly shouting. "I wrote to you about my brother Shamus. He's missing in the gold country."

The old man frowned. "You say your brother's missing?"

"Yes!" Sheridan said loudly. "He struck gold."

"Well, good fer him. Good fer him. Always glad to hear of it. So many don't, you know. Go home empty-handed."

"No, sir. You don't understand." Sheridan raised her voice. "I say my brother's disappeared."

"You don't say."

"I wrote to you. Do you remember my letter?"

"Eh?"

"My letter. In my letter I asked you to find a detective for me. Someone to help me find my brother."

"Detective work, you say?"

Sheridan nodded vigorously.

"I'm sorry, child," his voice dropped. "I'm too old and too tired to attempt work like that. I can barely lift the frame into the press anymore. I'm sorry I can't help you." His old face looked sad. "I wish I could, child."

She took a deep breath, her shoulders drooping. "I do, too, sir. Aye, that I do."

"Eh?"

"I said I wish you could help." She shook her head forlornly.

The old man patted her hand.

"Thank you," Sheridan mumbled and backed toward the door.

"Eh?"

"I said thank you," Sheridan shouted and attempted a smile. "Good luck with your paper."

He nodded and gave her a feeble salute with his hand. "God bless you, child," he said, going back to his work.

"I'll be needin' it," Sheridan muttered as she closed the door behind her. Clutching the latest edition of the *Gazette* in her hand, she allowed the driver to help her into the carriage.

Across the street, Marcus Jade stepped backward into the shadows as Sheridan's vehicle pulled away. It had been a close call. Moments earlier he'd been about to stride into the *Grizzlyclaw* to speak with his father, when Sheridan alighted from her carriage.

Catching his blunder in time, he faded into the darkness, watching Sheridan's animated visit with his father. At first he was amused. But the amusement quickly turned to shame. Marcus knew he needed to make amends, and he intended to do it tonight at supper. He'd come clean, then try to convince her that he still wanted to help her find Shamus. His offer wouldn't even include a private detective fee or a payback with stories sent to his father for printing. Unless, of course, Sheridan didn't mind about that part.

His father knew nothing of Marcus's dealings with Sheridan or his plans to deceive her. No, and if he did, he'd disapprove. In fact, he'd be downright livid.

Marcus watched Sheridan's carriage disappear into the darkness. What if she said no to his offer to help? He might not see her after tonight. Ever. And that would bring a much greater sadness than anything else he could contemplate right now.

Yes, he thought, *I have to tell her who I am. Tonight. Before it's too late.*

Three

At the elegant California Palace, Sheridan stepped from the carriage. The entrance lamps that earlier burned so brightly now were veiled in a heavy mist, casting an eerie glow into the deepening night. Shivering, the young woman clutched her cloak and hurried through the ornate, wood-carved doors and up the winding staircase to her room on the second floor.

Sheridan sighed contentedly as she entered her room and tossed her cloak at the foot of the tall, spindle-posted bed. The place seemed to reach out and welcome her in its coziness and warmth. A cheery fire crackled in the fireplace across from the bed; a glossy mahogany table flanked by two high-backed chairs graced one corner. A mirrored washstand with a floral bowl of scented water, a small dish of soap, and fresh towels stood in the other corner. Stretching across the room's far end were french windows that opened to a small upstairs porch. On a clear day, the desk clerk had said, the place afforded a stunning view of the city.

Unfastening the glass-paned doors, Sheridan moved onto

the balcony. Fog had rolled in from the bay and shrouded the scene below.

Just like my life right now, she thought, peering into the darkness. *I wish I could see beyond my own clouded uncertainty. Should I hire Marcus Jade, even though I've not had a personal endorsement from the* Grizzlyclaw Gazette *editor? Or should I find someone else, maybe wasting days of precious time in my search?*

She thought about simply striking out on her own, heading for the gold country, nosing about with no one's help.

That's what Callie would do, she thought suddenly, remembering her brave friend. When they were working in the Underground together, Callie always seemed to have the answers — knew exactly when to act and where. Strong-willed and courageous, Callie was born to lead.

Sheridan sighed, missing her friend. Oh, if Callie and her new husband, Hawk, could only be with her now! Though Harvard-trained as a doctor, Hawk, with his Mandan Indian mother and trapper father, was the best detective a person could ask for. He'd even found Callie and Sheridan months after they'd disappeared without a trace from Oberlin College.

Sheridan raised her eyes heavenward. "Oh, heavenly Father," she breathed. "What am I doin' here in this place, half a world away from home?" A hot sting of tears filled her eyes. "I'm the least brave of all your children, yet here I am, ready to cast body and soul into the unknown, chasin' after my brother.

"I'm scared, heavenly Father, I am! No matter what this Marcus Jade says about my capabilities and determination. I'm tremblin' inside, even when I'm actin' like I'm filled with courage."

She looked into the heavy fog. It reminded her of the mists of the Irish coast that crept inland from the sea. "When you can't see your next step," she remembered her grand-ma'am saying about the gloomy, low-lying clouds, "that's when it's time to look heavenward and ask for God's help. And it's the same in life, child. It's his strong arm of grace that will keep you steady even when you can't see ahead."

Then Grandma'am had added with a smile. "Sometimes he allows tryin' and confusin' times just so we'll look to him. Then he scoops us up into his arms — just as your pa does when you raise your wee arms to be lifted. But God wants us to ask for help, he does, child. He wants us simply to raise our arms up like a wee child and ask."

Sheridan dried her tears and again looked heavenward. "That's what I need now, heavenly Father. I need you to scoop me up into your arms, hold me fast, and calm my fears."

She thought of her brother, and fresh tears traced down her cheeks. "Forgive me, Father, for thinkin' more of myself, my own tremblin' fears, than for my brother's safety. Help me remember that even though I don't know where he is — or even where to begin looking — you're with him. Keep him safe in your arms, and help me find him."

Feeling better, Sheridan blew her nose and again dabbed away her tears. She came inside, washed her face in the rose-scented water, and brushed her dark hair until it gleamed in the lamplight. She hummed a little song with words she'd made up when she first sailed from Ireland. The tune was from a family lullaby that had been passed along the genera-tions, and her words formed a prayer, speaking of her deep love for God and his for her. "I love you, dear Jesus…," she breathed to the lullaby's meter.

When she was a child, a cousin had taught her to play an Irish harp. Now, as she hummed her song, she wished she still had that wooden instrument.

It was nearing eight o'clock when Sheridan finished dressing for dinner. She'd changed from her traveling suit into a dark velvet skirt and a white, high-collared lace blouse. Around the collar, she fastened a cameo on a black velvet ribbon. She'd swept back her hair from her face and tied it high so that it hung, sleek and shining, down her back.

Promptly at eight, Sheridan descended the wide staircase to the lobby. There, at the foot of the stairs, stood a smiling Marcus Jade. As she neared the final steps, he reached up to take her hand.

Sheridan caught her breath in surprise. This was not the disheveled, stubble-jawed, wild-and-woolly-looking man who'd left her just hours before.

That man had all but disappeared. In his place stood the most debonair and dashing, rawboned, handsome creature she'd ever seen. The cut of Marcus Jade's dark suit, the pressed and spotless shirt, the felt hat he swept from his blond hair as he greeted her — all spoke of a *savoir faire* that had been nonexistent in their earlier meeting. Sheridan was stunned at the transformation.

She blushed as she caught herself staring open-mouthed at this new Marcus Jade. She hadn't yet stepped from the last stair to join him, and he, watching her with amusement, still held her hand lightly.

"Mr. Jade," she finally managed with a hard swallow, "I…ah …I almost didn't recognize you."

He merely tilted his head with a half smile but didn't comment. Her hand still in his, he said simply, "Our table is waiting." Then he led her to the dining room.

A few minutes later, the couple was seated at a small table set with pewter warming plates and polished silverware. At the table's center, a lighted candle adorned a small basket of roses.

Sheridan asked Marcus for his recommendations about the menu, and he suggested the poached salmon served with oven-roasted venison and candied apples. Noting her surprise at the sophisticated offerings, he went on to tell her that the California Palace was known far and wide for its epicurean bill of fare. After ordering and speaking for a few moments about the hotel, its history and clientele, they turned to more serious matters.

"There are some things I need to explain to you, Miss O'Brian," Marcus began.

"Please, call me Sheridan," she interrupted, fully aware that until this moment she hadn't intended to drop their formalities.

"It would be an honor," he said, a gentle — though somehow sad — smile crossing his face in the candlelight. "Though you may withdraw your request when you hear all I need to tell you."

"Sir?" Sheridan said, wondering what was coming next.

He chuckled softly. "Until then — why don't you call me Marcus." He paused. "'Sir' makes me feel like you're speaking to my father. And he's a very old man."

Sheridan laughed, and her table partner's eyes brightened at the sound. "Aye, Marcus it is then, at least until you bestow your ominous-sounding news."

Marcus didn't laugh with her. His eyes held hers earnestly. "I want you to know how sorry I am about our meeting this afternoon."

She nodded, considering his humble demeanor, the pensive look on his face.

"I behaved poorly. I'm sorry."

"You're forgiven, Marcus." She spoke from the heart.

"But there's more." Marcus was interrupted by the waiter who stepped to their table with great fanfare. A moment later, he was joined by another young man who set their dinners before them.

Marcus cleared his throat. "As I was saying," he began just as the waiter returned to pour their wine.

Smiling benevolently, the man poured the sparkling liquid into pewter goblets, set them by the plates, then offered the couple warm slices of sourdough bread from a linen-wrapped loaf, which he left on their table. He set a small dish of whipped sweet butter near the thick-crusted bread and asked if they cared for water.

Marcus sighed and shook his head. When the waiter left, Sheridan was pleased to see Marcus bow his head in a moment of humble thankfulness to God for their meal. Then the couple lifted their forks and ate for a few minutes in silence.

"Delicious," Sheridan murmured.

Marcus nodded, and swallowed a drink of wine, ready to begin again. "There's something besides the apology that I must tell you," he finally said.

Across the table, Sheridan leaned forward, again captivating him with her lively blue eyes, their crystalline depths as clear as any gently flowing mountain stream. The beauty and goodness he saw there emanated from someplace deep inside. Marcus could think of only one thing as his gaze met hers. He didn't want this young woman to walk out of his life.

He cleared his throat.

"Sheridan," he said, "I've done some things in my life that I'm not proud of."

"We all have."

He sighed deeply. "Well, you see, this involves y —"

Just at that moment a commotion erupted from the kitchen, directly opposite their table.

First a shout, then a child's scream carried from the kitchen into the dining room. There was a loud clatter, followed by another.

"Someone's throwing things," Sheridan murmured.

Marcus stood and threw his napkin onto the table.

Another yell pierced the air — again from a child.

Then in a split second, a boy — perhaps ten or twelve — emerged from the kitchen, running around the corner, slipping and sliding in his haste. He tripped, then tried to regain his footing just as a heavyset cook appeared, waving a wooden spoon and shouting profanities at the child.

The boy rolled into a ball and covered his head, preparing for blows from the spoon-wielding chef.

"This'll teach you, you little ruffian." The man grabbed the boy's dirty, ragged collar, yanking him to his feet.

The child tried to shield himself as the chef raised the spoon to deliver the first blow, all the while dragging the boy back into the kitchen, away from the silent and gawking diners.

"Stop!" In a heartbeat, Marcus was beside the child, a firm

grasp on the chef's arm. "Let go! Now!"

The man dropped the long spoon. "You defending this lyin' little thief?" the big man growled, looking in disgust at the thin, cowering boy.

"You have no right to beat a child — no matter what he's done."

"Yeah? My heart's bleedin', mister. You gonna pay for the ruin to my kitchen, too?"

"What'd he do?"

The chef, still breathing heavily and his face flushed, glanced at the boy, then back to his kitchen. "He stole food, and while he was at it, he ruined the rest of tonight's fare with his dirty, thievin' hands." The big man tried to raise the spoon again above the boy. Marcus held his arm fast.

"I'll pay for the damage," he said quietly. "It appears the boy is hungry. I'll take care of that, too."

The big man shrugged and dropped his hand. As Marcus led the boy back to their table, his eyes met Sheridan's. She smiled her approval and signaled the waiter for another chair.

As soon as the boy was seated, Sheridan touched his small, dirty hand. "What's your name?"

For a long time the boy stared into his lap. Then his wary eyes met hers. "Duncan," he finally said bravely. "Duncan Kelly."

I should have guessed, Sheridan thought, *with the child's bright red hair and dark freckles.* "Aye," she said softly. "'Tis a good Gaelic name you've got. And where are you from, Duncan Kelly?"

The boy tightened his lips and pulled his hand out from under Sheridan's.

41

Marcus spoke up. "Excuse us for not introducing ourselves," he said seriously. "My guest," he nodded toward Sheridan, "is Miss Sheridan O'Brian. My name is Jade. Marcus Jade." He considered the boy for a moment, his ragged appearance, his thin, dirty face. "We just want to help you, son. Tell us where you live, and after you have a bite to eat, we'll see that you get home."

The child's eyes widened; he looked frightened. "Don't need no help."

Sheridan opened the cloth-covered basket of sourdough bread. "Would you like some of this?"

The child grabbed the basket and placed it in his lap. With both hands he reached for the breadloaf and held the whole thing to his mouth.

Sheridan exchanged glances with Marcus. He nodded slightly. The child had been without food for a long time.

Abruptly, Duncan stood, still holding the basket in one hand, the breadloaf in the other. He looked at their half-finished plates. "I've gotta go now," he said. "Could I have what's left on yours?"

"Not so fast," Marcus said, placing his hand firmly on the boy's arm. "I'll buy you as much food as you can eat, but first, tell me where you live." He paused, searching the child's face. "And tell me why it's been so long since your last meal. Your pa out of work?"

Duncan dropped into the chair. "I ain't got no pa."

Sheridan reached for the boy's hand again, but, still clutching the bread, he ignored her gesture.

"How about your ma? Where's she?"

"Dead." Duncan took another bite of bread.

Sheridan drew in her breath audibly. "You're an orphan?"

The boy shrugged, ravenously chewing another bite of bread. "I guess," he said between swallows.

"No other family?" Marcus's voice was gentle.

The boy shrugged again, then took a deep breath. "I got a sister," he said finally. "She's six. Her name is Evangelia."

"That's a pretty name," Sheridan offered.

"I call her Lia. She likes that," the boy said proudly, tearing another bite from the loaf. "I take care of her. Do a pretty good job of it, too. I'm eleven," he added, sticking out his thin chest. "Each other's all we got. That's why I need food. Lia hasn't eaten since this morning when I stole some smokefish down by the wharf."

"Where do you live?" Marcus tried again.

The boy looked at him suspiciously, seemed to consider his options, then finally said, "Sydney Town."

"You're from Australia then?"

Duncan nodded.

"You came here with your parents?"

The boy squirmed in his seat, then let out a deep sigh. His little shoulders sagged as if some internal conflict was over. He shook his head. "Nah, I brought Lia here myself. My ma died on the schooner, coming from Sydney. She was bringing us here to find my pa's brother, Sonny Kelly. He'd written her about finding gold."

"And your pa?" Marcus asked, though he had a feeling he knew what the boy would say.

"He died in prison."

"In Australia."

The boy nodded, then looked solemnly at the empty bread basket.

Marcus signaled the waiter and ordered a setting for the

boy with more bread, a tall goblet of milk, and a bowl of beef stew. He added that the boy would need an identical order packaged to take with him.

"Have you tried to find your uncle?" Sheridan's heart ached for the child. "What was his name again?"

"Sonny Kelly."

"Have you tried to find your Uncle Sonny?" Sheridan pressed.

Duncan nodded. "Yes, ma'am. But last anyone heard tell, he'd struck it rich in a place called Everlasting Diggins. I just haven't been able to find my way there yet."

Sheridan's eyes widened, and Marcus groaned inwardly, guessing what she was thinking. She looked heavenward, a small smile playing at her lips. Marcus thought she must be praying, even with eyes wide open, though he'd never seen anyone pray quite that way.

And she was. *Sometimes,* she was telling God, *when the mists are too heavy to see clearly and you scoop us up into your arms, we think it's only us you're rescuing. But the strange and wonderful thing is, we never know who else is going to be there. We never know who you've scooped up to be with us on our journey.*

She looked at Duncan with shining eyes. "Isn't that a coincidence?" she said. "That's exactly where we're headed. Mister Jade is a private detective who specializes in findin' lost people. And do you know, Duncan, what I'm thinkin'?" She winked at Marcus. "I'm thinkin' that it's one of God's sweet, mysterious wonders that we all met here tonight!"

"Hear, hear," Marcus said weakly, lifting his goblet of wine toward Sheridan. "Here's to the search."

She smiled happily at him over the rim of her pewter goblet.

Four

❧

Later that night, after Marcus Jade had placed Duncan in a hired carriage to fetch his sister from Sydney Town, he met Sheridan in the hotel foyer.

Sheridan noted Marcus's grim expression as he nodded toward two high-backed velvet chairs near the room's ceiling-high stone fireplace. He escorted her across the room, then, still frowning, seated himself in the chair opposite hers.

"You can't seriously be thinking about taking the children with us."

Sheridan patiently settled into her chair as he continued.

"We're heading into mother lode country. We'll be facing some of the most dangerous terrain in California. Not to mention the thugs we'll meet up with. It's no place for children."

Sheridan shrugged. "That doesn't matter. It's not a coincidence that we met the dear child tonight — with him and his sister trying to find their way to Everlasting Diggins. It's Providence." She smiled sweetly. "With a capital P."

Marcus shook his head slowly and stared into the fire.

"Providence or not," he muttered, "the mother lode's not even a place for women. And when you've got a couple of street urchins tagging along," he let out an agitated sigh, turning toward Sheridan again, "who knows what trouble lies ahead?"

"Nonetheless," Sheridan said, her voice taking on a brittle edge, "they're going." She paused. "And, may I ask, if you think a woman isn't up to the task, why are you sitting here?"

He didn't answer.

"This is the second time you've hinted at such a thing, Mister Jade. You must be in anguish over the chore ahead — takin' care of this poor little Irish lass, keepin' her out of trouble and imminent danger." She adopted a thick Southern accent, an exaggeration she had perfected while in Natchez. "Perhaps you'd better find yourself other employment. I wouldn't want to compromise your sensibilities."

"No, no," Marcus said quickly. "You've jumped to conclusions again."

"Have I?"

"I'm merely looking out for your welfare, and for that of the children. I have no doubt that you're up to the trip ahead. But the children?" He paused, his brow furrowed. "There are safer places for them to be than in the back of a mule-drawn wagon heading into the mother lode. We can find them a place here in town, perhaps a convent, if there's one here. I'd be happy to see about their —"

"A convent?"

He nodded, noting her expression. "Or maybe an orphanage?"

Sheridan shook her head. "No."

"Just like that? No?"

"No convent. No orphanage."

"You're absolutely sure?"

"Aye."

"I can't let you do this —"

"*You* can't let *me* do this, Mister Jade?" Her voice was a whisper, an angry whisper.

Marcus swallowed hard. "I'm sorry, Sheridan. I merely meant that I strongly recommend that you — rather, *we* — not take on this added responsibility."

"Then there is no *we*, Mister Jade." The words fell from her mouth before she realized what she'd said. Without Marcus Jade, she'd be heading for the dangerous mother lode country — with two wee ones in tow. She sighed softly, but didn't take back her words.

"You're firing me again?" He looked incredulous.

Suddenly mute, Sheridan merely nodded. It was too late to retrieve what had already been said. Besides, she'd show him what a woman could accomplish in the wilds of the mother lode. She decided without a second thought that she would not hire another detective. She'd show Mr. Marcus Jade exactly what a woman could achieve on her own.

Marcus stood, his face grim, yet still the gentleman, he helped her from her chair. "All right, then," he sighed as she stood and straightened her skirt. "But may I help you find another detective?"

Sheridan laughed. "Of course not. I'm not of a mind to be waitin' around San Francisco one day longer than necessary. Besides, I see now that I'm fully capable of continuing on without a guide."

"Then you're planning to go on alone?"

"I'll not be alone."

"Oh, yes. You'll have the children with you." He looked angry. "You really plan to take them."

"Aye. I told you I wouldn't be goin' without them." Then with her chin tilted upward, Sheridan swept past him, heading toward the stairs leading to her room.

Marcus caught her arm, gently turning her toward him. "I'm sorry for what I said." His eyes searched hers. "As you must realize by now, I often speak in haste and regret it later. Please, Sheridan. Let me go with you."

She considered his stricken face and weakened somewhat.

"You can't go out there without —"

"Without a man, Mr. Jade? Is that what you were about to say?"

Marcus stared at her for the briefest moment, his expression icy. "I was going to say, without a *partner*, Miss O'Brian. A partner."

Before a surprised Sheridan could answer, Marcus had turned for the exit, leaving her standing alone in the hotel lobby.

She considered his words a moment too long. When she finally started through the door after him, a retort in mind, Marcus Jade's dark brougham was already careening down the cobbled drive. It sped past an arriving carriage, nearly forcing it from the road.

Sheridan stood in the outer courtyard, hands on hips, chin in the air, watching Marcus's disappearing rig. "Aye," she muttered, "you're thinkin' this Irish lass will be backin' down, aren't you now, Mr. Jade? You're thinkin' I'll not go without you." She lifted her chin a bit higher. "I'll be showin' you a thing or two, just won't I?"

Seconds later, Sheridan heard Duncan's voice call out from inside the still-swaying vehicle that pulled up to the hotel portico.

"Miss Sheridan, Miss Sheridan. This here's my sister, Lia." The carriage door flew open and two small figures emerged. Duncan grabbed his sister's arm with one hand, dragging a heavy satchel behind him with the other.

Sheridan stooped so that she could look into the younger child's face at eye level. "Good evening, Evangelia," she said softly.

The little girl popped a dirty thumb in her mouth and regarded Sheridan solemnly.

Sheridan reached for her hand. But the tiny child stepped behind her brother. Evangelia's movement was so silent and natural, yet so graceful, that she reminded Sheridan of a frightened fawn seeking cover near its mother.

"I'm glad you've come, Lia."

Evangelia's large, serious eyes never left hers. The thumb stayed in her mouth. Sheridan sensed that beneath the layers of dirt and tattered clothing was a child who had seen more heartache in her six years than some adults experienced in a lifetime. Duncan had said his sister was six, but she appeared to be no more than four years of age. Though her brother had done his best, Lia probably hadn't had proper food since her mother died. But then, neither had Duncan.

"Come on, Lia," growled the boy. "Don't be bashful." He gave her a gentle push forward.

Evangelia shrugged her shoulders, keeping her luminous eyes on Sheridan. Again, she reminded Sheridan of a little fawn, hair of the palest red-brown, limbs of such delicate and fragile grace, eyes that seemed to hold a bewildering world within their depths.

Finally, Sheridan stood and gave her a quick hug. "We'll have time to get acquainted later," she said, leading the children to the hotel entrance. "For right now you both need a bath and a good night's sleep. We've a lot to do come mornin'."

"A bath?" Duncan looked fearful.

"Aye." She held the door open for the children to enter. Evangelia's eyes widened as she considered the opulent furnishings of the lobby. Even the thumb briefly fell from her mouth.

Sheridan asked for an attendant to prepare the bathing room. Then she ushered the still wide-eyed children up the spiral staircase.

"A bath with water and everything?" He clung to the banister with one hand and held the dirty satchel with the other. Evangelia trudged behind him, holding onto the tail of his shirt. "With soap?"

"Aye."

"Aw," he grumbled, "water *and* soap?"

"Aye." Sheridan winked conspiratorially at Evangelia. She was rewarded by a knowing look from the little girl. "And perfumed bubbles."

Duncan shot a pained glance toward Sheridan.

"Aye," Sheridan said solemnly, then paused before adding, "for Evangelia."

A few minutes later, Duncan sprawled into the high-backed chair near the fireplace. "So, where's Mister Jade?"

"Mister Jade will not be accompanying us."

Frowning, the boy pushed a lock of his red hair from his forehead. "Why not?"

"I've decided we don't need him."

"I thought you said that he's the best in finding lost people."

"I did."

"Then why?"

Sheridan cut him off. "As I said, we don't need Mister Jade." Noticing Duncan's perplexed expression, she added gently, "If you and your sister would rather not come along without Jade, I'll understand. But if you do, I promise we'll search for your uncle at the same time I'm lookin' for my brother Shamus. You'll be safe with me — probably safer than if you stayed here livin' on the streets in Sydney Town."

The boy nodded slowly. "What's Mister Jade gonna do?"

Sheridan sighed. "I have no way of knowin' that."

Staring into the crackling fire, Duncan considered her words. He turned again to Sheridan. "Aye," he finally said with a half smile. "We'll go with you."

"Aye?" Sheridan wondered if he was poking fun at her use of the word.

"My mother was always sayin' 'aye.' She was from Dublin — before she married my pa and they left for Australia." He looked at the floor. "It's good to hear it again," he mumbled shyly.

Sheridan nodded. Ireland! No wonder the child had captured her heart. She sighed contentedly, feeling an even stronger sense of responsibility for the two little orphans.

A few minutes later, the bath attendant knocked on the door, telling them their tub was ready in the bathing room down the hall.

Duncan let out an exaggerated groan and looked relieved

when Sheridan took Evangelia by the hand, indicating she would be first.

"But don't be goin' out, Duncan Kelly," she said with a warning look as they left. "We'll be savin' the most fragrant bubbles for you."

A small giggle escaped from behind Evangelia's thumb as they stepped from the room and headed down the plushly carpeted hallway.

Early the following morning, Sheridan left the children sleeping and went downstairs to hire a carriage. Little more than two hours later, she returned with packages filled with calico dresses, bonnets, aprons, petticoats, and leather high-low boots for Evangelia. For Duncan, she had found two pairs of Kentucky jeans with galluses, some bright print shirts, and ankle-boots like Lia's, only several sizes larger. She bought everything too large so they'd have room to grow.

The children hadn't moved from Sheridan's bed where they had spent the night.

"Wake up, you sleepyheads." Sheridan pulled back the drapes and sunshine flooded the room. Rubbing their eyes, they blinked in confusion when they saw the bundle of packages in Sheridan's arms.

"These are for you. Hurry. We'll need to see if they fit."

Duncan went first. He whooped with delight when he saw the boots. "Like a man's." He pulled one onto his right foot and pronounced it a proper fit. His fingers gently felt the smooth leather. His freckled face lit up as he tore open the other packages, whistling softly with each new article of clothing.

Evangelia watched her brother solemnly as he opened his packages. Finally, she gingerly untied her first parcel. Her dark eyes widened in disbelief, then slowly she lifted the red calico to her face. Rubbing it softly against her cheek, she popped her thumb in her mouth and regarded Sheridan quietly.

"There's more," Sheridan encouraged. "Open the others."

The little girl untied another package and held up a lace petticoat. For the first time, Sheridan noticed a hint of excitement in the child's expression.

"Come on, Lia. Open this one." Duncan thrust a heavier package into her lap.

Tiny fingers pulled the twine, releasing the brown paper to reveal the high-lows. She bit her lip in concentration and placed one delicate foot into a boot, then held the other boot out for the opposite foot.

Then Evangelia stood, grinning. Duncan knelt before her to fasten the buckles. "You look like a fairy princess, Lia," he said when he'd finished. "Fact is, even princesses don't have duds this nice."

Evangelia didn't answer, first staring happily at the boots, then into her brother's eyes as if trying to communicate something.

"It's all right, Lia," Duncan said, as if she'd spoken audibly. "These are yours to keep. No one will ever take them away." As if for confirmation, his gaze settled on Sheridan.

She nodded. "Aye." Suddenly, Sheridan was aware that something was amiss. How could she have overlooked it so long? Evangelia hadn't spoken. Not a word. A soft giggle over Duncan's bath. And a cry from a fearful nightmare during the night. She obviously wasn't mute, but since her arrival, the little girl hadn't uttered one word.

"Lia?" Sheridan spoke softly.

Evangelia looked up at her solemnly.

"How do you like your new clothes?"

The child shifted her gaze to the floor.

"Lia?"

"She likes 'em fine." Duncan answered for his sister.

"I was speaking to Evangelia."

He shrugged and turned away, but not before Sheridan noticed something akin to fear in his face.

"Lia?" she began again.

The little girl looked up at her, her light brows raised in a questioning manner. But she remained silent.

"Can you speak, Lia?"

Evangelia tilted her chin upward, her lips clamped together in a tight line. Her eyes were huge and dark.

"Duncan, can your sister talk?"

"Yeah, I guess."

"What do you mean, you guess?"

The boy sighed deeply. "She used to. So I know she can."

"How long has it been?"

"Since our ma died."

"How long ago was that?" Sheridan was aware of the little girl's penetrating gaze as she questioned Duncan.

"'Bout a year and a half, I reckon."

Sheridan considered the children standing before her — each dressed in her spare nightclothes and their new ankle-high boots. Their thin faces held expressions of fear and hopelessness.

"I s'pose you won't want us now." Duncan pulled at a lock of his red hair. His eyes wouldn't meet hers.

"Is that what you think, son?" She reached out for Duncan's small hand and pulled him closer, at the same time lifting Evangelia onto her lap. "I wouldn't be much of an Irishwoman then, would I? Desertin' you would be the same as desertin' my own kin."

She narrowed her eyes. "I don't ever again want to hear words such as you just spoke. God himself brought us together. He'll care for us all — see us through to our journey's end. I'm as sure of that as I am of being Irish."

Duncan grinned, and Evangelia snuggled closer to Sheridan, her thumb in its usual place. She lifted the toe of one big boot and turned it this way and that, admiring the look of it.

Sheridan smiled. The little girl's red-gold hair still smelled of roses from last night's bath.

"Heavenly Father," she breathed, "I know you've scooped the three of us into your lovin' arms. But I can't help wonderin' what you've got in store for us next."

CHAPTER

Five

After a hearty breakfast at the hotel, Sheridan hired a carriage and, with the children in tow, hurried into the city to buy supplies for their journey. After consulting a map detailing the narrow trails into the mother lode, Sheridan abandoned her plans to buy a wagon and settled instead on riding horses and pack mules.

At the livery she chose a spirited Appaloosa named Shadrach for herself, and for the children, she asked to see some older horses. They were led to a small corral. Evangelia ran ahead of Sheridan and her brother to pat the neck of a gentle palomino near the fence. It was love at first sight.

"We'll take that one," Sheridan announced to the stable hand.

"Lia wants to name her Buttermilk," Duncan said solemnly after watching his sister for a moment.

"How do you know that?"

The boy shrugged. "I just do."

Sheridan hesitated, studying the little girl's face. "Lia, do you like this one?

Evangelia buried her hair in the horse's mane, but not before Sheridan had seen a small smile.

"And what you do think about the name Duncan picked?" Lia peeked through the silky mane, her smile wider. "Then Buttermilk it is," Sheridan pronounced.

"And I'd like this one." Duncan had let himself through the gate and strode toward a lively sorrel. "He'll be Blaze — for the white spot on his head."

Sheridan noticed that the boy seemed very sure of himself around the horses, the way he patted them, ran his small hand up and down the muscled forelegs. "Sounds like you've had these names picked out for awhile."

"Maybe." Duncan rubbed his horse's neck and nodded. "This is a good piece of horseflesh," he announced in a grown-up voice.

Sheridan squinted at a small corral filled with a few swayback pack horses and several mules. She picked three pack mules to round out her caravan. When the bill was totaled, Sheridan raised her eyes toward heaven in thanks for dear Aunt Fiona's generous covering of the trip's expenses.

At the mercantile, Sheridan purchased three Hudson's Bay blankets for bedrolls, a canvas tent, and a dutch oven. The food supplies included smoked pork, beef jerky, flour, sugar, Irish oats, and sourdough starter. At the last minute, she added two pounds of exorbitantly expensive coffee, a needed luxury in her opinion. Tough days lay ahead, but at least she could start those days with a decent cup of coffee.

Just before leaving the mercantile, Sheridan inquired about keeping grizzly bears from raiding the camp's food supply. Following the shopkeeper's advice, she purchased a strong length of rope for wrapping their food and hanging it from trees.

The wide-eyed children listened attentively. But a few minutes later, at the gunsmith's next to the mercantile, their mouths fell open as Sheridan concentrated on her next purchase. After some deliberation, she picked out for herself a French clasp knife and a Hawken muzzle-loading rifle. She surprised the gunsmith and the children by easily swinging the twelve-pound rifle to her shoulder, squinting down the barrel, and pronouncing the .53 caliber just what she was looking for.

"You know how to fire that?" Duncan's voice was filled with awe.

"Aye." Sheridan didn't elaborate, just continued sighting down her new weapon. Then she asked the gunsmith for a cinch-bag of balls and another filled with black powder. "Add to that a powder horn, ramrod, and pick," she said sweetly, "with some linen patches, a wormer, and another cinch-bag filled with shot. Place it all in a leather bag with a strap. I'll be wearin' it around my neck — just in case we meet up with some ornery bear," she added with a smile to the stunned children.

The gunsmith, seeming too astonished to reply, just nodded as he filled her order. Then Sheridan ordered all purchases — horses and mules with packed supplies — to be readied for travel by sunup the following morning.

At her final stop, Bourke and Monaghan's Clothiers in the heart of the city, Sheridan bought traveling clothes. For herself, she chose a butternut leather riding skirt, matching boots, and two soft woolen shirts. To go with the clothing she'd already purchased for the children, she chose trousers and jackets to keep the wee ones warm in the mother lode's mountain climate.

As the shopkeeper tallied the bill of sale, Sheridan picked up a lacy white blouse, touching the soft folds of its gigot sleeves. A foolish choice for the wilderness, but Sheridan couldn't resist, especially after the shopkeeper mentioned the lace was from Ireland. With a small sigh, Sheridan asked for the blouse to be wrapped with the others.

Satisfied with the day's success, Sheridan again ushered the children into the waiting carriage, and they made their way along the cobbled roads leading back to the hotel.

"There is no stoppin' a woman, Mr. Marcus Jade," Sheridan breathed to herself as she settled into the vehicle's leather seat. "There is no stoppin' us when put to a proper task. No stoppin' us at all."

They rounded the top of the hill near the hotel, and she could see the hills east of the city, toward the mother lode. The sun hung low in the sky and cast a golden glow over the scene. Shamus could be just beyond those mountains. And she would find him. Aye, she would. She raised her chin a bit, thinking about Marcus Jade. The next best thing to finding her brother and the children's Uncle Sonny would be watching Marcus's face when she returned to San Francisco with the news of her accomplishment.

Just to see his expression will be worth it all, she decided as the carriage pulled by the portico of the hotel. *Sure, it will.*

Just as dawn began to lighten the mist-covered city, Sheridan and the children arrived at the stables. The three saddled horses whinnied softly, their warm breath visible in the early chill. Nearby, the mules stood quiet as statues, the heavy supplies tied to their backs. Long ears twitching and tails flicking, the animals were led from the corral and roped together.

"All right, now," Sheridan said, taking a deep breath. "Here we go." She helped Evangelia onto the palomino, placing the little girl's hands on the saddle horn. "I'll be holdin' the reins till you're used to ridin'."

The child nodded, her face pale.

Duncan, however, climbed onto the sorrel as if he'd been around horses every day of his life.

"Have you ridden before?" Sheridan wondered where he'd gained his experience.

"Yep." He jutted his chin in the air. "Lots of times." But he said no more.

After asking the proprietor about the departure schedules for the Bay ferry, Sheridan, with Buttermilk's reins in her hand, led the small caravan from the livery. Duncan followed behind Evangelia, and behind him, the three mules.

The sun broke through the bay mists just as they arrived at the wharf to catch a ferry. By midday, they were ashore at a place called Nettie's Landing. Within minutes, Sheridan led the small group away from the bay and onto a trail into small rolling hills covered with scrub brush and live oaks. They had passed only a few miles when Sheridan spotted the trail-head for the mother lode, exactly where the map had indicated.

Reining her horse to a halt, she turned to face the children. Duncan had seemed abnormally quiet since they left the livery, and she thought it best to say her piece before they traveled any farther.

"This is your last chance to change your minds."

Both little faces stared at her, eyes large, faces pale.

"We can't turn back after startin' down this trail." She certainly didn't want to get halfway to the gold country, only to have to return to San Francisco. "If there's any reason why you can't go on with me, you need to tell me now."

Evangelia popped her thumb into her mouth. With the other hand she twisted a strand of Buttermilk's mane. She wouldn't meet Sheridan's gaze.

Duncan's horse whinnied and danced sideways. The boy looked up at Sheridan, his freckles darker than usual on his worried face. "There is somethin' I forgot to tell you," he said.

Back in the city, Marcus Jade propped his feet on his desk and leaned back in his chair at the *Grizzlyclaw Gazette* office. For the thousandth time in two days, his thoughts turned to Sheridan. He wondered if she had begun to purchase her supplies. He pictured her pretty head spinning as she considered her needs for the journey, her dismay at finding no room on the mules for her capes and crinolines and beribboned shoes.

He'd spent the previous day biding his time to ride to Sheridan's rescue. At first he thought he'd give her at least three days to worry over the dilemma of choosing supplies. Then, like a knight to the rescue, he'd sweep in and offer his assistance. Now aware of her stubborn Irish ways, he'd not dare take over. He'd simply offer sage advice and the sound wisdom of his experience. It wouldn't really matter that he had no firsthand knowledge of traversing the mother lode trails. She, he figured, would be grateful for his help and probably wouldn't notice his lack of expertise.

But he found that three days was too long. He'd spent the first day turning over the operation of the *Gazette* to his father, figuring that as long as the paper continued to run, his traveling expenses would be covered. Marcus promised his father that, once he got there, he'd send hair-raising stories from the mother lode, boosting sales — and their income.

So, on the morning of the second day, Marcus was ready to plan his next move. Should he wait for Sheridan to come to him? Or should he drop by the California Palace, perhaps invite Sheridan for another supper in the Palace's elegant dining room?

Then a new thought struck him like a bolt of lightning: if Sheridan was as inexperienced as he figured, why hadn't she contacted him? She was in a hurry to leave for the gold country. That much was a fact. And he knew, from short but careful observation, that this was a young woman unused to twiddling her thumbs.

He swallowed hard. What if Sheridan had already left — had actually purchased her supplies and headed for the mother lode?

Just as quickly as the question came to mind, he discounted it. Two children and a woman untrained in the ways of the West? It was ludicrous to even consider it. Or was it? He tried to convince himself that Sheridan was probably still at the California Palace, trying to figure a way out of her dilemma. Maybe even trying to find a way to contact him.

He just hoped she'd come to her senses about the children. If Sheridan *had* been foolish enough to leave with them, he had a strong suspicion that they all could be in danger.

Something about the boy's story had bothered him. What was it? Duncan had said his father died in an Australian prison, his mother on a ship headed to San Francisco. Homeless, the boy had cared for his sister for a year and a half, living in Sydney Town, stealing food.

But what about shelter? Duncan never really said where they lived. San Francisco was too cold and dangerous a place for children to live outdoors — at least for very long.

Had the boy lied? Two children living on the streets for that length of time seemed unlikely.

It had bothered him the first time Duncan told his story, and now even more so, that the children's Uncle Sonny was seeking gold in the very place where Sheridan was headed. What a strange coincidence. How could Duncan have known?

Marcus was sorry now that he hadn't accompanied the boy when he fetched his sister in the carriage. At least there would be no mystery about the children's living arrangements.

He sat for a few more minutes, considering Duncan and Evangelia Kelly. With a deep sigh, he swung his long legs from the desk, realizing that his curiosity had gotten the best of him. He stood and grabbed his coat.

Minutes later, Marcus headed along the wooden sidewalk to a nearby livery. He didn't own a horse. Never had. Not many people knew how he detested them. His father accused him of fearing the beasts — said horses can smell a man's fear a mile away. Marcus didn't agree. He didn't acknowledge fear of anything: persons or animals. At least that's what he told himself.

He turned into the livery and hired a carriage. As the

vehicle clattered along the city streets, a brisk breeze began clearing the ocean mist and sharpening the afternoon shadows. By the time his hired rig pulled into Sydney Town, the shadows were stretching long and dark, casting foreboding images across the shanties and narrow, dirty roadways.

Marcus paid the cabbie and strode through the swinging doors of a seedy-looking tavern. He'd learned that innkeepers usually knew the goings-on about the neighborhood.

"Evenin'." The barkeep, standing atop a ladder and reaching for some mugs on a high shelf, nodded as Marcus entered. "What can I get you?" He lifted a shaggy brow above a leathery face. It appeared he'd once spent some time in the weather.

Marcus sighed and swung onto a high stool. "Just information. I'd like to ask you some questions."

At the far end of the bar, two unkempt miners looked up. He could smell them from where he sat. They didn't look friendly. Marcus ignored them.

"Nothin' here's free," the barkeep drawled. Frowning, he stepped down from the ladder and moved toward Marcus.

"Know any Australian orphans here in Sydney Town by the name of Kelly?"

"Who wants to know?"

"I do. Otherwise I wouldn't be asking."

"Don't get smart, mister. It won't get you anywhere."

Marcus could feel the miners' hostile eyes boring through him. He didn't turn, just kept his gaze steady on the man before him. Then he sat back, squaring his shoulders, hoping to appear tough. "So what's it gonna cost?"

"A fiver."

Marcus guffawed. "Hey, nothing's worth that." He stood to leave.

"Then make me an offer." His eyes narrowed. "I do have news of the boy, if that's your worry."

"You know where he lives?"

"I might."

Marcus pulled a coin from his pocket.

The barkeep stared at Marcus's palm. "That's not gonna buy you an address."

Marcus added two more coins, and the barkeep's eyes brightened. His bushy brows turned upward in the middle. "Boy's been around here," he said. "Did odd jobs for me once in a while."

"And?" Marcus prompted.

The man shrugged.

Marcus pulled out another coin. He was rewarded with a toothy grin.

"All right. You go on down to the next corner and turn right. You'll be goin' uphill — past the big sycamore. There's a livery on the left. Behind the feed yard in back, you'll see a shack about yea tall. That's where the boy used to live."

"What about the girl?"

"What girl?"

"His sister."

"Don't know anything about any little girl."

With a deep sigh, Marcus dug into his pocket. He slapped the coin on the counter. Quick as a wink, the money disappeared under the barkeep's chubby fingers.

"Oh, yes. The boy did mention once about his sister. Leah, I think he called her."

Marcus tried to be patient. "You said 'used to live.' How long ago did they leave the place?"

"Goin' on two years ago, I suppose."

"Know why they left?"

The man shrugged. "To live in an orphanage, I heard."

Marcus cocked his head and squinted. "Then that's where they were last living?"

The barkeep ignored his question. "Until they went into the orphanage someone said the boy's baby sister was near starving, sickly. They both near froze in that little shack during winter. The boy was always on the streets, begging for odd jobs or just for food. Before long I heard that he finally took his sister to the orphanage. Lived there himself, too. Until lately."

"Until lately?"

"Yup."

"What happened?"

"Someone paid to get 'em out."

"What?"

"Yeah. The one that bought 'em got a real good deal."

"What do you mean?"

"Seven years work from them both in exchange for room and board, and, of course, what he paid the orphanage."

Marcus let out a low whistle. "What's the man's name — the one that bought them?"

The man's eyes glittered, but he remained silent, an expectant half-smile playing at his lips.

"Come on, man," Marcus said, exasperated. "These children need help."

"Guess it don't make much never-mind to me."

Marcus again dug into his pocket for another coin. The man was getting more than the original fiver. He narrowed his eyes and sat forward. "Who bought them?"

"You coulda saved yourself some money, mister." The barkeep sniggered. "I gave you the address right off. It was the owner of the livery that bought 'em." He nodded slowly. "Man named Titus Roderick. He took 'em in all right. After the legal papers were signed, sealed, and delivered to a bank vault, he moved those poor orphans into the same shack by the feed yard. And he worked the boy from dawn to midnight. Little girl was still too small. I heard tell he figured he'd get his money back from her later." The man shook his head slowly. For the first time a hint of sympathy crossed his face. "At least they got food. Probably not much more than pig slop, but it was somethin'."

"You're talking like they're no longer there."

"They aren't." The man grinned. "Heard they disappeared just a day or so ago."

Marcus kept his expression passive.

"Seems there's quite a price on their little heads."

"What?"

The barkeep seemed to consider holding out, then changed his mind. "Titus Roderick figures he wants 'em back, no matter the cost. Figures he's got at least another six-plus years they owe him."

"What kind of a reward?"

"More'n what you got, mister, or could ever dream to have." He stooped down and stared, eyes again glittering, at Marcus. "Unless, of course, you got information about these two orphans you ain't lettin' on." He frowned, leaning forward. "Why you comin' around here snoopin', anyway? How'd you find out about this boy and his sister? You know somethin' you're not tellin'?"

Marcus stared at him a moment, then stood. "You got a fiver?" he asked, a half-smile playing at his lips. When the man didn't answer, he went on. "You've set a precedent, you know, for question and answer exchange."

The man stared at him dumbly, his leathery nose wrinkling.

Marcus didn't comment further. "Good day, then," he finally said pleasantly and strode across the saloon floor, but not before he noticed the two surly miners had slipped out ahead of him. As he exited the swinging doors, he saw them turn right and head up the hill, past the sycamore, toward the livery the barkeep had earlier described.

Marcus hailed a cabbie. "To the California Palace," he called to the driver as he climbed inside. "And hurry."

Six

❧

The swaying carriage rounded the last curve before coming to a halt at the portico in front of the California Palace. After slapping a coin into the cabbie's hand and asking him to wait, Marcus sprinted, coattails flying, into the lobby and rushed to the registration desk.

"Miss Sheridan O'Brian — is she still a guest here?" He tapped his fingers impatiently as the bespectacled man behind the desk squinted at the names on the register.

"No, sir," he finally said. "I'm sorry. She and the children checked out two days ago."

Marcus drew in his breath. "What?"

"I said, sir, that the young lady in question checked out of our establishment the day before yesterday —"

"Where did she go?" Marcus interrupted. "Did you make arrangements for her to move elsewhere? Another hotel?"

The man scratched his balding head. "No. She asked for our carriage to take her into town before sunup. We, of course, accommodated her request."

"Where was she taken?"

"I don't know, sir. You could check at the carriage house in back. Perhaps the driver who accompanied her will remember."

"Yes, yes. I'll do that. Thank you." Marcus muttered as he headed for the door.

A short time later, he had the information he sought. Sheridan and the children, trunks and satchels in tow, had been deposited at a livery in town. The driver had seen the waiting horses and pack mules. He also remembered the exact location. Within minutes, Marcus was again heading into the city, shouting directions at the cabbie as they raced down the curves, the carriage rocking and clattering.

At the livery he found a stablehand, a young man who called himself Kitt ("with two *ts* so's no one mixes me with Mr. Carson," the man explained), who recognized the pretty Irishwoman's description. He gave Marcus a detailed account of her purchases and trail plans. Kitt also confirmed Marcus's fears.

"They've got at least a two-day head start on you." Kitt looked as if he could read Marcus's mind. "At least if you're of a notion to catch them," he added with a wink. "I can give you a map. I can show you an alternate route. A shortcut. With a fast horse you'll catch her in no time. What kind of a mount you got?"

"I…ah…" Marcus hesitated, looking around at the corrals. He sighed. "I'll need to buy a mount."

"Take your pick."

"And a saddle, of course. Whatever one needs when riding horseback."

"Leave it to me, sir." Kitt grinned. "We'll fix you with the works." He set about outfitting Marcus with a big stallion as black as obsidian. Its neck was elegantly — or arrogantly, depending on one's view — arched, and its eyes held a spit-fire that caused Marcus to swallow hard and take a deep breath.

"Name's Desperado." Kitt looked amused.

"I beg your pardon?"

He rubbed his beard and chuckled. "I said his name is Desperado."

Marcus looked into the horse's fiery eyes. "Fitting," he muttered, suddenly wondering how he'd landed here — soon to be atop this wild beast, chasing after a woman he barely knew, daring to ride to her rescue when he didn't even know if he could rescue himself.

He sighed. Just a week ago his only ambition was to make his *Grizzlyclaw Gazette* the best paper in northern California. He'd fashioned a sensible life for himself, selling what he thought was quality information and pleasing his readers with tales of the wild West. Tales he'd dreamed up, not lived.

And now because of the beautiful Sheridan O'Brian, he was about to experience those very stories. Or worse. All because of this woman whose eyes — sometimes violet, sometimes midnight blue — reflected a soul that drew him into an inner place of sweetness and light.

She had awakened something deep inside him. Something so wondrous, he could scarcely consider her without his heart turning somersaults. He was just beginning to realize that he'd gladly ride to the ends of the earth just to be with her, protect her, and help her care for the little ruffi-ans. Ends of the earth? The mother lode had been called worse. And he'd willingly face greater dangers than those in the gold country just to see her again.

Kitt broke into his thoughts. "If you'll go next door and purchase your supplies, I'll be happy to help you load up," Kitt said, scratching his beard.

Within minutes, Marcus returned with a bedroll and pouches of pemmican and jerky. Kitt asked about firearms as he tied the bedroll onto the back of the saddle.

"I don't carry a weapon."

Kitt grinned. "Well, from what I heard, your little gal bought one plenty big enough for the whole family."

Family? Marcus was first struck by how much he liked the word. He'd never thought about himself in that context. His mother died years ago. He and his father were partners, friends. Both had ink in their veins instead of blood. But Sheridan, the little ruffians, and Marcus a family? He sighed, considering the notion.

Suddenly his mind latched onto Kitt's other words. "She bought what?"

"A weapon." The stablehand tightened the rope around the bedroll and pulled it snug. "For the last two days it's been the talk of this end of town. The gunsmith can't keep his yap closed about it."

"About what?"

"The way she flipped that big Hawken to her shoulder as if it was nothing." He reached down to tie another knot. "Then sighted down the barrel. Said somethin' about needing it for grizzlies." He chuckled. "Seems she's been shooting all her life." Then, finished with his chore, Kitt slapped Desperado on the rump, causing the stallion to snort and dance sideways. "Well, sir, sixteen hands high and he's all yours. You just need to pay up and be on your way."

Within minutes, Marcus led Desperado from the stables and into the street. He hadn't dared to mount the horse in the livery. He feared he'd replace Sheridan's Hawken purchase as the topic of conversation among San Francisco merchants. Holding the reins gingerly and hoping above all hope that the beast wouldn't bolt, Marcus stuck a foot in the stirrup and swung across the saddle.

Desperado whinnied nervously and, nostrils flared, craned his neck and looked back. Marcus wondered if it was his imagination or if he really could see pulsating blood in the animal's eye. For a long moment, they stared at each other, then Marcus gently nudged Desperado's flanks. The horse reared, causing folks on the sidewalk to turn and gawk. Marcus briefly wondered if someone in the stable had fed the stallion a bucket of crazy weed. With an indignant snort and stamp of the hoof, the stallion headed down the center of the cobbled street, Marcus leaning low and hanging onto the saddlehorn.

Marcus reined the beast toward the *Grizzlyclaw Gazette,* where he would stop to tell his father his plans and pick up a change of clothes. At least, that was his intention if he could get the blasted beast to stop.

"You've got something you forgot to tell me?" The bright morning sun had risen higher and was beating down on Sheridan and the children. She nudged Shadrach into the shade of a nearby live oak. Duncan and Evangelia followed on their horses.

Sheridan's horse skittered sideways and she reined it closer to the boy's sorrel. "What do you have to tell me?"

The child bit his lip, and he looked down at the ground. Next to him, Lia clamped lips over thumb and fixed her eyes on something distant.

Sheridan touched the boy's arm. "What is it you're hidin'? You need to tell me. Now."

"I wasn't hidin' anything. I just thought it might be better to wait till now to tell you."

"Till now? And tell me what?"

He nodded, then answered only the first question. "Until we were out of the city."

"Why?

"Most likely we'll be followed." His eyes briefly met those of his sister. His expression softened, as if trying to convey a bit of comfort. Then he turned again to Sheridan. "I can't say for sure, but it's more'n likely." He swiped at his nose with the back of his hand, and Sheridan wondered if he might be thinking of crying.

She drew in a deep breath, frowning. "You still haven't told me why. Are you running from the law? Did you do something wrong?" The boy swallowed hard and looked down. "Are you really orphans?" she whispered, suddenly fearing she might have run off with someone else's children. She grabbed his arm and held it fast. "Tell me the truth. I've got to know." She put her fingertips under his chin and tilted his face toward hers.

The child's eyes were bright. She could see he fought against crying. He pushed her hand away and swiped at his nose again. "We ran away." His voice was barely a whisper.

"From home?"

Duncan shook his head. "No. We don't have a home. Just like we told you. Our ma and pa are both dead."

"Then who — or what — did you run from?"

The boy told her about the past three years, explaining to Sheridan in detail about their lives on the street, the move to the orphanage, how he and his sister suffered after they'd been taken in by Titus Roderick, and especially how they owed him years of work.

Sheridan let out a deep breath and tried to gather her thoughts. The boy was right. From everything he'd told her about Titus Roderick, the man would be hot on their trail.

"Did anyone see you leave the night you came to me at the California Palace?"

"I don't think so." His horse swished its tail at a pesky fly, and all around them bees hummed and butterflies flitted among the wildflowers.

"Then no one will guess where you've gone, will they?"

For the first time, the boy looked hopeful. His clear eyes met Sheridan's. "You're not mad?"

Sheridan noticed that Evangelia had moved the palomino closer and was watching her intently. "I'm disappointed you didn't tell me sooner — disappointed that you didn't trust me enough to tell me everything. Especially something like this. My knowing could have made the difference in whether or not we got away safely."

Around them the sounds of scrub jays and insects rose into the morning sky like a wild, soft music. After a moment, Duncan said, "You're not gonna send us back?"

"Of course not."

His freckled face broke into a wide grin. "Then we can stay?"

"As sure as we're all part of God's family, Duncan Kelly, you'll be stayin' as long as you and little Lia like." Sheridan reached for the little girl's hand, gave it a squeeze, and kissed her rough knuckles. Evangelia studied her solemnly but didn't pull away.

"It's our heavenly Father who's brought us together." Sheridan let the tiny hand go. "And he'll be takin' good care of us, too. You just wait and see." Then she nudged the Appaloosa to a slow walk, the children moved their horses behind Shadrach, pack mules in tow, and the small caravan started down the mother lode trail.

As they emerged from a thicket of fragrant sage and buckthorn, Sheridan gazed across the gently rolling foothills ahead. The autumn grasses shimmered in the soft winds like spun gold in the sunlight. The sky, a canopy of a nearly purple blue, stretched endlessly beyond the hills, touching the faint outline of the majestic Sierra Nevada in the distance.

"Ah, my Father," she breathed, feeling quick tears sting her eyes. "What beauty you've created! Your glory seems to stretch from here straight into the gates of heaven itself. How can I worry that a God of your power and magnificence might forget to watch over this little band?

"If you could create a world such as this, with the same power can you not care for the smallest part of your creation?" She looked down at Evangelia, then moved her gaze to the boy, following close behind. "And I think you love these innocent little ones more than any other," she prayed. "Help me care for your lambs. Help me do your bidding on their behalf, Father." Then she smiled to herself. "Though perhaps you'd better start by helpin' me figure out exactly what that bidding is."

They rode two hours, stopped for a quick midday meal of smoked pork and hardtack beside a nearly dry stream, then remounted and rode on through brush, now growing more dense than before.

Shadows lengthened, and the land took on a somber, ashen look in the fading light. Sheridan spotted a long stand of sycamores a few miles ahead. "Let's head over there." She nodded toward the place. "Looks like water nearby. It will be a good spot to camp."

After they dismounted, Duncan led the unsaddled horses and unpacked mules to a grassy meadow to graze, then set up a makeshift corral near camp. A bit later Sheridan watched the boy check the animals for chipped hooves or sore muscles. The palomino seemed to have a sensitive spot on its left shoulder, and Duncan rubbed it down with liniment.

"We'll put on a warm compress after I get the fire goin'," he announced as he led the animals into the corral.

Sheridan whispered a prayer of thanks for the boy's familiarity with livestock care. At least some good had come from his years with the liveryman, Titus Roderick.

Then she took Evangelia by the hand and led her to a forested place by the water to look for dry twigs and branches. A few minutes later, Lia skipped among the grove of sycamores, humming to herself as she picked up small pieces of firewood, examining the turn of each dry leaf and crooked twig. She stooped to look at a clump of nearly spent lupines, picked one, and held it to a patch of sunlight. She stepped toward Sheridan and lifted the flower.

"It's pretty," Sheridan murmured, watching Lia intently.

But Evangelia shook her head vigorously.

Sheridan tilted her head and frowned. The little girl again lifted the purple-blue blossom and placed it on Sheridan's cheek near her eyes.

Then Sheridan knew. "My eyes are the same color?"

Evangelia nodded and, with a small smile, placed the wilting wildflower in Sheridan's palm, then went back to gathering firewood.

Duncan finished watering the horses and mules, then helped Sheridan pitch the tent and lay out the bedrolls. Sheridan raised her eyes heavenward, thankful for his help and, as darkness fell, for the company of both children.

After supper, Duncan leaned against a small boulder and Evangelia curled up close to Sheridan. Before them, the fire crackled and danced into the starry sky. The woodsmoke drifted among the leafy oaks and sycamores.

Sheridan began humming an Irish ballad, and before long, Duncan joined in.

"My mother sang that song to us," he said quietly after a bit. "She'd sit between our beds. Sometimes she'd hold our hands while she sang. Other times she'd play a little harp and want us to sing with her."

"I'm sorry. Did my singin' make you lonely for her?"

Duncan stared into the fire, his expression sad. "Yes," he finally said. "It made me miss her, but don't be sorry. When you were singin' I suddenly remembered what she looked like." He paused and turned away. "I've been so scared because for the longest time, I haven't been able to remember her face."

"But my song made you remember?"

The child nodded.

"What did she look like, Duncan?"

"She was pretty — like you, and her eyes were just the same." Duncan studied Sheridan's face.

"You're meanin' the same color?"

"Nah. It wasn't that. Hers were green. But there was somethin' inside that was different than most people's."

"What do you mean?"

The boy seemed embarrassed. "I dunno." He shrugged. "You've got somethin' different in yours, too."

Sheridan smiled softly. "I do?"

Again he looked away as he spoke. "Yeah, somethin' like carin' or love or somethin'."

"Your ma was a carin' person?"

Duncan turned back. "Yeah."

"And people loved her, too, I'd imagine."

"Yeah."

"I bet you loved her a lot. You and Lia." Sheridan noticed that the little girl had turned away and was staring into the sky. "And you probably still do. Love her a lot, I mean."

"Yeah."

"You know something, Dunc? I noticed something about your eyes."

"Yeah? What's that?"

"There's something special in them, too."

He watched Sheridan carefully.

"They've got a soft light that I bet was just like your mother's."

"Yeah, that's it. A soft light — that's what hers had."

"I know just what you mean. Because I see it in your eyes and in Evangelia's too."

The boy's freckled face lit up in the firelight. "You do?"

"There's definitely something special there that you don't see in just everyone's eyes. I'm sure yours are just like your mother's."

His face spread into an even wider grin. "Yeah?" He poked a stick at the fire, the pleased expression still on his little freckled face.

"Aye," Sheridan said with a happy sigh. Then she reached out and pulled Evangelia close. The girl's thin shoulders were rigid, her mouth set in an angry line. She refused to look up as Sheridan cuddled her. But Sheridan didn't let go, just held her and gently stroked her arm. After a moment, Lia buried her face in Sheridan's lap. Sheridan gathered her closer, feeling her heart would break as she listened to the child's soft sobs.

CHAPTER

Seven

❧

Inside the tent, long after the children slept quietly on their bedrolls, Sheridan stared into the darkness. An owl hooted, its lonely call drifting from the top branches of a nearby oak.

Sheridan thought about the journey ahead, now more certain than ever that caring for the Kelly children must surely be part of God's plan. There was her mission to find Shamus and, of course, the children's Uncle Sonny.

Uncle? Her eyes widened. The children hadn't told her the whole truth about their running away. What if they had lied about their dear father's brother? Maybe it was no coincidence, his being in Everlasting Diggins, the same place she'd planned to look for Shamus. What if Duncan, in his desperation, had somehow found out about her mission, somehow "arranged" the meeting in the hotel dining room? What if…? Sheridan frowned, deciding not to go on with her internal guessing game. She would wait until the time was right to ask the children.

Her thoughts went to Marcus Jade. No matter what, she'd

never admit that he might have been right — that she had no business heading into the wilderness with two young children. No, she decided, it didn't matter how the children got here, how they ended up in her care. They were here, and just like a mother grizzly, she'd protect them with her life. Uncle or no uncle. Marcus Jade or no Marcus Jade.

She let out a small sigh, considering him. What a work he was, as Grandma'am would've said. Exasperating, yes. But a fine work. She pictured his wide, strong shoulders, the way he combed his fingers through his sun-streaked hair, the hint of humor in his expression, and his eyes: they were exactly the color of Irish seas on a misty day.

Sheridan pictured Marcus that first night they met. She remembered how he'd reached for her hand to help her down the stairs at the California Palace. She'd looked into his face, wondering how it could be that she'd not known him forever, yet at the same time feeling something fresh and beautiful awaken within her. For all his arrogant ways, there was also a sweet humbleness about him. She'd seen it when he'd bowed his head in prayer the night they dined. Aye, he was a work, all right. No man had ever touched her heart in such a way.

How many times during this, her first day on the trail, she had regretted her swift action, firing him the way she did. Grandma'am had often cautioned her about her temper, and sure enough, it had again pointed her down a path she really hadn't intended to take.

About to drift off to sleep, Sheridan heard a rustle in the brush. The hairs on the back of her neck stood on end. Footsteps, she thought. She listened carefully. Were they from man or animal?

She sat up and squinted into the midnight darkness of the tent, not daring to breathe. The sounds seemed to come from a stand of buckthorn near the other side of the corral Duncan had made. The rustling grew louder. Grizzlies, she suddenly remembered. Or savages. Her heart skipped a beat. She didn't know which was worse to consider.

Sheridan reached for the Hawken, pulling it to rest across her lap, glad she'd cleaned and loaded it earlier. The feel of its cold metal and heavy wood didn't make her feel any braver. Outside, one of the horses whinnied. Another snorted. Then the mules started in, bawling and kicking. A horse neighed in fright. She worried the lot of them would bolt and run into the night.

Well, as her grandma'am used to say, no good ever came of sittin' still and doin' nothing. A wrong decision was better than no decision at all. Sheridan's heart seemed to thud so loudly she worried it would surely wake the children.

She took a deep breath, stood, Hawken in hand, pulled back the tent flap, and stepped outside. The embers of the nightfire cast a pale glow around their campsite. Beyond the small area, though, midnight's black canopy obliterated everything else from view.

The rustling in the brush stopped abruptly, but the still-frightened mules continued their braying and bawling. And the horses snorted and kicked.

"Who's there?" Sheridan forced a low, strong tone into her voice.

An owl screeched, and Sheridan shivered. But no one answered.

"Identify yourself. Who's there?"

No one answered. Maybe it was a grizzly. Or a mountain

cat. Sheridan's imagination began to run wild. She grasped the muzzle-loader tighter. Just one shot would probably frighten the beast off. She'd aim at the treetops. The sound would reverberate through the night, loud and mighty. A warning if the midnight visitor was human. A signal to flee if the visitor was not.

Of course, she'd have to reload. Fast. There wouldn't be much time if the midnight visitor decided to come after her.

Sheridan lifted the Hawken to her shoulder.

In the distance, Marcus Jade halted Desperado atop a small knoll. Since darkness fell, he'd been heading toward a pin-prick of light on the gentle slope of the foothills ahead. He hoped it was Sheridan's campfire, but of course, he wouldn't be sure until he arrived.

The stallion had kept up a brisk but steady gait since they'd found their way through the city to the mother lode trailhead. Marcus had given the animal its lead, figuring the horse would set its own pace anyway. But after nightfall, with only a star-spangled sky to light the trail, they'd slowed con-siderably. For the first time, Marcus appreciated Desperado's sure-footedness. He even patted the animal on the neck and told him so. The big beast didn't seem to appreciate the kind gesture, however, and simply laid his ears flat in reply.

Marcus squinted into the dark, measuring the distance to the campfire. Riding hard, they'd make it in just a few hours. But at their present pace, they'd probably not overtake Sheridan until daybreak.

He let out a long sigh and rubbed his lower back, trying not to think of the blisters he'd acquired. Nearby, a mockingbird warbled its nightsong, and a spotted owl called from atop a distant branch, then lifted silently into the starry sky. Desperado danced sideways, impatient to continue.

"Well, come on, old man," Marcus muttered, clumsily patting the horse's neck and nudging its flanks. "Let's be on our way."

The horse sniggered and, with a toss of the head, stepped gingerly into the deep night.

For two hours they rode slowly. Desperado seemed to sense the watering holes and, without waiting for a signal from Marcus, headed from creek to stream, then back to the trail. Often the stallion stopped to nibble at a low-growing sage, leaving Marcus tapping the saddlehorn impatiently. If Marcus attempted to move him forward, the horse merely flattened his ears and continued chewing.

From time to time, Marcus lost sight of the distant campfire and peered uneasily into the darkness. Then they'd round a curve or cross a hill, and he'd spot it again. They rode on through the night, and another hour or two passed. Sometimes the dimming campfire appeared ahead to guide them, other times only bleak darkness lay ahead.

Then the small light disappeared completely.

Marcus urged Desperado to a hilltop slightly off the trail. This time the horse obeyed. Marcus dismounted and stretched his sore muscles while the horse nibbled on some underbrush. Perhaps he should camp for the remainder of the night. Ride again at sunup.

No, he needed to hurry to Sheridan's side. Nothing would stop him. Not a headstrong horse. Not even the lack of his little guiding light. Not with what he'd discovered about the children and about the reward for their return. All three could be in great danger. He might not be the only person hot on their trail. He had to get there first.

He patted Desperado's shoulder, preparing to mount. The horse moved away and eyed him suspiciously, ears back.

"Okay, mister." He sighed heavily, glaring at the beast. "Don't put on that loftier-than-thou attitude with me. You just hold still so I can get on." Surprisingly, the ears twisted forward, and the animal held steady while Marcus swung a leg over the saddle.

They'd ridden only another mile or so when Marcus heard the shot. It rang across the hills, echoing like distant thunder.

He thought about Kitt's words — how Sheridan's purchase of the Hawken had all the merchants in town abuzz with the gunsmith's word of her expert handling.

The Hawken. It had to be. He frowned. The muzzle-loader was big enough to take down a buffalo. And it certainly was big enough to sound like thunder.

This time he kicked Desperado hard in the flanks, almost daring him to ignore the command. But the horse, somehow sensing the urgency, seemed to fly into a gallop, a fluid movement of raw power and grace.

Sheridan took the Hawken from her shoulder and, after her heart stopped its mad pounding, smiled nervously, her knees weak.

A large raccoon waddled out of the brush. Behind it followed a family of three nearly grown kits. The four animals stopped and peered at Sheridan, their black masks giving them a comical appearance.

"What happened?" A sleepy Duncan joined her. Beside him, Evangelia rubbed her eyes and squinted at the raccoon family. The little bandits stared back, still as statues.

Sheridan chuckled. "We've got some night visitors. I was thinkin' an animal was maybe gettin' after the livestock, so I fired to scare it off." She took Lia's hand and led the children back into the tent. "I'm sorry I woke you."

After the children slipped once more under their covers, Sheridan placed a few more sticks of wood on the fire to keep it burning until morning. In its bright glow, she reloaded the Hawken. She carried the gun inside the tent, then lay down, resting her hand on its heavy wood stock.

But she couldn't relax. Outside, the night sounds continued, the owls' hoots, the bats' high-pitched squeaks, somehow more ominous than musical. The horses and mules remained restless, their nervous bawling and snorting magnified in the stillness of the night.

A twig cracked near the tent.

Sheridan grabbed the Hawken and pulled it closer. Biting her lip, she took a deep breath. It had to be her imagination. Or another furry masked bandit.

Then another twig popped.

Suddenly all was silent, the horses, the mules, the nightbirds. Too silent. Except for the unmistakable sound of heavy footsteps moving closer to the campsite.

Faster than lightning, Sheridan grabbed her weapon and flew from the tent. Again swinging the Hawken to her shoulder, she sighted down the barrel, pointing it to the place where she knew someone waited in the shadows.

Through the low-hanging branches of a sycamore, Marcus Jade saw Sheridan step from her tent. The glow of the night-fire illuminated her perfectly, her porcelain face framed by raven hair, her lacy chemise looking more silver than white in the starlight. And — he gulped — the Hawken by her side.

Before he could react, even call out, she raised the rifle and pointed it straight at him.

"One move closer, mister, and I'll be firin'." Her voice was barely more than a whisper. But she didn't sound scared. Marcus could see her finger on the trigger.

"Sheridan," he called out, though not daring to move for fear she'd fire. "Sheridan, it's me."

She held the rifle in place. Marcus knew he was still in her sights.

"Who?"

"Me — Jade. Marcus Jade."

Finally, she lowered the weapon and leaned it against the tent as Marcus stepped out of the shadows.

"You gave me quite a fright, Mister Jade." She looked stricken. "You shouldn't be creepin' up on people like that."

He moved toward her and reached for her hands. "Are you all right? I heard gunfire earlier."

She tilted her head in that way that nearly drove him to distraction. He swallowed hard and went on. "I worried that you'd been hurt."

"How long have you been following me, Mister Jade?" She pulled back her hands, looking disappointed in him.

"Not long," he said, mildly irritated at her thinking. He knew what was coming next.

"You didn't believe me when I said I could take care of myself? You've been lurking behind, waitin' to ride to the damsel's rescue?"

Marcus let out an exasperated sigh. His backside hurt; his blistered legs had been nearly rubbed raw. The blasted horse had tried his patience nearly to a frazzle. He was tired and hungry. And this was the gratitude he got. Marcus set his lips tight and stared at the beautiful woman before him.

"Lurking?"

"Aye. Lurking."

Marcus shook his head slowly and turned away. For a moment he studied the dying embers of the fire. "We'll talk about it in the morning," he finally said. Without another word, he headed toward Desperado.

"Mister. Jade." Her voice was so soft he nearly didn't hear it. "Mister. Jade," she said again before he was out of sight.

He turned.

"I'm sorry."

He stared at her without answering.

"My grandma'am always said I too often speak from the place of my temper — without usin' my mind. Or my heart."

Sheridan looked so fragile, standing there in the golden glow of dying nightfire, her eyes wide with an emotion he couldn't fathom. A gentle breeze brushed against the lace on her nightclothes and lifted a strand of hair across her face. She pulled it back, twisted it daintily with her fingers, and hooked it behind an ear.

"Please be forgivin' of me, Mister. Jade." The soft Irish lilt in her voice touched him.

Marcus's voice was gruffer than he intended when he finally answered. "As I said, we'll speak more of my

89

intentions in the morning," he said.

She turned to enter the tent.

"One more thing." He let out a deep sigh.

Sheridan looked up at him.

"Could you please quit calling me Mister Jade?"

She nodded. "Marcus," she said softly with a small smile. Then she picked up the Hawken and pulled back the tent flap.

"Oh, and there's something else."

Her gaze met his expectantly.

"There's nothing to forgive. I acted unkindly back in San Franciso the last time we met. You were right in suspecting the worst."

"I shouldn't have doubted that you'd simply come to help, Marcus, no matter how long you'd been followin' our little band."

"I rode out this morning — actually yesterday morning," he said, looking east where the faintest glow of dawn announced the new day. He smiled gently. "But I'll explain it all later. For now, let's try to get some rest. We've got a long day ahead."

Sheridan nodded and daintily covered a yawn.

Marcus headed back to the place he'd tied Desperado, only to find that the horse had disappeared, saddle, saddle-bags, and bedroll still on the animal's back.

With a grumble that spoke not too kindly of the beast, Marcus returned to the campfire. He lay down without cover against the early morning chill or even a saddle for a pillow.

His eyes closed, and Marcus fell, aching and exhausted, into a dreamless sleep. A bit later he turned over and moved closer to the dying fire.

Marcus paid little attention to the sounds of approaching horsemen from the west. He merely yawned and drifted back to sleep, sure that the hoofbeats were those of the returning Desperado.

Eight

༂

"Wake up, Miss Sheridan!" The boy's voice was a frantic whisper.

Sheridan opened her eyes, momentarily forgetting where she was. Then she focused on the tent, the bedrolls and scattered children's clothing, and finally the two frightened faces leaning over her.

"Please, wake up," Duncan whispered again, his voice choked with fear. Beside him, a wide-eyed Evangelia noisily sucked her thumb.

"What's wrong?"

"Someone's outside."

"I know, Duncan. It's Marcus Jade. He rode in during the night."

Duncan nodded vigorously. "I know his voice, but there's other folks out there. I hear 'em. They're mean-soundin'."

Sheridan quickly sat up, signaling the children to be silent. Creeping to the side of the tent, she knelt near the closed flap, listening to snatches of the conversation.

"I'm trying to find them, too." Marcus's voice was a low

growl. "But you could've asked me that back there. I certainly don't know why in tarnation you'd follow me clear out here just to find that out."

Someone answered, but Sheridan could only make out a word or two. Something about a tavern, then a mention of Titus Roderick. She glanced at the children. Their eyes were large with fear.

She reached for Evangelia and cuddled her close.

Then Marcus spoke up again, his voice sharp. "I'm as interested in finding the orphans as the next person, but I hit a dead end. I decided to give it up for now. Besides I've got better things to do."

"Like what?" the guttural voice muttered.

But Marcus didn't answer. A few more words were spoken, then Marcus spoke up again, his voice angry. "No," he said. "You're not going in there!"

Sheridan heard the crunch of footsteps coming toward the tent.

"I wouldn't go in there if I were you."

A low guttural laugh was his only answer.

"My wife's in there."

Sheridan heard his words and her eyes widened. His wife?

"So's, what's the problem?" the guttural voice went on. "I just want to see if'n she's got any company."

"That's what I was referring to earlier. She's not feeling well right now."

The footsteps halted.

"What's she got?" The question came from a higher pitched voice. "Is it catchin'?"

"Don't matter," the lower voice said. "You git in there and have a look-see."

Sheridan motioned to the children to move to the back of the tent. Then she took a deep breath and let out a low moan followed by a cough.

Outside, all was silent.

She winked at the children and moaned again. Duncan covered his mouth to stifle a giggle. Even Evangelia smiled behind her thumb.

"What's she got?" The high-pitched voice asked, sounding worried.

"Came on like wildfire," Marcus said. "We don't know what it is. Though cholera sometimes comes on sudden like this."

"Cholera?" the high-pitched voice squeaked.

"I've heard of recent cases around here," Marcus began.

"Water," Sheridan called out weakly. "Bring me some water. I'm thirstin' to the point of near dyin'." She wailed again, waited a moment, then coughed. "Please, hurry."

There were scuffling sounds around the campsite. After a moment, the sounds of hooves could be heard pounding the earth as the men rode off.

"They're gone," Marcus called out.

Sheridan grabbed her robe and pulled back the tent flap. She was met by Marcus's dazzling smile.

"Your wife?"

He grinned. "Are you sure you're well enough to be up and about?" He laid down the wood he'd gathered for the morning fire. "I was about to go for water."

"I did it for the children."

"I know."

"I don't believe in lyin'." The children were in the tent pulling on their britches and shirts and combing their hair.

Sheridan figured it was better to speak of the early morning visitors out of their hearing. "I fear for the wee ones, Marcus. Those men sounded like animals."

Marcus looked up from the firewood he was setting, tepee style, into the cold firepit. "What you did protected the children, Sherrie. You convinced the men to leave. That was a whole lot better than shooting at them."

Sheridan liked how he'd called her Sherrie. No one but her family in Ireland and her dear friend Callie had ever called her that. It reminded her of home and the people she loved. She blinked away the unexpected mist in her eyes.

Marcus suddenly frowned. "Did Duncan tell you why they ran away? Why Titus Roderick is hunting them?"

"Aye, the boy did." Sheridan sighed and sat down on a nearby log. The morning sun cast dapples of light across the man in front of her. His hair held glints the color of ripe wheat.

Marcus finished with the fire, stood, brushed off his pants, then sat down on the log with her, stretching his long legs out in front of him. "I found out yesterday that Titus has offered a hefty reward for the children," he began.

Sheridan caught her breath. "A reward, Marcus?"

He nodded. "For their return. Seems he's determined to have them back." He paused and squinted west, seeming to consider the place where the riders had just left. "The men who were just here heard me make inquiries yesterday in Sydney Town. They thought I knew something about the children." He turned back to her. "I'm sorry. I didn't think about being followed. I should've been more careful."

"That's why you came? To warn me?"

"Yes. And to help you and the children — if you want me."

Sheridan smiled. "Of course you're wanted, Marcus. And needed. I'm sorry for the unkind things I said about you before. We really do need help — especially from someone like you."

"Like me?" At first he didn't understand.

"A detective. Finder of lost persons."

"Oh." He looked toward the now blazing cookfire, unable to meet her admiring gaze. He waited a few minutes before again turning to her.

She looked more lovely than she could ever know, the early morning light gently touching her face, the dimple in her chin, her dark, silken hair. And when she lifted her violet eyes to meet his gaze, his heart nearly stopped beating. But it was her trusting expression that rendered him nearly speechless.

"What is it, Marcus?" She frowned, understanding he had something else to say.

"I've got," he began, then decided he couldn't continue. He needed to gain her trust first, prove to her that he cared for her, for the children. A few days down the trail he'd confess the deception. Or perhaps when they got to Everlasting Diggins. Then he'd tell her everything and ask her forgiveness.

"I'm worried about others coming after the children. The two old miners who just left here will probably spread the word that they heard me asking around in Sydney Town. It won't take long for someone else to head out here after us."

Just then the tent flap opened, and the children raced out. Sheridan put her fingers to her lips, and Marcus said no more.

"Mister. Jade!" Duncan, delighted to see Marcus, ran to his

side. "When did you get here?" Evangelia climbed into Sheridan's lap and cuddled against her.

He patted the boy on his back. "Just before sunup."

"You gonna stay?"

Marcus's eyes met Sheridan's, and she smiled. "As sure as God made Ireland, he is," she said happily.

Duncan tugged at his hand. "Come with me to the corral. I'll show you the livestock." As they walked, the boy told Marcus all about the horses: Buttermilk, Shadrach the Appaloosa, and especially Blaze, his sorrel. "And we've got mules," he added excitedly. "Wait till you see 'em. And I'm in charge of carin' for 'em all."

"Then maybe you can help me find my stallion," Marcus muttered to the boy as they left camp.

After a breakfast of hotcakes, baked apples, and coffee, the small band packed up and headed down the mother lode trail. Desperado had been found grazing in the tall grass by the creek, saddle, saddlebags, and bedroll still strapped on. The animal seemed only mildly surprised to see Marcus again. As usual, he stared, fiery-eyed, at Marcus when he mounted.

For three days, the little caravan traveled east, making their way slowly toward the gold country. Every day the sun beat down from a deep blue sky. At night the heat quickly disappeared, though, as mountain breezes chilled the land.

Usually, Sheridan kept the lead on the Appaloosa. Close behind followed Evangelia, then Duncan and the mules. Finally Marcus trailed at the end, keeping an eye out for unwelcome riders who might be following, but also glad no one would notice his horse's irreverence for its rider.

As they moved eastward, the countryside changed from rolling hills to mountains of considerable height, covered with tall, dry grasses. From a distance, Sheridan noticed, the mountains appeared soft as velvet, but up close they were as rugged as any she'd ever seen. The forests of oak were thicker now, no longer simply dotting the landscape, and the sycamores had all but disappeared. In the distance, the towering Sierra Nevada rose majestically.

As they rode, Sheridan pointed out colorful birds, so different than those she had known in the East. There were scrub jays and mountain bluebirds, woodpeckers that reminded her of butlers dressed in fancy black suits and white shirts. Even Evangelia giggled when Duncan found he could draw a flock of scolding jays by gathering acorns and throwing them in the air for the birds to catch. But Sheridan's favorite was a tiny gray bird called a titmouse for its cocky topknot of feathers. Often hawks circled above them, gliding, dipping, and almost dancing in the air, red tails reflecting the sun.

From time to time they passed Indian women gathering the seeds of wild sunflowers. Sheridan was in awe of the exotic women, with their dark and shining skin, their lithe limbs and graceful figures. Even the large baskets the women carried were delicate and appeared to be light in weight, beautiful works of artistry and function.

One night at their campfire, Sheridan commented to Marcus about the small bands of Indians they'd seen nearly every day. He explained that the women gathered the flower seeds to mix with pounded acorns and grasshoppers to make bread flour.

"Grasshoppers?" Duncan stuck out his tongue and made a face. "Ugh!"

Evangelia wrinkled her nose and buried her face in Sheridan's skirts.

"It's probably very good," Marcus said.

Duncan interrupted. "Have you ever eaten any?"

"No," he said with a laugh. "I've just read about it."

"You read a lot?" Sheridan's admiration was clear.

"Yes. It's part of my job." Marcus realized his mistake as soon as he'd said it.

"I wouldn't think a private detective would have much time to read," she said with a smile. "Seems to me that you'd need to be out lookin' for lost people."

Marcus swallowed hard. He didn't answer.

The following morning, they started out again. As usual, Sheridan took the lead on Shadrach. This day, however, Evangelia, on the palomino, lagged behind, taking her place near Marcus on Desperado.

"You're going to ride back here with me today?"

Evangelia nodded, holding onto Buttermilk's reins with one hand and twisting a strand of the palomino's mane into a curl with the other.

Marcus was concerned that Desperado, with his skittish, spirited ways, might spook the child's horse. "You'll have to ride slowly and quietly, staying close by me."

The little girl nodded that she would.

"That's somethin' you don't have to fret about," Duncan called back from in front of the mules. "Her makin' noise." He pushed his carrot-red hair out of his face, frowning. "I just wish she'd make more. Bein' quiet's worse'n yellin' once in a while."

Marcus figured the boy had been Evangelia's champion for so long, he couldn't let go of his worries about her. "She'll be fine with me," he called up to the boy, and he hoped that it would be true.

He looked again to Evangelia. "And we'll be eating mule dust."

She shrugged and gave Marcus a shy smile.

"All right then, you're officially my partner for today."

The smile grew wider, then the ever-present thumb popped into her mouth. The sun gleamed on her pale red hair that Sheridan had earlier plaited into two narrow braids. He was suddenly aware of her fragile appearance. How could the little girl have survived in this rough country without mother or father? Her brother had somehow kept her safe, but not without emotional scars — her unwillingness to speak told Marcus that. The tragedy she'd seen was probably nearly too much to bear, too much to speak of. Someday maybe she'd feel safe enough to talk. At least Duncan had made it possible for his little sister to survive.

As they moved out, Marcus watched Duncan, sitting as proud as any man atop his horse, driving the mules, facing the unknown future, acting braver than most adults. And all the while, playing guardian angel to little Evangelia.

Marcus considered the children, wondering what lay ahead for them. They deserved better than the hardships life had offered them so far. Much better.

Sheridan had been right to gather them into her arms. And he felt ashamed that he hadn't done the same.

They wound deeper into the foothills. From time to time

they passed miners, usually alone with a pack animal or two, heading out of the mother lode. Most of the grizzled men looked disheartened, some even defeated. Marcus wondered if they were moving on because of dreams that hadn't worked out.

Near midday, the caravan entered a deep gorge that led to the Stanislaus River. Sheer cliffs of granite and sandstone dropped from heights of several hundred feet.

"We're nearly into the mother lode," Marcus called up to Sheridan. He didn't mention he'd only read about the area in books and seen it on maps. "This is the beginning. From here we head north up the canyon, cross the river, then it's only a short distance to Everlasting Diggins."

Sheridan nodded and signaled the others to halt. Marcus nudged the stallion closer and followed her gaze toward the winding trail up the cliffs.

"It's not very wide," she breathed in awe. "I'm wonderin' if we can go up side by side."

Marcus swallowed hard, thinking of Desperado and his mean-spirited tricks. "Maybe in some spots," was all he could muster.

"Wow," Duncan said softly, craning his neck upward. "Look at that."

Evangelia moved Buttermilk closer to the others, reached for Marcus's hand, and held on tightly.

By the time the band reached the cliffs, the sun cast long shadows across the canyon walls.

"Don't look down once we start climbing," Marcus admonished. He'd read that somewhere. He was surprised his voice sounded braver than he felt. Then he smiled widely at Sheridan. "Do you want me to lead?"

She bit her lip. "No, no. Let's keep on in the same order. You'll keep behind Buttermilk?"

He smiled at Evangelia. "We'll be fine, won't we, Champ?"

She giggled softly behind her thumb.

"We're ready back here."

Sheridan suddenly turned. "Do you think we should wait till morning — I mean, maybe the animals would be fresher. And it might be dark by the time we reach the top."

Marcus gazed at the narrow trail ahead. "No," he said, thinking of other things he'd read. "The morning mists from the river might make the walls more slippery than ever. It's better we go now." He hoped he was right.

"Aye," Sheridan answered, her voice sounding small. "Let's be on our way then." She took a deep breath and nudged Shadrach into action. The Appaloosa scrambled up the steep trail. Loose rocks clattered down the incline behind her.

"Hah!" Duncan kicked his horse, and the beast clambered upward, followed by the tethered mules.

"All right, Champ." Marcus smiled at Evangelia. "Your turn — oh, and you'd better hold on with both hands."

She leaned over the palomino's neck, holding the reins tightly. When she was set, Marcus swatted the horse's rump, and with a movement of grace and agility, Buttermilk leapt forward up the trail. With surprising strength, the little girl hung on, braids flying behind.

"Okay, Desperado, it's just you and me," Marcus muttered, patting the horse's neck. The stallion's ears flattened. "You may not like the looks of this any better than I do, but if we go over the side, you're as dead as I am. Keep that in mind."

Marcus could see the others up ahead, their horses now picking their way along the terrifyingly narrow trail, shining granite cliffs on one side and a sheer drop-off on the other.

Drawing a deep breath, Marcus kicked Desperado's flanks. The horse snorted and reared, and for a heartbeat, Marcus thought the animal would leap over the side. Then with a movement as fluid as quicksilver, Desperado clambered upward, hooves clattering, small rocks bouncing down the cliff behind them.

Marcus fought the urge to simply close his eyes and wait till the horse had borne him to safety. Instead, he hunkered over the stallion's neck and watched the trail ahead, leaning as if one with the animal.

Within moments they'd caught up with the others as they slowed on the precarious and winding path.

Then Marcus noticed Evangelia's eyes were scrunched closed, and she'd let go of the reins and clung instead to Buttermilk's mane.

"Champ," he said softly. "You need to grab hold of the reins. Easy now, just reach down and find them."

She didn't move. Her little face was white.

"Lia, do as I tell you. Now. It's important."

Evangelia shook her head, clamping her lips together. Her eyes remained tightly shut.

Up ahead the path widened a bit and Marcus nudged the stallion closer to the girl. Then, leaning forward as far out of his saddle as he dared, Marcus made a grab for the palomino's reins. He missed.

"Champ," he said calmly. "Please. Reach for the reins."

But she seemed paralyzed with fear.

Marcus swung forward and made another grab.

Then his heart stopped at the sound he'd worried about hearing since leaving San Francisco.

A rattler! Close to the trail.

It rattled again.

One of the mules brayed in fear. The other two bawled. At the same time, the horses reared, whinnying.

Desperado bolted upward, front legs kicking, back legs fighting to hold fast to the trail.

Buttermilk bucked sideways. The child flew off the horse, a tumbling bundle of calico and red-gold braids.

The last thing Marcus saw before he fell backwards from his saddle was a tiny boot-clad foot twisted in the stirrup and the palomino scrambling madly for its balance at the edge of the cliff.

Nine

❧

Tucking his head, Marcus rolled with the fall, taking most of the blow with his left shoulder. Near him, Desperado caught his balance and, scuffling and snorting, backed onto the trail. Eyes wild with fear, the palomino still bucked and whinnied. Evangelia lay in a crumpled heap, dangerously close to the cliff's edge. Her foot had obviously been thrown loose from the stirrup.

The rattlesnake buzzed wildly just inches from her leg. It had slithered into a coil.

"Don't move, honey." Marcus spoke softly, holding her gaze, willing her to believe him and obey.

In her fear, the child's eyes seemed too big for her small, white face. She held perfectly still.

Several yards farther up the trail, Sheridan had halted the other horses and the pack mules. She and Duncan silently watched Marcus and Evangelia. Just before he started moving toward Evangelia, Marcus thought he saw Sheridan's lips moving in silent prayer.

Letting out a breath, Marcus grabbed a long manzanita

branch and held it as he scooted closer. "Don't move, Champ," he whispered again. "No matter what happens, don't move." He knew the snake would strike if she so much as blinked or, even more likely, popped her thumb into her mouth. "I'm coming. Everything will be all right. I promise," he murmured. "I'm almost there. Remember, don't move."

The snake, in a coil, rattled again, sounding louder than thunder to Marcus. He wished he'd read something about fighting rattlers. Even if he'd brought a weapon, it would do him no good. The snake was too close to Evangelia to shoot.

"Okay, now. Here goes." Marcus was within a few feet of the child.

Her unblinking eyes never moved from his.

In one fluid motion, Marcus leapt to his feet, swinging the branch forward.

The rattler struck just as Marcus hit it. Dead center. The snake flew into the air. It sailed upward, almost seeming to float in the air. Then it plunged into the deep gorge, disappearing into a clump of granite rocks hundreds of feet below.

Evangelia reached for Marcus just as part of the dirt and stone cliffside gave way. Rocks clattered downward, bouncing off the walls of the gorge. The little girl slipped toward the edge. She frantically grabbed a clump of turtleback brush. It stopped her from falling, but Marcus could see that the small plant would not support her weight for long.

"Keep still!" Marcus commanded.

She swallowed, her eyes never leaving his.

He flattened onto his stomach, crawling toward her, feeling for loose rocks as he went. Somewhere on the trail above, he could hear Sheridan speaking softly to Duncan, telling him to stay put.

"Now, reach out your arms. That's it, honey. Slowly, now, grab my hand."

Evangelia did as he told her.

As soon as he had a good grasp, he scooted her gently away from the edge. Closer. Ever closer, until she was safe in his arms. For a long minute, he knelt on the rocky trail, holding her close while she sobbed silently, clinging to him as if she would never let go.

"It's over," he said gruffly. "It's all right, now." He awkwardly patted Evangelia's hair and rocked her gently. "Everything's going to be all right, little champ." Over the top of her head, he could see Sheridan's and Duncan's worried faces. "She's going to be all right," he called up to them. Then he checked her limbs. Nothing was broken, but the ankle that had been caught in the stirrup was beginning to swell.

The child flinched when he touched it. Marcus pulled out a handkerchief and wrapped it tight. He'd once read that it kept down swelling and reduced pain. "And we'll get cold water on it as soon as we find some," he added knowledgeably.

She smiled softly when he'd finished, finally popping her thumb into her mouth.

He'd also read that if you fell off a horse, it was best to get right back on. But he knew that climbing back onto the palomino was the last thing this little girl needed. It was going to be hard enough for him to remount the blasted Desperado. "I think you need to ride with me," he said with a grin, hoping he looked braver than he felt. "You up to it?"

She nodded, and he set her on the stallion's saddle. He noticed that for once the big animal's ears didn't flatten. "Good boy," he said, patting the horse's neck. The horse danced slightly away from him, as usual, as Marcus swung a leg over the saddle behind Evangelia.

He lifted one hand in a salute, signaling to Sheridan that they were ready to continue. She gave him a shaky smile, then turned forward in her saddle and gently kicked the Appaloosa in the flanks. Dark mane flashing in the sun, the horse snorted, shook its head, and clambered up the trail. Duncan nudged the sorrel and yelled "gee-up" to the mules. Marcus soon followed, leading the empty-saddled palomino by its reins.

The small caravan once again trooped slowly up the narrow trail. Within minutes, Evangelia fell asleep, resting her head against Marcus's arm. She didn't wake until they reached their night campsite.

That night, after the children had gone to bed, Marcus asked Sheridan to accompany him on a walk to a nearby creek. She smiled and took his hand.

A full moon cast a shimmering silver light across the pines and oaks, enough light to walk without a lantern. A gentle breeze rustled the leaves of a nearby cottonwood. As they drew closer to the creek, its bubbling joined the soft hooting of owls and the occasional sounds of frogs to create the most beautiful night music Sheridan had ever heard.

Marcus stopped near an outcropping of boulders by the creek and leaned his back against it, crossing his ankles. Sheridan sat near him on a slightly rounded rock. The autumn night was crisp, and she was glad she'd pulled on her cottage-cloak; its hood draped down her back, adding extra warmth on her shoulders.

"It's beautiful," she said reverently, pulling the cloak close and staring into the sky.

"It is." Marcus was looking at Sheridan, not the moon.

She smiled at him. "Marcus, what you did today was wonderful. You saved Lia's life." Sheridan hadn't been able to erase the scene from her mind. He could have died trying to save the little girl.

"I only did what anyone would do."

"Aye, but you were there. And you knew exactly what to do — how to reach her, how to get rid of the snake." She sighed softly. "You comforted her, made her feel safe after it was all over. Not everybody knows how to do that."

Marcus looked out at the bubbling waters of the creek. For a long moment, Sheridan didn't think he was going to answer. A sadness seemed to settle in his expression. He frowned and turned back to her.

"What is it?"

"I've got something I need to tell you. It will probably change the way you feel right now."

She shook her head slightly. "I can't imagine —"

He interrupted. "I've deceived you."

"What do you mean?"

He let out a deep breath, the unhappiness on his face etched deeper than before. "I'm not who you think I am."

She tilted her head, confused. "Whatever are you meanin'? You're not Marcus Jade?" Her voice was a whisper.

"Oh, yes. I'm Jade. It's what I do that I've lied about."

"You're not a private detective?"

"No. Well, not exactly. I mean, I do investigate mysterious disappearances from time to time, nose around for stories, try to figure out mysteries."

"Aye?" Sheridan asked. "Then who are you, Mr. Jade? What *do* you do?"

"I'm a newspaperman."

She narrowed her eyes at him, beginning to understand.

"A newspaper publisher," Marcus continued.

"And editor." Her voice held no emotion.

"Yes," he said simply.

"Editor of the *Grizzlyclaw Gazette*."

"The same." He looked away as if he couldn't bear to see her disappointment.

"You're the editor I wrote to from the East?"

"Yes."

"Why didn't you tell me? I mean, right from the beginning, why didn't you just say so?"

He let out another long breath and turned again toward her. "I smelled a good story. I'd been writing about the gold country — that's why you'd heard of me. My *News Travels* editions were being sold in New York, Boston, Charleston, and heaven only knows where else. People were lapping up the stories like cats after fresh milk. Especially stories of drama and intrigue about the gold miners."

She stared at him, trying to take it all in.

He nervously combed his fingers through his hair. "The gold fever's died down. Folks weren't buying my paper the way they used to."

"What does that have to do with me? With Shamus?"

"I thought if I told the story firsthand — went along with you on the search, sent the stories back for printing...." He let his voice die, swallowed hard. "Each week there'd be a new installment. I was hoping to sell more papers." He turned to her, his eyes meeting her level gaze. "Can you understand?" He reached for her hand. She pulled it away.

"Aye, you were hopin' to cash in on my poor brother's plight."

"That was before I knew Sheridan O'Brian was you."

"It wasn't a dishonest thing to do to a man?"

"No, no. Of course it was."

"Answer me this, Marcus Jade. Are you still writin' your stories? Sending them into your *Grizzlyclaw Gazette* for your accomplice to print?" Sheridan thought she might cry.

"My partner happens to be my father. And he's not an accomplice."

Sheridan remembered the sweet elderly man she'd met at the *Gazette* office. "Your father?"

Marcus nodded slowly. "He doesn't know anything about my plan." An owl called out softly, and Marcus looked up into the top branches of an overhead oak. "He'd be ashamed if he did."

"And the stories?"

"I put aside the idea, Sheridan, that night at the California Palace. I decided I couldn't go through with it."

Sheridan tried to comprehend all he'd told her. She gazed into the moonlit night. A few minutes ago it had been so alive with promise. Now, the silvery light had turned to the color of ashes. Marcus wasn't who he'd said he was. He had deceived her. And now he expected her to tell him it was all right between them. He'd done everything he could to help her, to prove his worth. He'd even saved Lia's life today. Shouldn't his actions tell her more about who Marcus was than anything he'd just said? She sighed, again feeling close to tears.

She knew he watched her expectantly, wanting her to

assure him of...of what? What could she say? She couldn't begin to define how she felt. To herself. Or to him.

"Why did you tell me now?" She turned again to him, struck by the clarity in his eyes, the depth of emotion that reached out to her, threatening to hold her fast no matter what.

"Why?" she repeated, suddenly fighting the urge to turn her back and run from this place, run back into her tent, leaving Marcus standing there, stewing in the knowledge that he'd hurt her. Then she thought of Grandma'am's words of caution about speaking — and acting — from her place of bad temper instead of her heart. Sheridan whispered a silent prayer that she would stay rooted to the spot until she'd heard him out, and spoken to him from her soul.

"Don't you know, Sheridan?" he asked simply. "Can't you guess?"

She shook her head, slowly, sadly. "How can you be expectin' me to read your mind, Mr. Jade?"

"Sherrie, please listen. Don't turn away." He reached for her hands and lightly kissed her fingertips. "Since I met you, everything inside me has turned upside down. I've seen myself against a different measure." He paused as if trying to find the right words. "Your goodness, your honesty, your compassion —" Swallowing hard, he searched her eyes. "Everything I saw in you touched me someplace deep inside. I couldn't bear to...to lose being close to you. A thousand different times in the past few days I wanted to tell you; I just couldn't."

He let go of her hands and brushed his hair from his forehead. "You asked why now. Because I'm falling in love with you, Sherrie. I didn't expect it to happen, but from the first time I saw you on the wharf," his voice dropped, and he sighed, "I haven't been able to get you out of my mind. I could no longer deceive the one I love."

Sheridan couldn't answer. In her confusion, she turned her back and for a long moment watched the bubbling waters of the creek, shimmering in the moonlight and creating the illusion of sparkling diamonds. Tiny, glittering, dancing lights. Without reality. Without substance. Love? She felt the heat of tears forming behind her eyes. She drew in a shaky breath. No, she couldn't bear to think about love now.

"You said that you don't believe in lying." Marcus had moved behind her, though he didn't reach out touch her. "I knew when I told you that you'd send me away."

For a moment neither spoke. She turned again to face him. "You said you've seen goodness, honesty — compassion — in me, said Sheridan."

"Yes, and more. So much more."

"What about forgiveness? You didn't see that in me? Or understanding?"

Marcus placed his hands on her shoulders and drew her closer. She looked up into his eyes and saw his pain. "I'm not perfect, Marcus. Far from it. I've needed forgiveness so many times I've lost count."

For the first time, Marcus laughed softly. "I find that difficult to imagine." He caught her hand, lifted it to his face, and kissed her palm. "Sheridan, can you forgive me?"

"Aye, 'tis already done, Marcus."

His voice was hoarse when he spoke again. "There's something else."

She gazed up at him, feeling her heart sink. "Another deception?" she whispered shakily.

"Oh, no," he quickly assured her, gently squeezing her hand. "It's about us, about my feelings for you. I care deeply, Sherrie. Just being with you —"

"Don't," Sheridan interrupted, stepping back from him. "Don't be speakin' of such things, Marcus. Not now. Not after what you've just told me —" Her voice broke off.

For a moment Marcus said nothing. When he spoke again, his voice was flat. "I understand. I'll not speak of it again."

"Please leave me now," she whispered, unable to meet his gaze.

"You shouldn't be out here alone —"

"I'll be all right. I'm just needin' some time to think."

After he returned to the campsite, Sheridan stood in the moonlight, considering the now somber voice of the brook and watching the cottonwood leaves turn in the wind. Listening to the gentle music of the night, she tried to sort out her feelings.

There was something about Marcus that touched her heart. He had begun to invade her thoughts as she rode on the trail with the children, as she lay on her sleeping pallet at night — even before he had so miraculously appeared at their campsite.

Sheridan let out a deep sigh. Perhaps that was why his deception hurt so much. But her feelings for Marcus were deep and mysterious. She couldn't deny or ignore them. She cared deeply. She thought about the boyish way he brushed back his shock of sun-blond hair, the way his eyes seemed to burn with the light of a thousand candles when his gaze met hers, the tender way he had lifted Lia into his arms after her fall. If she had ever doubted his kindness, his compassion, that brave act had erased it.

She sighed again. Aye, she cared deeply for the man.

Later, on her bed, Sheridan pulled the covers up under her chin. She stared into the dark of the tent. The memory of standing near Marcus, of listening to him say, "I care deeply, Sherrie," made her breath catch.

She loved him! Her heart leapt with the sudden and joyful realization. *Aye! I love him,* she whispered into the darkness. *I do!*

Tonight by the creek, she had been unable to listen to his words of caring or speak to him from her heart. But tomorrow, she mused happily. Tomorrow was another day. She would find the time, the place, to tell Marcus Jade that she cared for him. Cared deeply. Aye, she would tell him first thing in the morning.

Sheridan woke to Duncan's shouting from outside the tent.

"Where's Mister Jade?" he cried. "Everything's gone — his bedroll, his saddle. Even Desperado's gone from the corral."

Sheridan threw back the tent flap, and she saw that the boy was right.

Marcus Jade had ridden out during the night.

A wind had kicked up overnight, and dust and ashes from the campfire circled in the air. When Sheridan emerged from the tent, her hair whipped across her face. Near the corral, she could hear the nervous horses whinnying and snorting.

She glanced around the campsite. Duncan was right. There was no sign of Marcus Jade. His bedroll, his gear — all traces of the man — were gone.

"Did he leave anything?" Her voice was shaky. "A letter?"

Duncan sadly shook his head "No, ma'am. He didn't. Even Desperado is gone."

"Maybe Mister Jade rode on ahead to make inquiries about Shamus and your Uncle Sonny," she managed with a weak smile. "Perhaps he believes he can better help us from a distance."

Both little faces fell. They cared for Marcus.

"I don't care about that." Duncan frowned. "I just wanna know why he run out on us."

She knew about Marcus's pride, and affection for them both, and she told them again how he felt. Duncan's chin trembled. "He's always doin' that — takin' off when we need him." He swiped at his nose with his sleeve.

The boy probably felt deserted by his own father, not understanding that death is not chosen. She'd seen the way Duncan watched Marcus at night by the cookfire, especially when Marcus entertained them with tales of the West. She noticed how Marcus would ask the boy for advice about the livestock, causing the boy's eyes to shine with pride. She saw how Duncan always sought Marcus's approval no matter what chore he was performing. The boy would glance at Marcus to see if he was watching.

And now, without a word to the boy — to either child — Marcus Jade had disappeared. No wonder the boy was angry. She was angry too. Sighing, she watched Duncan's stiff shoulders as he turned abruptly and marched toward the corral to ready the horses and mules for the day's trek.

Sheridan turned her attention back to Evangelia and gathered the little girl into her arms. "Mister Jade called you his little champ. Don't ever forget how proud he is of you." She gave the little girl a gentle hug as around them the wind again kicked up and whistled through the trees.

Wispy strands of the child's sun-gold hair blew across her face. Sheridan tucked them into Evangelia's tiny braids, then kissed her cheek. Evangelia smiled shyly, put her arms around Sheridan's neck, and gave her a squeeze in return.

No matter what, Sheridan decided, Marcus had given the child a special gift the previous day. And it wasn't just that he'd saved her life. He'd touched her with love.

Marcus Jade halted the stallion at a small creek and dismounted, filled his hat with water, and let it pour over his head. Then, lying on his belly, he scooped up the sweet liquid with his hands and drank his fill, glad he remembered to do so upstream from Desperado's watering hole.

It was Indian summer in the Sierras, and the ride had been long and hot. Marcus had pushed the horse hard, riding nearly twenty miles since dawn's first light. Afraid he'd change his mind and turn back, he'd wanted to put as much distance as possible between himself and Sheridan.

He'd spent the night searching his soul, wondering how he could remedy his ill-timed words. When he finally reached the conclusion that he must leave, he'd gritted his teeth and made himself saddle up and get out of camp before Sheridan or the children arose.

It hadn't been a difficult decision. He couldn't undo the deception or his brazen words. If he could have figured out a way to simply ride into the sunset, out of Sheridan's life forever, he would have done it.

But there was the matter of honor. He'd pledged his help, and he would keep his word: not to win Sheridan's affection — he figured it was too late for that — but simply because keeping his word was the honorable thing to do.

He thought about the letter he'd left for her and pictured her reading his parting words. It had taken him hours to decide what to say, and even now his letter was practically engraved in his mind:

Dear Miss O'Brian,

 I apologize for my intimate words of last evening. I realized as soon as they had left my lips that I should not have spoken of my feelings for you. Upon reflection, I added "insult to injury," as they say and, for that, I am extremely sorry. It was quite enough for you to hear of my grievous deception without the added declaration of affection, taken (I now realize), as too forward and insensitive.

About my pledge to help you find your brother, I will abide by that commitment, though from a distance. I will also make inquiries about Sonny Kelly, the children's uncle. Please ask at the Wells Fargo office in Everlasting Diggins for communication from me in regard to either matter.

I see in you a contagious joy — a compassion for others, for life itself. Perhaps, Miss O'Brian, it was that which I mistook for love. Again, I apologize for my arrogant assumptions. Please forgive me.

I have two requests. Would you please give the little champ a sweet embrace from me? Tell her that I am proud of her brave heart. Please, too, tell Duncan for me that if his own father could see how he's caring for his sister and for you, he would burst his shirt buttons in pride — just as I am.

Marcus hoped that Sheridan, in reading his missive, would realize that he'd left because of his high regard and deep respect for her. He wondered if she would ever know the depth of his feelings for her.

Running his fingers through his wet hair, Marcus replaced his hat and remounted Desperado. The horse bucked slightly sideways, ears flat, nostrils flaring, seeming as determined as ever to show Marcus who was in charge. Sighing, Marcus nudged the big black in the flanks, and Desperado, ears still horizontal, ambled up the creek bank and headed back onto the oak-lined trail.

As they rode, Marcus thought of Sheridan's sweet, trusting face. He pictured the way her expression had changed from admiration when she'd spoken of his bravery, to anger when he'd told her of his deception, then to confusion when he declared his love.

He closed his eyes, wanting to erase everything about their conversation the night before. Instead, he wanted to hold dear the memory of her wide, violet eyes that seemed to hold in their depths the warmth of a thousand kindled fires; her velvet skin that made him want to brush her cheeks with his fingertips; her graceful way of moving, as if her soul danced to music that only she could hear.

He considered for a moment that inner peace he'd seen in her. He knew that it had something to do with words he'd heard her say to the children at night, words about God.

At night, lying by the campfire, looking up into the star-spangled heavens, he'd listen to Sheridan. She was just a few feet away inside the tent, tucking the children into bed. In her musical, lilting voice, she spoke about God and his Son Jesus. She told them stories from the Bible before they fell asleep.

One night she told them about God being their Father, that he loved them and would never desert them. She used the word Abba, and he remembered the reverence in her voice as she whispered the word to the children. "You may call your heavenly Father, Abba," she'd said. "It means Daddy or Papa. It also means that you have a special and close relationship with him — something that no one can ever take from you."

She told Duncan and Evangelia that God had known them always — from the time they were wee babies. He knew their heartaches and sorrows, their deep sadness when their own mama and papa died. He'd also brought them to

Sheridan. It was all in his plan, she'd said. He'd scooped them into his arms together — Duncan, Evangelia, Sheridan, and even Marcus.

Marcus had never heard God spoken of in such a personal way. He'd thought of him as distant, uninvolved in people's lives, someone you acknowledged during Sunday services, then promptly set aside for more pressing matters during the rest of the week.

But something Sheridan had read to the children one night had stayed with him for days. She'd read a verse from the book of Jeremiah: "I have loved thee with an everlasting love."

Everlasting love? When she'd said the words, Marcus had been lying by the campfire, staring up into the starry universe. He tried to comprehend such eternal, deep, and abiding love. He felt lost in the immensity of the thought. How could God love him — or anyone — with that kind of love? A person would have to be either a child or a saint to deserve it. And, heaven only knew, Marcus had done nothing to earn that kind of regard from God.

Marcus dug his heels in Desperado's flanks and reined the horse toward a small outcropping of granite boulders in the distance. As they rode through a grove of oaks, he thought about Sheridan, her inner peace and strength, even her passion for life. She seemed utterly secure in the love and care of her heavenly Father, the one she called Abba.

Marcus let out a deep sigh as he halted Desperado at the top of the rocky hill. *Abba,* he breathed, looking into the azure heavens, *if only I could know such peace.*

Then, with his hand shielding his eyes from the sun, Marcus squinted into the distance. It was a magnificent sight.

First the taller pines towered among the gray-green live oaks. Then farther into the valley cottonwoods and quaking aspen, now in their autumn garb, splashed the landscape with shimmering golden hues. A small river twisted along the valley floor, a sparkling ribbon weaving in and out of the dappled green and red-gold forests.

Fom this side of the river Marcus could see the buildings of Everlasting Diggins — log houses and shops as tiny as toys in the distance — tucked among the trees. Curls of wispy smoke rose into the crisp fall air from dozens of chimneys.

A short time later, Marcus rode toward the south end of town. The place was a beehive of activity. Miners, with picks, shovels, or noisy rockers and long toms that separated their gold from the soil, worked their claims, most too busy to look up as he rode past. Their tents, or tent houses, stood nearby; the more permanent dwellings told of the obviously greater yields of the mines.

Hundreds of such claims were visible from the trail as Marcus neared the mining camp. Though he'd recently read that Everlasting Diggins was the fifth largest town in California and that some three to five thousand miners were employed there, it was startling to see firsthand, especially considering the place had nearly burned to the ground barely two years before. It had literally been rebuilt from the ashes.

A stream ran through the middle of Everlasting Diggins, but even before Marcus reined Desperado onto Main Street, he could see flumes running in almost every direction, some seeming to interlace each other in a maze of ditches and connecting wooden boxes. Water from the stream obviously had been diverted for the miners' use in the sifter-rockers and long toms, a necessity for sluice-washing the soil from the gold nuggets. Some miners worked alone. Others seemed to have as many as six or seven partners.

Marcus finally reined Desperado down Main Street. He spotted a hotel at the south end of town, the Falcon, next door to the town's newspaper, the *Herald Star.* The rooming house appeared to be clean though noisy, apparently because of a downstairs theater. After registering and placing his gear in his room, he headed to the livery stable at the corner of Main and State Streets with Desperado.

A few minutes later, Marcus arranged for the horse's care, telling the stable hand to carefully check Desperado's hooves and give his weary muscles a good rubdown. That was the least he could do for the beast; Marcus had to admit Desperado had borne him faithfully to his destination. The stallion snorted and lifted his head arrogantly as Marcus left the stable.

He walked directly to the newspaper office, let himself in, and immediately felt at home, greeted by the smell of ink and the sounds of someone running the printing press downstairs.

A balding and bespectacled man looked up from behind his desk. "Can I help you, son?"

Marcus smiled. "I hope so, sir. Name's Jade. Marcus Jade." He strode across the room and stuck out his hand.

The man shook it. "Laramie Burkett here," he said. "Editor of the *Herald Star.*"

"Laramie?" They were a long way from Wind River country.

The older man grinned. "Most folks ask." He chuckled. "I was a guide out of Fort Laramie before I came to California.

Guess I talked about my adventures one too many times out here. Folks got to callin' me 'Laramie Tales.' The moniker stuck. I decided I liked it better than my Christian name." He laughed again. "Horace. Now do I look like a Horace P. Burkett III?"

"Laramie's a better fit," Marcus agreed, liking the man more all the time.

"Glad to make your acquaintance, Marcus Jade," Laramie said, pumping Marcus's hand again. "Now what can I do for you?"

Marcus told him about his paper, the *Grizzlyclaw Gazette*, noting Laramie's obvious delight at meeting a fellow newspaperman, then went on to ask about Shamus O'Brian.

Laramie shook his head slowly. "I've been here four years now, and I don't recollect anyone by that name."

"Know anyone who might know of him? Maybe someone working directly with the miners?"

The editor rubbed his shiny head, frowning. "A grubstaker by the name of Carter Bainbridge is one who might remember. He runs the largest mercantile in Everlasting Diggins — supplies most of the miners' equipment. Grubstakes them from time to time."

Marcus nodded. "I can find him at the mercantile?"

"Across from the livery."

"I know the place." After thanking Laramie, Marcus started to head for the door, then turned. "By the way, what kind of a man is this Bainbridge? Will he be open to telling me what he knows?"

Laramie hesitated, frowning. "Mostly he's highly thought of in town. He's powerful. But be careful how you question him, son. You don't want to get on his wrong side."

"What do you mean?"

"He befriends folks as long as they don't cross him."

"What's he got to hide?"

"You get right to the point, don't you, boy?" Laramie smiled. "A good nose for diggin' up the truth goes with the ink in your veins."

"Takes a newspaperman to recognize another."

"Maybe you ought to come on part-time with me — that way you can poke around without asking any specific questions. Keep yourself outta trouble that way."

"A bit of detective work." He grinned.

Laramie nodded. "Might find out more that way than any other."

Marcus considered the offer. "Why not just tell who I am — a newspaperman from San Francisco, working on an assignment about missing miners?"

"Folks in these parts are suspicious of city folk. Especially San Franciscans."

The younger man frowned. "Why's that?"

"Many've gone to San Francisco to spend their hard-earned gold, only to be cheated or robbed. They come back ready to kill the first San Franciscan they see."

Marcus swallowed hard. That wasn't something he'd read about. "All right, then. Let's do it your way. You can introduce me around as your new assistant editor."

Laramie agreed. "I'll say you're starting a column in the *Herald Star* about miners who didn't strike it rich and went on to other work. We'll print some innocuous stories telling about those who left Everlasting Diggins and then hit it big — say in banking or in the mercantile business or by raising Amazon parrots." He shrugged and winked. "We'll have these miners in a tizzy, thinking they can strike it rich raising parrots."

Marcus chuckled. "I like your style."

"The sad truth of it is, Jade, that they probably would make better wages in some other line of work."

"I've heard that."

The old man's eyes twinkled. "How soon can you start?"

"How about first thing tomorrow?"

With a wide grin, Laramie Burkett stuck out his hand. "Welcome aboard, son," he said. "I can't tell you how glad I am that you've joined the editorial staff of the *Herald Star*." He pulled off his spectacles and rubbed them with his handkerchief. Placing them back on his nose, he squinted at Marcus. "And, of course, you know your first assignment?"

"I can guess."

"You'll be meeting with Bainbridge at the mercantile before he turns over the 'open' sign. I might even go along to make the introductions." Then Laramie frowned, keeping his gaze on Marcus. "There's one more thing, son." Now he was all business. "I'd like a favor in return for takin' you under my wing this way."

"Name it."

"Give me the story, the real story, when you've finished diggin' up the dirt. Ready for print."

Marcus didn't hesitate. "It's yours, Laramie. You'll have it before it goes to print in the *Gazette*."

"I'd appreciate that to no end, son."

"But," Marcus hesitated, thinking of Sheridan. "There's one problem."

Laramie raised an eyebrow.

"I'll need permission from the young woman on whose behalf I'm investigating."

"Go on."

"It's her brother, Shamus O'Brian, I'm searching for. It's only right that we notify her of our intent when all is said and done."

Laramie nodded. "That's only fair."

"But when she grants permission, the story is yours. Exclusive."

"She'll grant it. If the story has a happy ending, she'll likely be happy to tell of your success. If it doesn't, she'll still want to spread the news of the culprits involved in the crime to see that justice is done."

"You sound as if you know the young woman better than I do."

"I know human nature, whether it's male or female, young or old. If you're telling the story for the sake of justice, it's one thing. If you're telling it just to sell papers, it's quite another." He grinned. "Of course, when both work together — that's the miracle we always hope for: stories that bring about justice *and* newspaper sales."

Marcus had an idea the old editor hadn't found many newsworthy stories in Everlasting Diggins for a long time. Laramie's thoughtful, eager look made Marcus figure the man wasn't that different from himself. They both could smell a good story a mile away. But he spoke of justice, and Marcus knew he could learn a thing or two about that from Laramie Burkett. If he had learned it earlier, Marcus would have been as open with Sheridan as Laramie had been with him.

"One more thing," Marcus said just before he left the newspaper office.

The old man looked up.

"Ever hear of a man named Samson Kelly? Goes mostly by Sonny Kelly, I believe."

A slow smile crossed Laramie's face. "Sonny Kelly? Who hasn't?"

Marcus raised an eyebrow. Notoriety in these parts wasn't necessarily good.

"Last I heard," Laramie continued, "he was set to swing. The hangin' was to be some time back. Somewhere over near Angel's Camp." He chuckled. "And if ol' Sonny didn't, he should have — at least that's the word around the mother lode."

It was nearing dusk when a weary Sheridan and the children, their mules in tow, rode their horses slowly down Main Street. They passed the Falcon Hotel, the *Herald Star,* a dry goods emporium, two mercantiles, a theater, and several saloons, on their way to the north end of town.

Sheridan spotted an elegant hotel called the Empress on the left side of the street. It was fashioned of bricks and whitewashed wood, its upstairs front balcony made of wrought scrollwork, looking more like something from New Orleans than from the Wild West. Two elms stretched their strong and graceful trunks skyward, framing the wide, forest-green front door.

"Aye, I think we've found a home," Sheridan breathed, swinging herself from the saddle. She helped Evangelia down, then tied both horses to the hitching post in front of the hotel.

Duncan stood with the sorrel and the mules while Sheridan registered.

"I'll take the room with the balcony," she said to the older man at the front desk. "With an adjoining room for my children."

The clerk nodded and gave her the register to sign. "There's a livery just around the corner. And I'll have someone help you with your things."

"Thank you. I'll tell my son." Evangelia watched Sheridan intently. Sheridan knew it was because of the words "my son" and "my children." She pressed the little girl's hand, and Evangelia squeezed hers in return.

While the luggage was carried up the stairs and across the central parlor to their rooms, Sheridan sent Duncan to the livery with the animals.

Minutes later, she stepped onto the balcony with Evangelia. A shout carried from the livery. They moved closer and squinted in the direction of the yell. She knew it was Duncan. Sure enough, a moment later, she saw the boy heading toward the hotel.

"Dunc! What's the matter?" Sheridan called down to him from the balcony.

He looked up. "Miss Sheridan," he breathed, panting from his hurry. He put his hands on his hips. "You won't believe who's in the stable."

"Who?"

"It's Desperado!" he shouted, nearly dancing in the street.

Sheridan caught her breath. "Marcus is here?" she whispered, wondering at her heart's sudden lightness.

Eleven

❧

That night, as Sheridan sat on the edge of Evangelia's bed, she told the children that she figured Marcus Jade might be in Everlasting Diggins nosing around, playing private detective, on their behalf.

Evangelia traced a cabbage rose on the floral wallcovering. She looked smaller than usual in the massive burled wood bed. A warm feeling of affection for the tiny waif washed over Sheridan as she tucked the bedcovers under the child's chin.

Across the room, in his own four-poster bed, Duncan frowned, considering Sheridan's words. "He's here to help us find Shamus and Uncle Sonny?"

"Aye, I think perhaps he is." Sheridan sighed. "I'm hopin' he is."

"If he's playin' private detective, maybe we oughta act like we don't know him."

"Why, Dunc?" She dimmed the light on Evangelia's bedside table.

"We might give away somethin' he's workin' on. If we're

askin' around and he's askin' around, askin' the same questions…." He let the thought drop, but Sheridan followed his logic.

"You mean he — maybe all of us — could be in danger?"

Duncan nodded. "Yeah."

"You could be right, Duncan." She knew it gave the boy hope to think Marcus was working on their behalf, and she didn't want to disappoint him. She only hoped, for all their sakes, the boy was right.

Evangelia watched her solemnly as Sheridan bent to kiss her cheek. "I only know he'll want to see his little champ again," Sheridan whispered gently, "and to tell you how proud he is that you helped him find Shamus, and of course, your Uncle Sonny." She was rewarded by a happy smile and an audible sigh of contentment as the child turned to the wall and settled under her covers.

From his bed across the room, Duncan looked uncomfortable. He buried himself under his quilts and changed the subject, asking Sheridan to tell them again the story of little David the shepherd boy and how he killed the giant.

At breakfast, as the sun rose the next morning, Sheridan ushered the children to a linen-covered table near a window. Sheridan told them to look outside.

Duncan pulled back a lace curtain so they could see better. A light frost had settled during the night. The slant of the early morning sun shone on the frozen crystals, creating a dazzling sight.

"It seems that God sprinkled a thousand wee jewels across the land," Sheridan whispered in awe.

"I wish it could stay that way forever," Duncan said as he

dropped the curtain back into place. "But the frost'll melt and be gone in no time."

Sheridan nodded. "Then we need to cherish it while it lasts. Cherish its beauty, then hold it dear in our memories." Her thoughts turned to Marcus. She already treasured his memory, his endearing ways, his expression when their eyes met. But she wondered if she had overlooked something of even deeper beauty and greater substance inside him, if in her quick judgment and her anger at his disappearance, she had let the growing love between them melt as quickly as the morning's dusting of diamond frost.

She glanced again through the window, and her thoughts turned to the children and how God had brought them together. She wanted to hold the little ones near, cherish them while she had the chance. If their quest for the missing Uncle Sonny was successful, she might not have that chance much longer. The thought saddened her.

Duncan rarely mentioned his Uncle Sonny, probably because he knew so little about the man. But if they were to find him, Sheridan needed to know more. She had remained suspicious of some of Duncan's story as told that night at the California Palace, but she had waited to ask about him, wanting the children to feel more comfortable with her, willing to trust her.

Now, as she looked at their fresh, rested faces across the table, she realized it was time at last to hear the whole truth.

The server stepped to their table and poured coffee in Sheridan's delicate porcelain cup. Sheridan ordered for them all: hot cooked oats, honey, a loaf of sourdough bread warmed with sweet butter, and milk. Then she turned again to the children.

"About Sonny Kelly," she began.

Duncan looked up sharply. Sheridan remembered the commotion the boy had made in the kitchen, the chef's threats, Marcus Jade's swift rescue, and Duncan's words about an uncle somewhere near Everlasting Diggins. "It's time for you to tell me more about your Uncle Sonny," she repeated.

The boy nodded. Evangelia popped her thumb in her mouth.

Their breakfasts arrived, and Sheridan nodded to the children to bow their heads. After a brief prayer of thanks for the food, she looked again at Duncan.

"Now," she sighed. "Tell me everything you know about your uncle." She sipped her coffee, watching him intently over the rim of her cup.

"Like I told you that night, he's my pa's brother. He went off looking for gold." Duncan lifted a heaping spoonful of hot oats to his mouth, then chewed slowly. Evangelia nibbled on a piece of warm sourdough bread.

"You said he'd come to Everlasting Diggins."

"I did?"

"Yes, Duncan, you did. Is that where he is?"

"I dunno."

Sheridan took a deep breath and reached for the boy's hand. "Duncan, look at me." His gaze met hers, his face pale beneath the freckles. "Why did you tell me that night that your uncle had come to Everlasting?"

"I heard you an' Mister Jade talkin'."

"When?" Sheridan tried to remember speaking of their journey in the hearing of others. She drew a blank.

"At the wharf that day you arrived."

Sheridan narrowed her eyes in thought. "I don't remember ever seeing you before that night at the Palace dining room."

"Well, I saw you. I was at the wharf tryin' to find some smokefish for my sister. I was hidin' behind some trunks near Mister Jade. I heard you talkin' about comin' here." He looked sheepish. "I even heard you fire him 'n' everything."

She frowned. "But how did you know where I was staying? Mister Jade didn't tell me until we were in the carriage."

"Oh, that was easy." The child looked proud of his sleuthing. "I asked the dockhand that hailed the cabbie for Mister Jade. He knew everything."

"So you caused the ruckus in the kitchen to get our attention?"

"Well, not exactly." Duncan stuck another bite of hot oats in his mouth.

She waited for him to continue speaking.

"I couldn't just come up to your table, so while I was waitin', tryin' to figure out what to do, I thought I might as well get somethin' for Lia to eat. She hadn't had much all day." Duncan looked down at his plate.

"You made up the story about your Uncle Sonny."

"No." He hesitated. "Not exactly."

"You do have an uncle."

"Yes, ma'am."

"But he's not here — here in the gold fields, I mean." She noticed that Evangelia had shifted her gaze to the window, as if no longer wanting to be part of the conversation.

"He's here, all right." His voice dropped.

"Tell me the truth, Duncan. No more lies."

"I never lied, Miss Sheridan." His eyes again met hers. "I just didn't tell you everything."

Sheridan drew in a deep breath. "So tell me everything now."

"My uncle's around here someplace. Before she died, Ma told us he was somewhere around Angel's Camp. She also mentioned Jamestown, even Everlasting Diggins."

"Aye. Go on."

"She also said to stay far away from him."

Sheridan swallowed. She could tell by the boy's expression that he was telling her the truth. "Why?" Her voice was barely more than a whisper. Evangelia placed her small hand in Sheridan's, then turned to watch her brother intently.

"Because," Duncan said, with an air of importance, "because Uncle Sonny is an outlaw."

Marcus Jade and Laramie Burkett walked along the rough boards of the sidewalk along Main Street, heading to the Goldstrike Mining Supplies and Mercantile. Most folks hadn't yet ventured into town, and the sound of the men's boots carried in the early dawn quiet.

The morning was crisp, cold enough for a man's breath to freeze in front of his face in gray puffs. Marcus buttoned his heavy wool jacket, glad for the long johns and woolen clothes underneath. Sunlight slanted between the buildings from the east, casting long shadows and intermittent splashes of warmth.

Marcus rapped his gloved knuckles on the door at the Goldstrike. It was dark inside, but the two men could see a light under the door of a back room office. He rapped again.

After a moment, a massive, well-dressed man moved toward the door and squinted through the glass. He raised an eyebrow in recognition when he saw Laramie.

"You're up and about early, Laramie," he said, frowning as he opened the door.

"This here's my new assistant editor. Name's Marcus Jade." Laramie nodded toward Marcus who stuck out his hand.

"Carter Bainbridge," the man said curtly as he shook Marcus's hand. "What're you two gentlemen up to this morning? Awfully early to be paying a social call." Marcus noted the broad-shouldered, aristocratic look of the man, and his impeccable clothing. He was about the same age as Marcus, with dark hair and gun-metal gray eyes.

"I've got my new assistant here working on a project. Have him tracking down miners who gave up minin' in pursuit of other ventures. He's to get their stories — whether or not they met success. Should make for some interestin' readin'. Not to mention, probably get the miners around here in quite a stir."

"What've I got to do with that?"

Laramie shrugged, a slow smile crossing his face. He removed his hat and rubbed his shiny head. "Just thought you might be able to point him in the right direction, Carter. I just came along to make the introductions before I cut him loose." He chuckled sheepishly.

Bainbridge seemed to accept the explanation. He invited the two men to join him in his office.

"Actually, I need to get back to the *Star*. But if you don't mind, Carter, I'll leave the two of you to chat a bit."

Bainbridge said he didn't mind, and after Laramie exited the gloomy mercantile, the two men stepped into the back office.

"Now, what can I do for you?" Bainbridge nodded to a chair opposite his desk, then settled into his own and leaned back, fingers laced behind his head.

"I heard about a young man who was looking for gold around these parts a few years back. Name's Shamus O'Brian. Do you know anything about him?"

Carter Bainbridge leaned forward. An expression hard as steel crossed his face. "I knew him. Lot's of folks did. But how did you get his name?" He frowned. "The boy's been gone for quite some time."

"His name's come up several times," Marcus answered, purposely vague. "Some say he struck it rich, then disappeared, just like that." He snapped his fingers with a shrug and a half-smile, trying to put Bainbridge at ease. "Could be an interesting story. Know anything about him — what might have caused him to pull up stakes?"

Bainbridge seemed to weigh his options, trying to decide how much to tell. Marcus wondered if it was because he was somehow involved in the man's disappearance. Then Bainbridge smiled, showing even white teeth below an expertly trimmed dark mustache.

He leaned back and sighed. "I haven't thought about Shamus in quite a while. He was mining near these parts up until maybe eighteen months, two years ago. I befriended the boy. At one point, I grubstaked him."

Marcus nodded, encouraging him to continue. Bainbridge shook his head slowly. "He borrowed against what he thought he'd find in the ground. Turned out to be phantom gold."

"Fool's gold?"

"Worse. There was nothing there at all."

"But he still owed the grubstaker — you — the money."

"That's right. But don't get me wrong." His steely gaze met Marcus's. "I wasn't pressuring him for payback. Nothing of the sort. I try to give these young miners as much help as I can. I think Shamus O'Brian was just too inexperienced to see it through."

"You think he left in defeat. He owed too much to make mining worthwhile — at least in his mind."

"That's about the gist of it." His apologetic shrug seemed genuine. "Not much of a story for your paper. I'm sorry."

They spoke for a few more minutes, Bainbridge mentioning other miners Marcus might use for his articles in the *Star.*

Marcus took notes, asked a few questions, then stood and thanked the man for his time. Bainbridge walked him to the front door. Marcus reached for the handle, then turned thoughtfully.

"One more thing, Carter. You didn't mention what happened to the gold mine. What was the name of it again?"

"Rainbow's End."

"Yes. That was it. Was it abandoned, or is someone still working it?"

Bainbridge looked uncomfortable. "It's being worked."

"Because of O'Brian's debts it now belongs to you, is that right?"

"That's right."

"Any gold in it?"

"What are you trying to say, Jade?" Again Marcus noticed the steely gaze, the hardened expression on the big man's face.

Marcus smiled. "I'm not accusing you of anything, Carter. It just strikes me as convenient that O'Brian disappeared and you get the mine. That's all." He chuckled. "But I suppose that's the nature of your business. After all, you're out to make money, not friends. That right?"

Bainbridge didn't smile. He reached for the door. "I think that ends your interview, Mister Jade. Good day." He gestured for Marcus to make his exit.

Marcus nodded affably, then stepped from the mercantile onto the sidewalk bordering Main Street. He headed back to the *Herald Star,* lost in thought. Bainbridge was smooth. Too smooth. If he did have anything to do with Shamus O'Brian's disappearance, he wouldn't have been so open about his business relationship with the young man. And of course, Bainbridge had no advance warning of Marcus's visit, no time to prepare a cover for his connection to O'Brian.

The sun had risen in a brilliant blue sky, and the earlier frost had all but disappeared. Marcus drew a deep breath, looking down the street at the brick storefronts, the bustling shopkeepers, and the folks beginning to mill about. A brisk energy seemed to emanate from the place. It might be a mining town, but the people here took pride in their storefronts, their hotels, and their theaters, built of brick and fancy scrolled iron.

Everlasting Diggins had been rebuilt from ashes at least twice since the gold rush began just a few years before. The folks had learned from their earlier mistakes. Now, few buildings were made of wood. Most had brick walls with doors of solid iron and windows with iron shutters to keep the flames inside in case of fire.

As he strolled down the street, Marcus admired the fancy buildings with their wood-carved signs. It was as solid a town as a person could want, if that person had a mind to settle down and raise a family. He'd even heard about Everlasting Diggins's new two-story brick schoolhouse built on a hill overlooking the town.

He was thinking about Duncan and Evangelia, how they would enjoy learning to read and write, when he rounded the corner near the Wells Fargo office.

He halted in surprise.

Sheridan had just stepped from the Wells Fargo office and turned toward him, flanked by the children. In earnest conversation with Duncan, at first she didn't see Marcus. His breath caught at her delicate beauty — the gleam of her dark hair, the velvet freshness of her face — as she stepped into a pool of sunlight.

Then she looked up and met Marcus's gaze. She continued to walk toward him, her eyes never leaving his. Even from a distance, her expression was as soft and tender as the sweetest embrace.

The children didn't see him. Duncan continued chattering at Sheridan's side and, as usual, Evangelia seemed lost in a world of her own.

Finally, Sheridan stopped only a few feet from him. Marcus hurried forward to greet her, fighting the impulse to gather her into his arms, to gather them all into his arms.

But before he could speak, Sheridan crossed the street, dodging horses and riders, hurrying the children onto the sidewalk.

Marcus thought his heart would break at the sound of their footsteps on the wood planks leading away from him.

Twelve

❧

Sheridan stopped and rested her hand on a railing, her knees weak from seeing Marcus. Though he didn't say a word, his eyes had spoken to her of his affection, his delight at seeing her. When he'd brushed back his blond hair and strode toward them, her heart had leapt with a joy so deep, so unexpected, it had nearly taken her breath away.

Then she thought about the way he had left camp. No matter how his presence affected her, she was angry with him for departing the way he did. Without a word, he'd simply disappeared. The children deserved better. And so did she.

A nearby shopkeeper opened his door, stepped out with a smile and a "good day" to Sheridan and the children. He swept the sidewalk in front of his establishment, whistling as he moved the broom across the wood planks. On the opposite side of the street, a stage pulled up to the Wells Fargo office and folks spilled out. Here and there, dogs barked and roosters crowed. The shouts of miners and the clanks of picks and the rumbles of the long toms added to the growing cacophony of the morning.

But since the trio stopped, Duncan and Evangelia hadn't moved their gaze from Sheridan's face. They hadn't seen Marcus, but they knew something was wrong.

"Children," Sheridan said, taking a deep breath. "Since breakfast I've been considering your circumstances." She needed to dwell on something besides Marcus Jade. The threatening tears were dangerously close to spilling down her cheeks. And she didn't want to frighten the children. They would speak of something pleasant. She smiled. "Children, I've come to some conclusions. And you need to know what I'm thinking."

Duncan nodded. "Yes, ma'am." He still looked worried.

Evangelia tightened her grip on Sheridan's hand.

"I saw a bench by a fountain around the corner. We'll go there and talk of some things I've been pondering." They nodded tentatively, and she ushered them to the place. When they were seated, one on either side, she explained her plan.

"The way I see it, the two of you have had enough vagrancy for a lifetime."

"Yes, ma'am," Duncan said softly.

Sheridan continued with a bit of a sigh. "It's time you two stopped runnin' from pillar to post."

Duncan frowned, not understanding.

"Aye," she said softly. "It's time we made ourselves a home."

"A home? You mean a house and everything? A barn? Horses?"

Sheridan grinned at his obvious delight. "Slow down, Dunc. We'll look for all that a bit later. Right now, I'm just insistin' that we stay put. I'd intended that we'd eventually go on to Angel's Camp. But with the news about your Uncle Sonny, I've decided we'll stay right here. You two need stability and love. You need someone watchin' over you to keep you safe and warm."

Duncan let out a deep sigh as if a weight had been removed from his thin shoulders. "But what about Shamus?"

"I can take a stage to Angel's camp — stay for a day or two to look for Shamus, then come back. It's the two of you we don't want runnin' into Sonny Kelly."

"What'll we do while you're gone?" Both children watched her carefully. She knew they were frightened of being abandoned again.

"You'll be busy." She smiled.

"Busy?" Duncan squinted at her in the sunlight. "Doin' what?"

"Goin' to school."

Duncan scratched his head. "School?" he repeated softly.

"Aye," Sheridan said resolutely. "If I'm goin' to be takin' care of you, it's my duty to see that you have a proper education. You'll both be learnin' to read and write."

"Aw, shucks," he said with a sigh. But Sheridan had never seen him so pleased.

"And what do you say about it, Lia? What do you think about goin' to school?"

Evangelia frowned as if worried. Sheridan lifted her onto her lap, gently rocking her and holding her close to her heart.

A shy smile lit Duncan's face as he watched them. "We're gonna be a family, Lia," he murmured. "A real family, with a ma an' everything."

Sheridan met his happy gaze and nodded. "A ma and everything."

As soon as Marcus could breathe again, he headed for the Wells Fargo office. He'd told Sheridan in his letter that he would leave her messages. She might ignore Marcus on the street, but surely she would be curious enough about the investigation to check with the stationmaster about mail left for her.

Now that she was in Everlasting Diggins, Marcus needed to warn her about Carter Bainbridge. He had to make it clear that, at all costs, she needed to stay away from the grubstaker. As had been his own experience, if Sheridan started asking questions around town, the trail would lead directly to Bainbridge. And Marcus's instincts told him the man was not to be trusted.

One question from Sheridan about Shamus might trigger a dangerous response from Carter Bainbridge.

Bainbridge would know that Marcus's questioning had involved something more than a follow-up on idle gossip for the newspaper. And, more important, he would immediately suspect that Sheridan herself was behind the investigation.

When Marcus reached the Wells Fargo office, he quickly scribbled a note asking Sheridan to meet him the following day. He drew a small map, instructing her to ride to a distinctive outcropping of boulders outside town. It was sheltered from the view of passersby and they wouldn't be seen. He would explain everything. Meantime, he warned her to stay away from Bainbridge. He also told her he had information about the children's uncle.

Marcus signed his name, folded the paper, and handed it to the stationmaster with instructions to see that it was given to Sheridan O'Brian when she called for her messages.

Within hours after her talk with the children, Sheridan arranged to lease the balcony rooms at the Empress Hotel. She wrote and mailed a letter to Aunt Fiona in New York, explaining about the children and her plan to live in Everlasting Diggins. She would need extra funds, she added, while searching for Shamus. After that, she planned to seek employment, possibly at the new schoolhouse, to care for herself and the children.

By late afternoon, she had enrolled the children in school, explaining to the schoolmarm about their upbringing, and especially about Evangelia not speaking. The woman had nodded in understanding and said that she would give the little girl extra help. Sheridan agreed with the teacher that being around other children might encourage Lia to talk.

The next day, as a light drizzle began to puddle the ground, Sheridan walked with the children to the school-house. Bundled in warm woolen coats and boots, Duncan and Evangelia each carried a small bucket filled with a lunch made by the Empress Hotel dining room cook.

After stooping to kiss Evangelia good-bye and tousling Duncan's wiry red hair, Sheridan watched the children walk up the steps and disappear inside the imposing brick build-ing. She whispered a prayer that their day would go well.

The heavy mist had now turned into a steady rain. Sheridan drew her cape close to her body, pulling its wide bonnet over her hair as she made her way through the deep-ening mud.

Earlier, she had decided to wait to begin her own investi-gation into Shamus's disappearance until the children were removed from any danger. Their school days would now give her the perfect opportunity for sleuthing. She headed to the Empress and within moments stepped onto the covered porch at the entrance. She would begin her questioning right there. The desk clerk had already told her he would be happy to help her out in any way he could. She scraped the mud from her boots and pushed open the door.

The bell at the top of the hotel door jingled as she entered the warm room.

Mr. Dickens, the clerk, looked up and smiled. "It appears that winter's on its way."

"Aye," she said, removing her cape. "Though I think it's already arrived."

They spoke for a moment about the school and the children's first day. Then Sheridan told the kindly man about Shamus.

"Did you know him?"

Mr. Dickens shook his head slowly. "Afraid not, child. But so many come and go around these parts...." His words fell off lamely. He shrugged. "I wish I could help you, but I don't even know where to tell you to begin."

"Where do the miners come when they're in town?"

Dickens scratched his head, frowning. "The saloons, of course. And they gather for the griz and bull fights."

"For what?"

He smiled sadly. "You've not heard of them?"

She shook her head.

"For entertainment, the miners pit grizzlies against bulls, or sometimes dogs or a man armed with a knife."

Sheridan felt sick. She noticed that Dickens had paled just talking about it.

"They're chained together until one is dead."

146

She swallowed hard. "I've never heard about such 'entertainment.'"

"It's not for the faint of heart, but it does draw a crowd. But back to your question about where the miners congregate in town." He thought a moment, then said, "They're always in need of supplies, so they spend time at the mercantile and such. And the claim office, too, of course." He grinned. "And there's those few who spend time at church, mostly praying to hit a vein."

"Aye," Sheridan sighed. "I suppose I should just start makin' my rounds. Perhaps the claim office should be my first stop."

Mr. Dickens nodded in agreement. "That would be my advice."

She thanked him, slipped on her cape, and headed out into the frigid rain. The claim office was two blocks down and over a few doors. She skipped over the puddles and hurried to the entrance.

She rapped on the door, then held both hands to the glass and peered in. The gloomy interior revealed that no one was inside. No sign hung at the window indicating whether the office was closed due to the rain or the early hour. Sheridan turned and hurried to the shelter of a nearby covered walkway. The rain fell harder, pounding loudly overhead and sheeting from the roof into the muddy street.

Across the street, she noticed a tall, broad-shouldered man unlocking solid iron doors at the entrance to a tall brick and stone building. She couldn't make out the sign through the rain; the place appeared to be a mercantile or dry goods store of some sort.

She smiled in relief. At last, perhaps she'd found someone

who could give her guidance, at least point her in the direction to begin her search. Once more she pulled her cape close, yanked its bonnet down to where it nearly covered her eyes, and headed through the rain for the mercantile.

The man who had just unlocked the doors turned when he heard Sheridan's footsteps sloshing through the mud and rain.

"Come in, come in," he laughed, holding open the door. "You're soaked through. Please come over by the fire. I was here earlier to get the place warmed up before opening for business." He led her to a potbellied stove across the room.

Gratefully, Sheridan slipped out of her cape, which the man placed on a coat rack near the stove. She held her hands out to the fire, thankful for its warmth.

"You're shivering," he observed. "Can I get you a blanket?"

She smiled at his kindness. "No, no. I'm fine," she said. "I'm just glad you had the foresight to have a waitin' fire."

He laughed lightly. And for the first time, Sheridan noticed his handsome good looks. His eyes met hers briefly, and in that moment, she saw a flicker of admiration. Flattered, she felt her cheeks color.

Outside the storm continued. The wind had picked up, producing a lonely-sounding howl and slanting the rain toward the windows. But Sheridan couldn't have been happier, with the fire blazing in the stove, this pleasant man at her side, and the shelves around her filled with picks and axes, shovels and pans, rockers and scales: mining supplies of every description. She'd obviously come to the right place.

"I'm sorry. I completely overlooked introductions." He gave her another dazzling smile. "I don't even know your name." His light eyes brightened, a nice contrast against his deeply bronzed skin, Sheridan thought. The cut of his clothing told her he enjoyed the finer things in life. She found herself studying the casual sweep of his dark hair, the trim mustache, the bold line of his jaw. She flushed again as he noticed her appraising gaze.

"Sheridan," she finally said holding out her hand. "My name is Sheridan O'Brian."

He took her small hand between both of his, warming it with a brisk but gentle rub. "I'm pleased to make your acquaintance, Miss Sheridan-with-the-beautiful-Irish-lilt." Again, his expression spoke of open admiration. "My name is Carter Bainbridge. And I'm pleased we've met. Very pleased."

For the longest moment, he didn't release her hand.

Thirteen

❧

"Carter Bainbridge," Sheridan said with a wide smile as she withdrew her hand.

The handsome man pulled a ladderback chair to a place near the stove, and Sheridan settled into it with a nod of thanks. He offered her coffee from the iron coffeepot atop the stove, and she gratefully accepted a mug of the strong and fragrant liquid.

"What brings you to Everlasting Diggins?" Carter asked as he brought another chair near her and sat, resting his elbow on a powerful-looking thigh. Sheridan was struck by his wide shoulders, his tree-trunk build. He seemed far too big for the spindly wood chair.

"I'm searching for my brother."

"He's missing?" He watched her carefully as he took a swallow of coffee.

She nodded sadly. "Aye, for quite some time now."

"Tell me what happened. Maybe I can help."

Sheridan sighed, hoping above all hope that he could. "'Tis my prayer that the search will end here, Carter. I've sailed around the Horn, trudged all over San Francisco, made my way through the wilderness to finally reach this place, yet I fear my search has just begun."

"Because this was the last place he was known to be?"

"Aye. He was here for a while, then moved to Angel's Camp. My aunt even had one letter from Jamestown. I figured I'd begin searchin' here because it's the largest of the mining camps. Maybe someone will have heard of him."

"Good thinking. He was a miner?" Bainbridge stood and, opening the stove's door, shoved in a small piece of oak. He brushed off his hands and sat down again on the stool.

"He struck gold somewhere between here and Angel's Camp. That much I know for sure." Sheridan lifted her mug with both hands, relishing its warmth. She took a sip, then held the heavy cup in her lap.

"There are thousands of miners who say they've struck gold between here and Angel's Camp." Carter lifted his mug to his lips, then took a long drink. "What's your brother's name?"

"Actually, he's my twin. His name is Shamus. Shamus O'Brian."

For a moment Bainbridge seemed to study Sheridan. His eyes narrowed. She couldn't read his expression, though it seemed to harden.

"You have heard of Shamus?" she prompted, confused.

"Yes," he said after a moment's pause. "I have." He sighed audibly, as if he had bad news.

"Tell me," she whispered. "Do you have bad news?" Her hands trembled as she clutched the mug.

Carter's eyes met hers, and he shook his head, almost imperceptibly. "It's been a long time since I've thought of

151

Shamus. I should have known the moment I saw you —" His voice broke off, and he regarded her thoughtfully. "He spoke of you often. And your aunt. What was her name again? It's been so long." He paused, then went on before Sheridan could speak. "Ah — Fiona, it was. Aunt Fiona and his sister, Sheridan. I should have realized who you were the moment I heard your name."

"Aye," Sheridan whispered, a catch in her voice. "Aunt Fiona." He must be telling her the truth. Otherwise, he wouldn't have known Fiona's name. "What else? Please tell me everything."

"Shamus was my friend."

"Was?" Sheridan could feel her heart thump inside her ribs. "Do you know what has happened to my brother?"

"I don't know, dear." Again, he shook his head sadly. "That I don't know."

"Then what?" She swallowed hard. "He was your friend. Surely you know something."

"I'll tell you everything I know of your brother's disappearance, Sheridan." He smiled gently and touched her hand. "And I pledge my help, if you'll allow me."

She nodded, wondering why his words didn't match the expression in his eyes. "Your help will be most welcome, Carter. Thank you for offering." Her hands still trembling, she lifted the coffee mug to her lips.

"Your brother was one of the most ambitious young men to head into Everlasting Diggins. Everyone liked him. I don't think he had one enemy among the other miners. And believe me, they can be an uncivil lot."

Bainbridge settled back into his chair, his eyes never leaving hers. "Right off he staked out a mine. Seems that he told

152

me his first claim was here in town. Got too crowded, he said, so off he went to Angel's Camp. Mined there for a while. Didn't hit anything big. Then he moved again. This time close to Everlasting Diggins." He leaned forward, narrowing his eyes as if in silent challenge before continuing.

Sheridan nodded encouragement. "Please, go on," she whispered.

"Your brother's last mine — the one he called Rainbow's End — was the place he'd been searching for. He took out several good-sized nuggets, enough to convince him he'd struck a vein."

Sheridan let out a shaky breath. "Aye, that's the one he wrote us about. He told us he'd finally struck it rich."

Carter nodded. "Shamus wanted to expand, buy better equipment, and hire workers to get the gold out of the Diggins faster. He thought the eventual payoff was worth going into debt — a mistake a lot of miners make."

"He borrowed against the mine?"

"It's called grubstaking." A flicker of cold emotion seemed to settle somewhere behind his eyes then quickly disappear.

"Using his mine as collateral," she said, taking another sip of coffee. She pictured her brother, his dancing eyes, his daring spirit and lust for life. He was a gambler by nature. The events Carter described were definitely in character for him.

Carter nodded. "Yes, using Rainbow's End."

"And he found no gold." Sheridan could guess the rest of the story.

"It just wasn't where he thought it would be." The handsome man shrugged his big shoulders. "The first year, he hired a couple of workers to help him. They operated the long toms and cradles from sunup to midnight. But after a while, the money ran out. They found some gold, but not the vein he'd expected. He finally had to let his helpers go. Shamus continued on alone for a few more months, convinced it would eventually pay off."

"Then he gave up?" That wasn't like Shamus. He wasn't a quitter.

"I'm afraid so. That's when he up and left town, never to be heard from again."

"But you said you were his friend. He didn't tell you where he was headed?" She considered Bainbridge thoughtfully for a moment, then widened her eyes. "He didn't come to you for help?"

Carter stood to stoke the fire, then turned with a sad expression on his face. "I did help him, Sheridan. I was the one who grubstaked your brother."

Her suspicions about the man were being confirmed, but she forced herself to remain calm and detached. "You loaned him money?"

He nodded slowly. "I did it to help him, Sheridan. Please believe me." Bainbridge sat beside her again. He took her hand. "We both had high hopes for the mine. When he started having trouble, I gave him extra time to pay me back. I even tried to excuse the loan completely." He shook his head. "But your brother wouldn't hear of it. He insisted that he would pay me back."

"But did he?" She folded her hands in her lap, not wanting to feel Carter's touch.

"No. He left before that happened." There was a bitter edge to Carter's voice.

"Surely you don't think he skipped out on you." She watched him carefully.

Carter's eyes met hers. "No. I think he was embarrassed because of our friendship. He left because he could no longer face me."

"My brother would never do that." And she was sure of it. Paying back one's debts was a matter of honor. "He would have made..." She faltered, just enough to disarm Bainbridge with her naiveté. "Arrangements of some kind."

"Sheridan, out here there's a different code. There simply are no 'arrangements' to be made. And as I said, I did try to excuse the loan. In fact, if you would like to take a look at my books, you'll see that the debt has been canceled. Shamus O'Brian owes me nothing."

For a few minutes neither Carter nor Sheridan spoke. Outside, the downpour continued, and the waters slid off the roof in gray sheets.

"What about the mine?" Sheridan finally asked. "What's happened with Rainbow's End?" She wanted to see the place, and she wanted Carter Bainbridge to be her escort. She needed to get close to the man, find out everything he knew about her brother.

"I took it over."

Sheridan wasn't surprised. She regarded the man carefully, meeting his gaze. "You're working it now?"

"Yes."

"So in actuality, my brother owes you nothing anyway. His mine was the collateral for your loan."

"That's true." He smiled benignly, almost as if to calm her thinking. "I understand how this may look to you. But you've got to believe me, Sheridan. I was your brother's friend." His eyes implored her to believe him. "Please trust me, Sherrie — that's what he called you, isn't it?" His voice softened, and he raised his eyebrows with the question. "Sherrie?"

"Aye," she whispered, remembering the lilt of her nickname when dear Shamus spoke it. She considered the dark and empty look in Carter's gray eyes. A shiver traveled down her spine. "Aye," she repeated softly. "He called me Sherrie. But only my family and dearest friends call me that."

He laughed lightly. "Then I'll have to earn the right, will I not, Miss Sheridan O'Brian?"

She nodded with a wan smile.

"And I should get started right away, shouldn't I?" He raised an eyebrow and grinned. "How about joining me for supper tonight at the Empress?"

"I am guardian to two young children. I'm sorry. Supper isn't a good time —"

"Why can't we all dine together?" he interrupted, leaning forward in his chair.

Sheridan laughed lightly, considering again her determination to get close to Bainbridge. "You don't know what you're in for. Today's their first day of school, and I'm afraid we'll be overcome by their exuberance, at least by Duncan's. My little girl is another story." She explained about Evangelia.

"I would love to meet them." He looked sincere.

"All right, then," she finally agreed. "Supper it is."

Carter suggested a time to meet in the hotel parlor as Sheridan stood to go. He held her cape while she slipped her arms into the sleeve openings, then walked with her to the door. The bell tinkled as he opened it. The rain had lessened to a light drizzle, and in the west a patch of blue showed between the clouds. Sheridan took a deep breath, enjoying the fragrance of woodsmoke and rain.

"I've enjoyed our meeting," Carter said as she stepped from the mercantile. "More than you know." He smiled.

She turned toward him. He was at least a head taller than she, and Sheridan had to tilt her face upward to meet his gaze.

"And I am serious about what I said about helping you find Shamus. In fact, I'm ashamed I didn't start looking for him myself much sooner."

"There is one thing you could do."

He arched a brow and touched her arm. "Anything," he said.

"I would like to see my brother's gold mine."

He nodded agreeably. "Of course. I should have suggested it myself. Would you like to ride out with me in the morning?"

"Aye, that I would, Carter, if it wouldn't be too much trouble."

He chuckled. "Trouble? Hardly, my dear. It will be my pleasure."

Marcus Jade strode from the Wells Fargo office and headed for Main Street. He was in a foul mood. Up at the crack of dawn, he'd ridden Desperado to the outcropping of rocks where he'd written Sheridan he'd meet her. Each mile further away from Everlasting Diggins, he became muddier and more drenched by the onslaught of rain. Though he wasn't surprised when Sheridan didn't arrive, he had been angered that she hadn't at least sent word to him back in Everlasting Diggins that she wouldn't be there.

He had turned the irritated Desperado back to the livery, instructing the stablehand to rub down the stallion. Then, heading for the Wells Fargo office, he planned the scathing words he'd leave for Sheridan in his next missive. "Insensitive" had a nice ring to it. He'd also work in "lack of concern" and "callous behavior."

But when he arrived at Wells Fargo, the place was empty, closed due to the inclement weather, he assumed. He banged on the door anyway, more because of his foul mood than because he thought he might raise someone inside. Silence answered him.

Marcus was about to head back to the *Herald Star* when he noticed a light inside the Goldstrike Mercantile and Mining Supply. Curious, he moved closer. He was directly across the street when the mercantile door opened. For a moment no one appeared.

He caught his breath as Sheridan stepped out and turned, looking up like a sunflower to the sun, into Carter Bainbridge's face.

Marcus stepped backward and tried to hide behind a post. But he needn't have worried. Sheridan and Bainbridge seemed lost in intimate conversation. Carter touched her arm and they laughed softly. She seemed to sway toward the big man, and the hair on the back of Marcus's neck rose.

What did Sheridan think she was doing? How could she so blatantly ignore the warnings in his letter? She seemed to have dismissed Marcus's words as if they had no meaning.

The rain had turned into a gray mist by the time Sheridan left the mercantile, her hood pulled over her dark hair. Marcus watched the dainty caped figure move down the covered sidewalk toward the Empress Hotel.

Overcome with loneliness and sad longing, he decided that he couldn't wait any longer to speak with her.

The streets were still ankle-deep in mud, but Marcus picked his way through the puddles to cross Main Street. He hurried to catch Sheridan before she entered the hotel.

He called her name, and she turned. Just at that moment, the sun broke through the clouds, and it seemed to Marcus that her turning had caused it. His heart caught in his throat, she looked so fresh and pretty. Her eyes seemed to shimmer in the light as he moved closer.

"Sheridan," he said again hoarsely. "We need to talk."

Carter Bainbridge stepped to the front window to watch the comely Sheridan O'Brian as she moved down the street.

A movement from across the street caught his attention and he narrowed his eyes. A man in a wool coat gingerly made his way through the puddled mud and headed directly for the mercantile. Just before he strode onto the sidewalk, Bainbridge recognized the face. Marcus Jade, the new assistant editor of the *Herald Star.*

He was about to turn away, when he saw Jade hurrying as if to catch up with someone. *Ah, yes,* he thought, squinting. *The woman. Sheridan O'Brian.*

Stepping closer to the window, he peered up Main Street toward the Empress. Sheridan turned. Bainbridge didn't miss her look of delight as she watched Jade stride toward her. It was obvious they had met before. Somehow he wasn't surprised.

Bainbridge pulled down the window shade against the glare of the sun, at the same time congratulating himself for acting so quickly in gaining the woman's trust. Taking care of the pretty Sheridan O'Brian and her nosy inquiries would be as easy as swatting a mosquito.

And immensely more pleasurable, he thought with a chuckle as he headed into his office.

Fourteen

❧

M arcus?" Sheridan's knees went weak again at the sight of him, and she forgot all about being angry.

The sun slipped in and out of the clouds. All around Marcus and Sheridan puddling rain dripped from tree branches and roofs. When caught by the sunlight, each droplet glistened like a dancing diamond. The air smelled fresh, and Sheridan sighed happily, looking up at Marcus. The look in his Irish-seas eyes made her heart beat faster.

She barely noticed when merchants began flipping over the "open" signs in their shops. Or when the miners headed out of nearby tenthouses, scratching their heads as they regarded the muddy streets. She was only vaguely aware when a few others wandered into a saloon next door and the tinny piano music started up and carried into the street.

"We need to go someplace to speak privately." Marcus's voice was low, insistent. He looked worried.

"All right." Her gaze never left his eyes. "Where?"

Marcus described the outcropping of rocks on the trail. She nodded and said she'd seen the place when she rode into town. He noticed that she said nothing about being sorry for missing their earlier meeting.

"Can you be there in a half hour?"

"Aye."

"I'm sorry we can't ride together, but it's really not safe." He looked around nervously.

"I understand."

Marcus smiled gently and touched her arm. "I'll see you there."

She nodded. "I'll be there."

And with that, Marcus turned back in the direction he'd come, and Sheridan headed to the Empress to change into her riding clothes.

A short time later, she reined Shadrach onto the trail, keeping to the rocky ledges and avoiding the muddier low spots. The Appaloosa whinnied and danced sideways, skittish at the roar of a nearby creek.

When Sheridan arrived at the outcropping, Marcus was waiting for her, standing beside Desperado.

He took her hand as she slid from the saddle. For a moment they took in the view of Everlasting Diggins and spoke of the storm. The town now lay in full midday sunlight, smoke twisting upward from dozens of chimneys, the shouts of miners and clanging equipment carrying toward them on the wind.

Though it was sunny, a winter wind sliced across the land, causing Sheridan to shiver. Back at the Empress, she had hastily pulled on her butternut leather riding skirt and boots, then wrapped around her shoulders an ivory-colored shawl, knitted by Aunt Fiona from soft Irish wool. She had quickly brushed her hair and pulled it into a loose plait at the back of her neck. The wind pulled a few wispy strands loose at her temple, and now she worked, without success, to tuck them into her braid.

She felt her cheeks burning and her eyes smarting from the chilly air. Finally, she took a deep breath and turned to Marcus. "Why did you leave me that night?"

"Surely you understood from the —"

She interrupted, her voice low. "Understood? Understood what? That you didn't want to even say good-bye to me or to the children? Is that what I should have understood?"

He regarded her solemnly, trying to understand her words. "But I thought I explained. I never meant for you to think I deserted you —"

She interrupted again. "What else was I supposed to think? We talked that night by the creek. You spoke of caring for me, and I —" Her voice broke off and she looked away from him, nibbling on her lower lip. When she spoke again, her voice was so soft he could barely hear it. "I turned away from you."

As her gaze held his, Sheridan's eyes were bright, either from the cold or from unshed tears. She reached for his hand, and at her touch, Marcus thought his heart would surely pound clear through his chest.

She went on. "I've always been too quick to judge, Marcus. I think I've mentioned this to you before. It's something my grandma'am always used to caution me about."

He squeezed her hand, and a small smile played at her lips as she went on. "That night, as I lay in bed, waitin' for the dawn, I thought about what you'd said, and my response, of course. My blithering idiotic response."

He didn't interrupt.

"And I prayed for the dawn to come quickly. Because, dear Marcus," she clutched both his hands, "I couldn't wait to tell you."

"Tell me what, Sheridan?" His voice was a hoarse whisper. Now he was sure the glistening in her eyes was tears.

"I couldn't wait to tell you how much I care." She sniffled and dabbed at her eyes with her fingertips.

Marcus pulled a handkerchief from his pocket. He cupped her chin with one hand and tenderly dabbed at her tears with the soft cloth. He wanted to pull her into his arms, but he could see by her expression that it wasn't the right time.

For a moment the only sounds that could be heard were those of a chipmunk skittering and chirping underneath a nearby buckeye. Overhead, a bluejay landed on a pine branch and cawed to its mate. A gray squirrel climbed an oak and darted among its limbs, nibbling at acorns.

And against the vivid blue sky, a red-tailed hawk caught the wind and soared heavenward, reflecting exactly the feelings in Marcus's heart. Marcus was so close to Sheridan that he breathed in the scent of her soap-scrubbed skin. Mixed with the fragrance of pines and rain-damp earth, the scent was sweeter than any perfume he'd ever smelled.

He started to speak, but she put her fingers to his mouth. "No, let me finish," she said softly. He nodded, and she let out a shaky breath. "I realized that night that I was judgin' you on what you thought about doin', not what you actually did." She was holding the handkerchief now. She dabbed again at her nose. "And that night as I lay prayin' and thinkin', I realized that I'd done worse."

"I don't understand."

She swallowed hard. "You see, all the way around Cape Horn, those endless weeks I spent on the clipper, I thought about the detective who was supposed to meet me in San Francisco."

Marcus nodded, feeling ashamed. "The detective I pretended to be."

"Aye. But it wasn't exactly a detective I was thinking about all that time, Marcus."

"It wasn't?" He frowned, trying to understand.

"No. I was dreamin' about a prince from a fairy tale." She laughed lightly, embarrassed. "I was expectin' someone else entirely."

"Then I showed up." Marcus had no illusions about being a prince, but he didn't know quite how to take her words.

"Aye. When I first saw you, I thought you were he."

"The prince."

"Aye."

"Then I disappointed you. I insulted you first by expecting a man named Sheridan O'Brian, then later by suggesting a woman couldn't face the wilderness alone."

"It wasn't you — your suggestions — that angered me. It was my thinkin'."

"How do you mean?"

"By the time I reached San Francisco, I was growing ashamed of my dreams about findin' a prince." She regarded him seriously for a moment. "Do you have any idea what I was doin' before I boarded that clipper?"

Marcus frowned. "Finishing school? You're obviously..." He started to recite all the wonderful qualities he saw in her.

She touched his lips again. "I was in school. I attended Oberlin College."

He was impressed. Oberlin was not a finishing school for empty-headed young ladies. But how was that connected to her thoughts aboard the clipper?

Taking a deep breath, she went on. "While there I became active in the Underground Railroad."

He let out a low whistle. "You what?"

"My friend Callie and I headed up stations in Ohio and in Mississippi. The reason I left Oberlin before the end of the term was because I was wanted by the law." She laughed softly. "Actually, I suppose I'm still considered an outlaw in Ohio."

"Sheridan, I had no idea." Frowning, he watched her intently.

"Imagine me — with all the dangerous scrapes I've been in and out of — wantin' a prince to see me through." She swallowed hard. "When you told me how you'd planned to deceive me for your own gain, I was reminded that my idea of a prince had been an idiotic dream."

"I'm sorry," he managed, unable to meet her eyes.

Sheridan touched his arm, shaking her head. Again their eyes met. "No," she said. "The eejit wasn't the prince, Marcus. The eejit was me." She reached for his hand and held it gently. Marcus smiled softly at her pronunciation of "idiot."

She went on. "My dream prince wasn't made of flesh and bones. That night in the tent, thinkin' about all you'd said made me realize it. You didn't carry through with your plans to deceive me.

"Instead, you went out of your way to help. And when you saved Evangelia —" Her voice broke off as she remembered how he had risked his life. "Aye, I knew then that you were a man of honor, Marcus. A man of bravery. And deep caring."

He lifted her fingers and lightly kissed them. Her lips curved into a trembling smile, and her violet eyes shimmered with emotion. She touched his cheek with her fingertips.

He drew her into his arms. But she pulled away from him slightly, tilting her face upward. "I should have told you all this before. Then maybe you wouldn't have left." She took a deep breath. "When you disappeared without a word, I didn't know if I'd ever have the chance —"

He broke in. "Wait. Did you say 'when I disappeared without a word'?"

She looked at him evenly. "Aye. You told no one."

"But I did, Sherrie. Didn't you get my note?"

Sheridan shook her head slowly. "There was no note, Marcus."

He gathered her close to his chest again, wrapping his arms tightly around her. His voice was gruff. "I would never have left you without saying good-bye, without telling you my plans."

"You left word for me?" she murmured contentedly, feeling the strong thud of his heart beneath the heavy woolen coat. It was as if the sun had just now slipped from behind the clouds. "You said you'd be back?"

"Of course. I left a letter for you. I'm no prince," he laughed quietly, "but I wouldn't have done that to you and the children."

She slipped from his arms and stood at arm's length, considering him solemnly. "I thought because of what happened, because of the words I said — or didn't say — that you'd left for good."

He shook his head slowly, and let out a deep breath. "We have a lot to catch up on. And not all of it is pleasant. I had asked you, in the note, to check for messages from me at the Wells Fargo office."

She shook her head. "I'm sorry, I didn't know."

He squeezed her fingers. "Don't apologize. I should have realized that the note could have been lost. Who knows what happened to it? But the point is," he turned her gently, and they sat on a flat granite boulder, "in my message I warned you to be very careful." He told her about his meeting with Carter Bainbridge, his suspicions about the man's past dealings with Shamus.

"Aye," Sheridan finally said, taking a deep breath. "I've got the same inclinations."

"I saw you with him earlier today."

She nodded. "I met him, quite by accident. But it didn't take me long to figure out that there is more to his association with my brother than what he told me." She went on to describe the information Bainbridge had given her.

"You know what this means, don't you?"

"Now he's suspicious of us both — first your questioning, then mine. He may figure we're working together." She touched Marcus's hand. "I'm meeting him tonight."

Marcus searched her face. "Why?"

"He asked me to dinner — with the children. I thought it would be good to spend some time with him, gain his trust."

"But now you can't — now that you know he suspects you."

She shook her head. "I disagree. I need to find out about his relationship to Shamus. I think I can regain his trust by playing...a certain role." She smiled and raised an eyebrow. "I've done it before."

Marcus figured she was referring to her work in the

Underground Railroad. But it didn't change the danger. He didn't like her thinking. "No," he said softly. "I can't let you do it."

She raised her chin, a bit defiantly. "I must. It may be the only way to learn what I need to know."

"For one thing, it's too dangerous. For another…" His eyes met hers. "For another thing, I can't bear the thought of you spending time with him. No matter the reason." He looked hurt as he brushed his hair from his forehead.

"It's only to gain information, Marcus. Nothing more. I'll be all right. Believe me." Then, with a quick grin, she daintily lifted her leather skirt a few inches and pulled down her boot top. Holstered at her ankle was a small, pearl-handled pistol. He remembered the Hawken, how she'd swung it to her shoulder as if she'd been doing it every day of her life. Despite her delicate appearance, Sheridan O'Brian was a strong, deliberate, and intelligent young woman. Still, Marcus worried. He'd already pegged Carter Bainbridge for a snake.

"I can take care of myself," Sheridan was saying. "Besides, it's only supper in the hotel dining room."

Knowing he couldn't change her mind, Marcus then told Sheridan of his work with the *Herald Star* and his plans to find out who worked Rainbow's End with Shamus. "I'm going to try to locate the men. They may be connected to Bainbridge. I'm wondering if he destroyed the mine's chances from the beginning — perhaps through the men Shamus hired."

Then they spoke of the children's Uncle Sonny, sharing the information they each had gathered. "I've got to keep them away from Angel's Camp," she said, telling him about enrolling the children in school.

Marcus agreed. "But don't get any ideas about going out there alone," he said. "It's a desolate area."

Sheridan nodded, thinking she should tell Marcus about riding out to the mine with Carter Bainbridge. Just as she was about to speak of it, Marcus stood and pulled her toward him. His expression was tender.

"My darling," he murmured, his voice low.

Sheridan sighed deeply as he gathered her into his arms. She had to tell him about going to Rainbow's End in the morning. "But there's something else I need to —," she began.

"It will have to wait, sweetheart."

"But Marcus —"

He interrupted her by cupping her face in his hands and tilting it upward. His lips brushed hers, at first as gentle as the touch of a butterfly's wing. Then he kissed her again, this time with a tender pressure that made Sheridan think her heart would never stop its somersaults.

She melted into his arms, knowing only that she wanted the moment never to end.

"Now, what was it you wanted to say?" He smiled into her eyes.

"I've forgotten," she breathed, circling her arms around his neck. And she kissed him again.

CHAPTER

Fifteen

❦

T hat night after dining with Carter Bainbridge in the Empress dining room, Sheridan ushered the children up the stairs, listened to their prayers, and tucked them into bed. They were tired from their first day at school and fell asleep almost before Sheridan reached the door.

Stepping from the children's room to the adjacent parlor, Sheridan smiled a greeting to the waiting Carter. He was seated in a brocade settee near the fireplace. He had poured two glasses of sherry from a crystal decanter that sat in a silver tray on a small lamp table. His gaze never left her as she moved across the room to join him. His scrutiny made her uncomfortable. Sheridan was suddenly glad she had chosen to wear a modest dark blue dress with a high lace collar; she straightened the skirt as she seated herself in a high-backed wing chair near him.

"Carter," she said with a friendly nod, taking the glass of sherry from his fingers. "I enjoyed our supper. Thank you for inviting us to join you."

"My pleasure," he said, meeting her gaze above the rim of his glass. "Your children are a delight. But I can see how you're going to have your hands full with that boy." He chuckled and related a tale about his own childhood. After a few minutes of speaking about Duncan and Evangelia, he glanced toward the balcony and stood. "It's a beautiful evening, Sheridan. A bit crisp, but one look at the night sky is worth putting up with the discomfort."

She nodded and rose. Carter held open the glass-paned door, and Sheridan stepped onto the balcony.

"About tomorrow —" Carter began, moving closer. She noticed he hadn't even glanced at the starry sky.

Sheridan smiled and stepped back, conscious of moving closer to the narrow, scrolled rail that bordered the balcony. She touched it with her fingertips, slightly alarmed to feel it wobble. "Yes?" she said, lifting her eyes to his.

"I figured we would leave after the children are in school."

She hesitated, thinking she would need time to find Marcus and tell him her plan.

"You're still going to the mine with me, aren't you?"

"Of course," she said too quickly.

"Good." He smiled. "We'll be heading into the mountains. The terrain is rugged, and the air will be frigid, possibly windy. You'll need to dress appropriately."

Sheridan nodded. "Aye." She shivered and wondered if it was from the damp night air or the man now standing too close.

"You're cold," Carter said, and draped an arm around her shoulders.

Sheridan took a deep breath. "I'm fine, Carter. Really."

She tried to move away from him, but his broad-shouldered body blocked her way into the parlor. And the loose railing behind her prevented her from moving backward.

"I...I really must be gettin' in now," she said, swallowing hard. She attempted a weak smile.

He held his arm around her a moment longer, staring into her eyes. His look was cold. She shivered again, and he pulled her closer. Sheridan could feel the iron strength of his upper body, and it frightened her.

She laughed into his eyes and pushed gently away. "Really, Carter. If we're goin' to be gettin' an early start tomorrow, I must go in."

He finally smiled, opened the glass doors, and cupped her elbow in his huge hand to help her through. Sheridan sighed, relieved to step into the warmth of the parlor.

"I'll call for you at 8:30," Carter said, his dark gray eyes meeting hers.

"We can meet at the livery."

He shook his head. "I would never let a lady go there unescorted."

She regarding him silently. "I've been there many times unescorted."

Laughing, he took her hand and locked his gaze on hers. "Not when you're planning to spend the day with me."

"We said nothing about the entire day, Carter."

"I thought I explained —" He raised an eyebrow expectantly.

"Explained what?" Sheridan felt her throat going dry.

"Rainbow's End is nearly a day's ride from here."

"It is?" Her voice came out in a squeak.

"Oh, yes, my dear. We'll be fortunate to get back by

nightfall." With that, Carter Bainbridge lifted her fingers to his lips, met her eyes once more, smiled, and was gone.

Sheridan tossed fitfully in the high, four-poster oak bed. Finally she rose, lit a candle, and, after pulling her cape around her shoulders, moved out to her room's private balcony.

She looked across to the adjoining parlor balcony, where she had earlier stood with Carter Bainbridge. If she'd had any doubts about the man's character, they were now gone. There was a darkness about him that made her shudder just considering it.

How could he have been a friend of Shamus? She wouldn't have believed it if Bainbridge hadn't mentioned Aunt Fiona and Sheridan herself. Puzzled, she stared into the midnight heavens. Perhaps he did befriend Shamus in the beginning, gained his trust. Then what?

Carter had openly admitted grubstaking Shamus and taking over the mine. But where had Shamus gone? If the events Bainbridge related were true, Shamus would have contacted her through their aunt. He might have been embarrassed over his loss and perhaps his ignorance or his misplaced trust. But he wouldn't have disappeared without a word.

Suddenly she thought about the cold look in Carter Bainbridge's eyes. Was there another reason Shamus had not contacted his family? Was Bainbridge a killer? The thought stabbed her with cruel clarity. Before speaking with Bainbridge, she had been sure that Shamus was alive; as his twin, she thought she would know if his heart stopped beating.

But now? She swallowed back a sob. What if she had

174

been wrong? What if Carter Bainbridge was her brother's murderer? She closed her eyes, trying to shut out the pain. Feelings of sadness, anger, and horror overwhelmed her.

Tears coursed down her cheeks. Sheridan cried silently into her hands; her shoulders convulsed with the nearly unbearable, crushing sorrow. After a moment, she lifted her face to God. "Oh, Lord," she breathed, "help me bear the pain. If Shamus is alive, help me find him. If he's dead —" She felt fresh tears begin. "If he's dead, help me find his killer and see that justice is done."

Sheridan prayed into the night, lifting heavenward every detail of her quest. Then she spoke to her Friend of the children, their needs, their futures. And finally, she told him about her growing feelings for Marcus.

"Dear Father," she prayed. "My heart quickens when I am near him. But I want to do your biddin' in my life. Grandma'am told me years ago that you have someone special picked out for me. When I was just a wee baby, she prayed for that child she knew you had set aside somewhere in the world.

"Is that dear one Marcus, Father? Was he the child Grandma'am prayed for?" She sighed and considered God's guidance, his wisdom and compassion. "Help me set aside my headstrong ways, because I know your ways are better than any I consider on my own. Gently guide me with your unfailing love."

Sheridan raised her eyes to the star-spangled heavens. She caught her breath at the sight. The stars created a blazing canopy of dancing jeweled lights in a black velvet heaven.

"Aye, 'tis a wonder indeed," she breathed, considering God's might and power and remembering, too, that the One who had created each star in the universe was the same God who had created her and Marcus, Duncan, little Evangelia, and dear Shamus. They were all in God's care! There was never a moment he forgot any of them. She smiled, remembering phrases from a Bible passage Grandma'am had taught her years ago about God's creation:

> Then the Lord answered Job out of the whirlwind.... Where wast thou when I laid the foundations of the earth?.... When the morning stars sang together and all the sons of God shouted for joy?

Grandma'am always said those verses meant that the stars and angels sang with God as he created the world and everything in it; that they sang when he created man and woman. Grandma'am told her too that she was certain they still sang today at each wee babe's birth.

Sheridan gazed at the stars and considered the idea. Then she sighed contentedly, feeling safe in the knowledge that she belonged to a God who cared for each of his created beings enough to cause the morning stars to sing and the angels to shout for joy.

"Aye, but I love you, Father. I love you so," she whispered in awe. "And I commit into your care all my confusin' thoughts and worries about tomorrow."

After a few minutes, Sheridan slipped under the heavy covers of her bed. She fell quickly into a deep and peaceful sleep.

The following day dawned brisk and sunny. After breakfast at the hotel, Sheridan walked Duncan and Evangelia to school, then hurried back to the *Herald Star*, careful to give a wide berth to the Goldstrike Mercantile and Mining Supply so that she wouldn't be seen.

Her heart fell when Laramie Burkett, after introducing himself as the editor, told her Marcus Jade hadn't yet arrived for work. After chatting about the weather for a few minutes, Laramie said to try next door at the Falcon Hotel. Sheridan thanked him. A few minutes later, the desk clerk at the Falcon gave her the bad news that Mr. Jade had ridden out before sunup. The gray-haired woman suggested that Sheridan leave a message for the gentleman, however, if she liked.

Deeply disappointed, Sheridan hurriedly wrote out a note, telling Marcus of her plan to accompany Carter Bainbridge to Rainbow's End. As she signed her name, she hesitated briefly, thinking she should apologize for not telling him sooner. She finally decided that such words could be better said in person. So she simply added that she would explain it all when she saw him, then folded the missive and handed it to the kindly clerk.

After leaving the Falcon, Sheridan turned down Main Street and hurried to the Empress. True to his word, Carter Bainbridge was waiting for her in the downstairs lobby.

There was a steely glint in Carter's gaze as he greeted her, and she had the feeling that he somehow knew she had been searching for Marcus. She felt cold inside and attempted to hide the small shudder that ran up her spine. If it hadn't been for Shamus, she wouldn't place herself in such danger. But she loved her brother, and for him, she would see this through. She gave Carter a tremulous smile and they headed toward the livery stable.

Minutes later she mounted Shadrach, and Carter swung his leg across the saddle of a tall gray. He pulled up beside her horse and said that he would lead the way.

"Aye," she said softly and, taking a deep breath, reined the Appaloosa through the livery doors and onto Main Street, following Carter to the north end of town.

They had ridden only a short distance when Carter halted the gray. Sheridan slowed the Appaloosa to a stop beside him. He explained that the trail they were on was the main highway between the northern mining towns and Everlasting Diggins.

"But we'll soon head off up into those hills." He nodded toward the northeast. "Your brother picked an isolated place. Most of the hills around here are crawling with miners. But not up there." He shaded his eyes against the morning sun and squinted into the shadowy hills. He laughed lightly. "He really knew how to find places off the beaten path; I have to give him that. We'll be lucky if we see another human being after we leave this trail."

Again, Sheridan thought she saw a knowing glint in his eyes. She lifted her chin and met his gaze. "Then we'd better get on our way, Carter. I need to be back for the children this afternoon after school."

He laughed. "I told you, Sherrie." She blanched at the presumed familiarity. "I specifically told you of that improbability."

"I'm afraid I have to insist, Carter," Sheridan said evenly, meeting his gaze. She nudged Shadrach in the flanks, and the horse headed down the trail. Carter kicked the gray and soon overtook her. Without a word, he again took the lead.

They rode without speaking for several miles. Lining the trail were miners working their claims. Sounds of long toms and cradles, braying donkeys, and barking dogs added to the racket of the picks and shovels. A few called out to Carter and tipped their hats to Sheridan as they rode by.

Too soon, Carter reined the tall gray off the main trail, and Sheridan followed him up a steep incline. The forests of oak and pine became sparser as they climbed. Sheridan spotted a few miners here and there, but after a time, she saw no one. Instinctively, she felt for the small pistol inside her boot. It was there, fastened securely.

The sun had risen high by the time Carter signaled Sheridan to halt the Appaloosa at the top of a rocky cliff. At the base of a small draw that looked to be a box canyon, he pointed out a spring where they could refresh the horses. She nodded and followed the gray into the deep canyon.

Once there, Carter dismounted, and Sheridan slid from the saddle while the horses drank their fill. The place was sheltered by a thick stand of aspen and a heavy tangle of underbrush. She was struck by the eerie sensation that no matter how loud a person might yell, there was no one around to hear.

"Beautiful country up here," Bainbridge said, though he was looking at Sheridan not the terrain.

She nodded. "God's country." And she meant it.

For a moment he didn't speak, regarding her with a frown. "I've noticed a change in you, Sheridan," he said. He rolled his big shoulders and flexed his arms as if tired from the ride. "I have the distinct feeling you don't trust me."

She tilted her head. "What do you mean?"

"The first time we spoke, that day you happened by the mercantile —" Carter gave her a half smile. "That day, you seemed perfectly at ease."

"Aye."

"Then something happened to change that."

Sheridan swallowed hard. "I still don't know what you're talkin' about."

"Then let me explain. Right after you left me, I saw you meet Marcus Jade on the street in front of the Empress."

Sheridan could feel her heart pounding, hard. She drew in a deep breath and gave him what she hoped was a benign look. "What does that have to do with —"

He interrupted, ignoring her question. "It struck me as odd that you asked me nearly the same questions that your Mister Jade asked the day before." Bainbridge pulled off his hat and gave his hair a swipe back from his face. "Mister Jade, the newspaperman," he mused thoughtfully as he replaced his hat. "Then when I saw you meet, I realized that you were attempting to play some kind of game with me."

"Carter, my brother disappeared two years ago. I'm tryin' to find him. There's no game involved. Why should I try to 'play' around with something that important?"

"My question exactly." He moved closer so that he was standing directly in front of her. The Appaloosa turned its head and seemed to regard the situation. The gray continued to drink from the stream.

"I'm thinking," Bainbridge continued, "that it must surely be because you suspect me of foul play." He lifted her chin, forcing her to meet his gaze. "Is that right?"

Sheridan shook her head and moved backwards a few steps. "No," she said softly. She wondered if she could reach her pistol before Carter again moved closer. She forced her gaze away from his cold gray eyes.

How foolish she had been to come out here with him.

Why hadn't she listened to Marcus's warnings?

"You know I don't want to hurt you, don't you?"

She swallowed and nodded.

"Look at me!" He'd moved dangerously close. His voice was a raspy whisper, and she could feel the heat of his breath on her skin. She lifted her eyes.

"I don't want to hurt you. And I would truly hate to hurt those little children of yours."

Sheridan gasped. "You wouldn't —" Her words faltered. "You wouldn't hurt them."

"I certainly wouldn't want to. After all, tiny little Evangelia couldn't even scream for help, if some…accident…occurred, now could she?"

"You animal," Sheridan hissed.

"Oh, no, dear. I'm no animal. Actually, I'm just letting you know where you stand. Many people have found that when they come up against me, they lose. It happens every time." He shrugged, and his lip twisted into a cruel smile. "I'm just giving you fair warning so that in the future nothing will happen to you, to your small wards —"

"Leave them out of it."

"You still don't get it, do you? It's too late, dear Sherrie. Last night at supper, Duncan told me all about his early life, his father, his mother, and of course, how he came to be with you. We had quite an animated conversation when you took Evangelia to the privy. He told me about Uncle Sonny — the outlaw whom I've actually had the delight to meet.

"Duncan also told me about running away from a livery owner in San Francisco. He said that the man would give anything to get the children back." Carter grinned wickedly. "Your young man gave me enough information in ten minutes to keep you all quiet for years to come, my dear." He brushed her cheek with the side of his thumb.

Sheridan clenched her teeth. "What do you want?"

Bainbridge threw back his head and laughed. "I knew you'd see it my way." Then just as abruptly, he fell silent. "For right now," he said, his voice cold and menacing, "I want you to listen carefully. And do exactly as I say."

Sixteen

❧

Marcus nudged Desperado's flanks and reined him toward an incline leading from the main trail. An ancient lava flow marked the place he headed for, an outcropping of boulders and obsidian at the highest peak above the still-sleeping Everlasting Diggins.

Dawn's gray mists still blanketed the town, but as Desperado, ears lying flat, climbed upward, the sky became clearer. In the east, a faint glow of the coming sunrise provided a lavender-rose backdrop to the mountain's dark silhouettes.

Marcus had risen that morning after a restless night — mostly, he knew, because of Sheridan. The previous evening as she dined with Carter Bainbridge, Marcus paced the floor of his room, checking his pocket watch every few minutes. He couldn't shake the feeling that Sheridan was entering a place of grave danger because of her association with Bainbridge. Several times Marcus stopped himself from leaving the Falcon for the Empress, striding into the dining room, and whisking Sheridan and the children away from the place.

Finally, in the predawn darkness, unable to shake his concerns, Marcus decided to ride into the hills where he could think through the events of the previous days. In San Francisco he often had walked to a place near the *Gazette* office, where he had an unobstructed view of the bay. There was something about the freshness of early morning, the sunrise glow on the waters, the lofty view from afar, that always cleared his perspective. Marcus clucked to the stallion as he nudged him onward. He hoped that by watching the sunrise from this mountaintop he would find the same clarity of thought and peace.

A few minutes later, he led Desperado to a small patch of autumn-gold grass to graze. The stallion eyed Marcus suspiciously as he strode to a nearby boulder and climbed to the top.

Below him, the trail leading from town stretched toward the northern mines, a winding ribbon of red-brown soil that disappeared into the morning mists. Reveling in the solitude of the place, the beauty of absolute silence, Marcus sat, stretched out his long legs, and crossed his ankles. A granite rock behind him provided a backrest. He settled back and let out a deep sigh of contentment.

His thoughts settled, as usual, on Sheridan. How had she so quickly touched his heart? Unknowingly, she had entered a place deep in his soul, a place where no one had been before.

He thought about her beauty. When she looked up at him with those deep blue eyes framed by dark, thick-fringed lashes, his heart never failed to miss a beat. But there was something inside her, an inner loveliness, that drew him even more strongly. It had something to do with her relationship with God. Sheridan faced life with an assurance, a contagious joy, from belonging to the One she called Abba who was far more real to her than any being made of flesh and bone. Marcus knew it to be true from listening to the nighttime stories she'd told the children; he knew it to be true just from being with her.

Marcus raised his eyes heavenward and thought again about the perfection this God required. In his eyes, Sheridan was perfect. No wonder God loved her so. But what about him? He was far from feeling loved by a God such as this.

But sometimes when Marcus faced nearly overwhelming problems, entanglements of deceit, dangers that threatened to swallow him in their complexities, he wanted to belong to a God such as Sheridan's. A God he could trust with childlike faith. A God he could call Abba, Father.

To the east, the sky brightened, and sunlight's first rays streamed through the tall pines. The forest's morning song, sung by a bevy of mountain quail, jays, titmice, and finches, lifted heavenward. The dawn sky gradually filled with the brilliance of the newborn sun spreading its palette of colors; changing from ashen to vermilion to gold.

How could one not believe in the God of such beauty, in the God who created the heavens and the earth? Marcus didn't consider it often, but in a moment of such exquisite solitude, he was absolutely certain of God's existence — and that there was something deeper about him that Marcus was missing.

The sleepy village below began to wake. The faraway voices of miners heading to their digs carried toward him on the breeze. Soon the entire valley was bathed in sunlight, and the dawn mists evaporated. The schoolbell rang, faint in the distance, and he could see dozens of children heading up the schoolhouse hill. He wondered if Duncan and Evangelia were among them.

After several minutes, Marcus stood, rolled his shoulders and stretched his arms. He glanced once more at Everlasting Diggins before beginning the climb down from his rocky perch.

Suddenly he frowned, spotting two figures on horseback, heading out of town. On an Appaloosa, a dark-haired woman in a blue cape followed a big man who looked suspiciously like Carter Bainbridge. If he didn't know better, he would have figured the woman to be Sheridan. He squinted as they disappeared around a bend on the trail.

He couldn't shake the image of the woman's dark cape from his mind. Sheridan wore one like it when riding in cool weather. Just the day before, he had gathered her into his arms and noticed the shade of blue nearly matched the violet in her eyes.

For a long time, Marcus kept his eyes on the trail. But it disappeared into thickets of evergreen oaks and pines, and he didn't see the riders again.

He had to be mistaken, he realized. After all, why would Sheridan ride from town with Carter Bainbridge?

As he mounted Desperado and headed down the mountain and into Everlasting Diggins, he couldn't shake the worry from his mind. What if it had been Sheridan? But by the time he rode down Main Street, his mind focused more on going after information about Bainbridge's connection with Rainbow's End than on whether the rider had been Sheridan.

He stopped at the claims office, dismounted, and looped

Desperado's reins over the hitching post.

A middle-aged man, graying at the temples, looked up as Marcus strode to the counter. "What can I do for you?"

"I'd like to see the Rainbow's End claim — was once owned by a Shamus O'Brian."

"What's your business with the mine?"

"I'm trying to find out what happened to O'Brian. Seems he disappeared a year or so after signing over his claim to a grubstaker."

The man merely raised his eyebrows and fixed an unblinking gaze on Marcus. "And you want to know who the grubstaker is."

"No. I already have that information."

"What then?"

"I'm hoping there'll be other information with the claim."

"Such as?" The man made no move to find the Rainbow's End file.

Marcus was getting impatient. "Is it possible to see the file?"

"Calm down." He smiled benignly. "I just need to know what you're after."

Letting out an exasperated sigh, Marcus began again. "I'm concerned about what happened to O'Brian. Perhaps the file will shed some light on what happened to him. That's all."

"You think the grubstake has something to do with his disappearance."

"Wouldn't surprise me."

"Now we're getting down to business. Who's the grub-staker?" He still made no move toward his file cabinet.

"Carter Bainbridge."

For a moment the man didn't speak. "He's an upstanding

citizen," he said with a frown. "You better be careful about your accusations." He looked at Marcus suspiciously.

"That's why I need to see the file." Marcus stared back. "Is there some reason you're not getting it?"

"No, no. Not at all." Finally, the man sauntered to his files, riffled through, and pulled out a handwritten sheet of paper. He placed it on the counter in front of Marcus.

Marcus scanned it. The original document gave the exact location of the mine. Nothing unusual was contained in its wording. Added to the claim was an informal note in the same handwriting detailing facts about a loan from Carter Bainbridge. It spelled out the terms of the agreement, ending with the statement that if the money owed was not paid off in a timely manner, the mine would go to Bainbridge. It was signed by Shamus O'Brian and Carter Bainbridge. Underneath were the signatures of two witnesses.

Marcus pointed to the "timely manner" phrase and looked up at the claims officer. "Is this usual wording?"

"What do you mean?"

"'Timely manner.' Seems a rather loose interpretation."

The man shrugged. "All I do is record 'em — how they're written up is anybody's business."

"How about these signatures?" Marcus pointed to the two witnesses. "You know these men?"

"Might." Marcus noticed the man had sweat beading on his smooth-shaven upper lip.

"I can't quite make out their names. One looks like Jackson Bent. The other —" Marcus squinted at the signature, unable to decipher it. Finally, he shook his head and looked up. "You know this one?"

"No, no. I don't." The man answered too quickly.

"You don't know if they're still around these parts?"

"No. I wouldn't." He nervously gathered up the claim and loan documents. "Now if you'll excuse me." Then he hurried to the file cabinet and dropped in the papers.

Marcus closed the claims office door behind him, remounted Desperado, and headed to the *Herald Star*. Minutes later, he was greeted by a smiling Laramie Burkett.

"Good to see you, son. Where've you been keeping yourself?"

Marcus grinned, glad to see his friend. He told Laramie about his unsuccessful stop by the claims office. "I'm curious about the witnesses to the loan documents. I probably wouldn't have given them a thought, except that the claims officer got nervous when I pressed him for information about the signatures."

"What was the one name you could make out?"

"Jackson Bent — you heard of him?"

Laramie shook his head thoughtfully. "No, but these miners come and go. You might try askin' around some of the saloons. You're right to suspect they might be connected to Bainbridge, though."

Marcus chuckled. "You read my mind."

"I could be wrong, but it stands to reason that if Bainbridge drew up the papers, he'd also handpick the witnesses to those papers."

"So these men might've been in cahoots with him from the beginning?"

"That's my thinking, son. And —" He polished his spectacles on his sleeve, then replaced them on his nose. "It also seems to me that Bainbridge might use the same men to keep an eye on our Shamus."

189

"What do you mean?"

"People like Bainbridge surround themselves with a few cohorts they trust. Very few. You found out that Shamus hired on a couple workers to help him with the mine after he was grubstaked. He thought Bainbridge was his friend — after all, the man loaned him the money he needed. Maybe Bainbridge also recommended the helpers."

Marcus nodded slowly. "How better to keep an eye on what young Shamus was up to?"

"How better to find out if the boy struck gold?"

"And get rid of him if he did," Marcus added sadly.

"You're on track, son. Exactly on track."

"*If* — and it might not be such a big *if* — these men worked for Bainbridge." Marcus saw the direction he needed to go. And his first step involved finding Jackson Bent.

They spoke about the search for Bent for a few minutes, then Laramie said he'd written Marcus's first article on the search for ex-miners. "After all, you gotta earn your salary," the older man added with a wink.

"Hope it's good."

"The salary or the article?"

"Both," Marcus said, grinning.

He was halfway to the door when Laramie stopped him. "I nearly forgot to tell you. That pretty little Sheridan O'Brian was by here earlier. Introduced herself." He shook his head appreciatively. "She's a beauty, she is. Warm as sunshine. And sweet as honey to boot."

Marcus spun around.

"You better ask her to our upcoming celebration before someone else does." He shook his head with a sly smile. "At least get your name on her dance card. I know I plan to."

Marcus looked confused, and the old man laughed. "You know about the new fire engine comin', don't you?"

He shook his head.

"Seems the hand-pumper was on its way from New York to Tahiti. Someone in San Francisco spotted it on the clipper, made the captain a better offer than what he was going to get in Papeete — so he made a deal. A deal for a whole lot of money." Laramie chuckled. "What they didn't know was that San Francisco was too hilly for that heavy iron mama. Everlasting Diggins bought it for a song. San Franciscans were so anxious to get rid of it — the pumper was quite an expensive embarrassment, you see — that they practically paid us to take it off their hands." He laughed again.

"About the celebration?"

"Oh, yes, back to that. It's to be held as soon as Pete arrives. There'll be a parade down Main Street in the morning. Of course, Pete will lead it."

"Pete?"

Laramie laughed. "Yes sir, Pete! Called that because the ol' hand-pumper was bound for Papeete. These folks think it's pronounced pa-pete — can you imagine that?" He shook his head, still grinning. "Anyway, the parade will be followed by a picnic barbecue in the afternoon. Games for the children.

"And that night…" Laramie raised his eyebrows and let out a low whistle. "Now that's gonna be something. It'll take place in the town square. The whole place is gonna be turned into an outdoor community hall. Highfalutin', too, so that women and children will feel welcome. No bear fights, nosiree. Or saloon hullabaloo. Just sweet bands playing and lots of candlelight dancing. You won't want to miss it, my friend — or to let that beautiful little lass outta your sight."

"Why did Sheridan stop by this morning?"

"I'm sorry, son, I almost forgot to say. She was lookin' for you."

The man could be exasperating. Marcus let out a deep breath. "Did she mention why?"

"No, I can't say that she did. But I sent her next door to the Falcon. Said she'd probably find you there."

Before the words were out of the old man's mouth, Marcus strode through the door and down the sidewalk to the hotel. Desperado lifted his head as Marcus passed, leaving the stallion tethered to the hitching post.

Moments later, Marcus unfolded the note that Sheridan had left for him at the registration desk.

His heart fell. It *had* been Sheridan he'd seen leaving town with Bainbridge earlier that morning. And she had gone to Rainbow's End, a place so remote — Marcus knew from seeing its location described on the claim — she would be in terrible danger if Bainbridge chose to exert his power and strength.

Angrily, Marcus crumpled the note in his fist and threw it down. Then he sprinted out the door of the Falcon Hotel straight toward Desperado.

Seventeen

W hat do you want?" Sheridan hissed.

"I just want you to listen carefully to what I propose. And please remember, your children's lives are in your hands."

Again Sheridan backed away from him, concentrating on getting to the pistol in her boot.

Carter gallantly patted a spot on a felled pine. "Here. Sit next to me and I'll explain everything."

Sheridan did as he instructed, pulling her cape close to stop her sudden trembling. "All right," she said, fighting to keep her voice strong. "You might as well put aside your pretense of civility, Mr. Bainbridge. Just tell me what you want me to do."

Laughing softly, he reached for her hand. She quickly withdrew it.

"It didn't take me long to figure out that you and Jade had come here to expose my operations. There've been others, and it always takes me some time to find their weaknesses, to 'convince' them they've come to the wrong place. But with the two of you, I hadn't yet decided how to handle the, ah — shall we say — situation. That is, until our lovely supper last night with your children.

"Suddenly I found your weakness, dear." He cupped his fingers under her chin and turned her head so that she looked into his eyes. "I found your vulnerability. You feel strongly about them — I saw that immediately. They've settled into a place in your heart where you'd like to keep them forever. Am I right?"

Sheridan didn't answer.

"Am I right?" he repeated, his voice low and angry.

She finally nodded. It was no use playing tough right now.

He dropped his hand. "Well, as I was saying, after listening to Duncan's delightful information, it didn't take me long to realize how we all can benefit." He smiled as if Sheridan should be pleased with the news. "You are going to help me with a bit of a charade, and I will help you keep the children."

"What charade?"

"I'll get to that in a moment. First I need to tell you about some things I want you to do for me."

Sheridan tilted her head. "What things?"

"I want you to stop investigating Rainbow's End. I want no one — you or your Mr. Jade — nosing around the mine or the claims office. I want no questions being asked in town. I want not so much as a whisper of suspicion cast in my direction. Do I make myself clear?"

Sheridan nodded. "Aye, sir. You do. Perfectly."

"Good."

"But what about my brother? Can you not tell me what

happened? My search really doesn't matter — if you'll simply tell me about Shamus."

"You don't need to be worrying about Shamus, dear. He met with an unfortunate accident. You'll not be seeing him again."

Tears filled Sheridan's eyes. "He's dead?" she whispered.

"There was nothing anyone could do. I'm sorry." His eyes were cold as he said the words.

"How…how did it happen?"

Bainbridge looked away from her. "Now that's one of those secrets that the dead take to the grave with them." He shrugged and said no more.

Sheridan clamped her lips together to keep from crying. Finally she whispered, "You said Shamus was your friend. You knew of our Aunt Fiona. He must have trusted you. Do you feel nothing about his death?"

But Bainbridge seemed not to have heard a word she spoke. He simply cleared his throat and went on with his list of her duties. "I want nothing said of our meeting here today. Not a word of our discussion, of our agreement. Is that understood?"

Again Sheridan nodded. "Aye." It was pointless to protest. The children's lives were at stake.

"That's all," he said with a shrug and a smile. "See, I'm a reasonable man. You do these things for me, and I provide insurance for your children."

"Insurance?" She frowned.

"If you live up to your end of our agreement, I will guarantee that your children will not be harmed — physically or emotionally." He lifted his palms in a supplicant manner and shrugged again. "As I said to you earlier, this is a cruel world where all sorts of harm could befall them. It will be reassuring to you, I know, to realize that I am on their side, helping you keep them safe." He smiled and took her hand in his. "Wouldn't you agree, Sherrie?"

She nodded, her mind already working at how she planned to escape this man's clutches. The fear that seemed to slice clear through to her heart seemed familiar somehow. The Underground Railroad came flooding back, her narrow escapes from slave hunters, the bitterness and hatred, the fear she'd seen on their faces. She remembered her friend Callie. Armed with only "southern belle" sweetness and iron resolve, she had helped hundreds of slaves escape. She had played the part with such aplomb that no one suspected her duplicity.

Sheridan took a deep breath. This was no different. She had learned well from Callie and the others in the Underground. Sheridan's strength and intelligence had been tested before. She turned to look deep into Carter's eyes. There was an innate weakness in him, a lack of character, of compassion, of anything good that would give him strength. Why else would he hide behind a young woman and two defenseless children?

Aye, she decided, the man was deficient in the areas of life that count. That didn't mean he wasn't dangerous. Oh, no. Far from it. Even her grandma'am said that often the weakest of men were the most menacing. Sheridan also knew it to be true from the slave hunters she'd met in her work with the Underground.

Suddenly, Sheridan was no longer afraid. She took a deep breath and smiled at the man sitting beside her. "I will do as you say, Carter. I understand."

His hard look seemed to soften somewhat. "Good. I was hoping that you would see it my way."

"The children — as you guessed — are very dear to me. I will do anything you say to keep them safe."

"I…I ah, didn't know if you would fight me on this, Sherrie — it *is* all right if I call you Sherrie?"

She laughed lightly and squeezed his hand. "Of course, Carter."

"There's something else you'll need to do to uphold your end of our —" He seemed to struggle with the words. "Our, ah, bargain."

"Aye?" She swallowed hard, somehow feeling he'd saved the worst for last. "And what would that be?"

He smiled, still holding her hand. "I feel that you need to show your support for me in town. If any of the folks in Everlasting Diggins suspect that you're investigating me, it could be, ah, shall we say, difficult for me in my business dealings."

She nodded, figuring what was coming next.

"I want us to be seen together."

Sheridan managed to nod pleasantly.

"Socially, I mean. We'll become, ah —" He looked hard into her eyes. "An item of conversation. Do you understand?"

"Aye." Again she smiled. "That will not be so difficult."

Bainbridge, surprised, lifted a handsome eyebrow.

She laughed lightly. "A few minutes ago, you frightened me, Carter. That I'll not deny. But I also need to tell you that since we first met, I've felt, well…" She allowed her cheeks to color — prettily, she hoped — and didn't finish.

He patted her hand, obviously surprised and pleased.

Sheridan wondered how he could be so naive as to believe her. Arrogance and vanity, as Grandma'am used to say, led many a man down the path to destruction. Samson wasn't the first, when Delilah cut his hair. Well, just as Delilah led the mighty Samson to his destruction, so would Sheridan work for Bainbridge's downfall.

"I would be most honored to be seen in Everlasting Diggins in your company," she finally said with a sweet smile. "Aye, 'twill be a privilege indeed."

"One more thing," he said, smiling back with cold eyes. "You are to stay away from Marcus Jade."

Sheridan tilted her head.

"I don't trust him. He asks too many questions. I want you to assure him that you no longer feel it necessary to pursue the investigation of Rainbow's End."

She nodded meekly.

"And you are to have nothing to do with Jade personally." He caught up her hand and held it to his lips as his steely gaze locked on hers. "If you do, those dear children will suffer from your indiscreet actions." He kissed her fingertips. "Aye, wouldn't that just be a shame, now?"

His last words mocked her Irish brogue. She bristled, but her smile remained frozen to her face. "Aye," she agreed.

There was no reason to go on to Rainbow's End after their conversation, according to Bainbridge, so they began their descent toward the main trail into Everlasting Diggins. Besides, he told Sheridan with a sly wink, she was the one who wanted to return before dark. Sheridan, astride the Appaloosa, dug her heels into the horse's flanks. Bainbridge rode close behind her. She could feel his eyes boring through her back, watching her every move.

They had nearly reached the valley floor and the main trail leading into town, when the Appaloosa whinnied and shied to the right, sensing another rider. Just then, the approaching horse appeared, a big black, galloping like wildfire.

Sheridan leaned back in the saddle, reining the Appaloosa hard to control the horse.

The black snorted and, nostrils flaring and eyes wild, reared.

Desperado! Sheridan's gaze moved to the rider struggling to stay seated on the big stallion. "Marcus," she breathed. His wheat-gold hair gleamed in the noon sun. Her breath caught as his eyes, blue as the Irish-seas, held hers in a brief moment of tenderness.

Marcus halted the stallion near the Appaloosa. The big horse danced sideways, still snorting. Shadrach whinnied softly but stood motionless beside Desperado. Before Marcus or Sheridan could speak, Carter Bainbridge rode up beside them on the gray.

"Greetings, Jade," Bainbridge said cordially. He stuck out his hand and nodded with a grin as Marcus shook it. "Nice morning for a ride — or maybe I should say afternoon." He squinted up at the high sun. "What brings you out this way?"

"I'm following a lead, you might say."

"Is that right?" Bainbridge glanced around the desolate terrain. "Well, I doubt that you'll find much to write about out here."

"Maybe not." Marcus met the man's gaze head-on, a cold

smile fixed on his face. Sheridan noticed a rugged strength in his expression. She was surprised she hadn't noticed it before.

"Ah, yes." Bainbridge chuckled lightly. "You were looking into Shamus O'Brian's mine. I suppose you're on your way to Rainbow's End?"

Marcus didn't comment.

"You're welcome to go there, of course. But I doubt that you'll find anything to help your story. In fact, we were on our way out there ourselves this morning, weren't we, Sherrie?" He smiled into Sheridan's eyes. "Then we decided it was a bit too far — and probably wouldn't have been worth the effort anyway."

Marcus met Sheridan's gaze as if trying to read her thoughts. She smiled gently, then remembered the children and looked away.

"And how is your story on O'Brian coming along, Jade?" Bainbridge looked genuinely interested.

Desperado snorted and arched his neck. Marcus patted the horse's shoulder. "I've still got some work to do on it. I'm checking into other miners' stories as well."

"You've not said anything about knowing Miss O'Brian here. She is in Everlasting Diggins looking into the same story." He chuckled, shaking his head slowly. "Seems quite a coincidence, doesn't it?"

Marcus nodded, again searching Sheridan's face. Finally he said, "Yes. We've met."

"So she told me." Bainbridge smiled fondly at Sheridan. She returned the look, aware that Marcus's eyes never left her.

"I see," Marcus said lamely.

"Maybe you don't, my friend." Bainbridge's voice was cold. "I believe Sherrie has something to tell you about her search, don't you, dear?"

Sheridan lifted her chin and spoke with what she hoped was convincing emotion. "The search is over, Marcus. Carter told me how Shamus died. It was a shameful death, but Carter kept it a secret to protect my brother's good name. And for that I'm grateful. It's enough for me just to know how it happened." Tears filled her eyes. "I've come to the end of a long journey, searchin' for my sweet brother. Now it's over. Carter told me everything." She drew in a deep, shaky breath. "Now I just want to put it behind me. I don't want to think about it anymore."

Marcus moved Desperado closer to Shadrach. He reached for Sheridan's hand. His eyes searched hers. "Is this true?"

Sheridan pictured Duncan, his freckled face and bright carrot-colored hair, how he was just beginning to live a normal life. And Evangelia, the precious baby who'd known too much tragedy and sadness. She thought about her wildflower fragrance after bath time as Sheridan wrapped her in a big towel and pulled her onto her lap. The children deserved to be happy and secure. Right now, Carter Bainbridge held their future in his hands.

"Is it true, Sheridan?" Marcus persisted. His expression spoke of compassion and concern. For the briefest moment, Sheridan was aware of nothing — not Carter Bainbridge or Shamus or the children — except Marcus and herself, the touch of their souls, the light in Marcus's eyes as he considered her. He expected honesty. And that was the one thing she couldn't, mustn't, give him.

Sheridan squeezed his hand, and again the hot threat of

tears stung her eyes. She finally spoke. "Aye," she whispered, "'tis true, Marcus." It nearly broke her heart to say it. She pulled away her hand and held it out for Carter Bainbridge to take in his. With a half smile, his gaze never leaving Marcus's face, Carter moved the big gray close enough to grasp Sheridan's fingertips.

Sheridan smiled up at Carter with what she hoped was a trusting expression, then went on. "I've decided that Carter did all he could for my brother. He even tried to protect me from findin' out about the way Shamus died." She turned back to Marcus and observed his hurt expression. "Carter has been more than generous, Marcus. And for that I am considerin' myself more than just grateful."

She could tell by Carter's pleased expression that her performance had moved him. But as Marcus reined Desperado back onto the trail and glanced at her once more before riding off, her heart was pierced with deep sorrow.

"Aye," she whispered, half to herself, as Marcus rode away. "That's done, now, isn't it?"

"An excellent performance. I especially liked the touch of your dear brother's shameful death." He chuckled wickedly. "But, of course, it must be my imagination that tells me you're much more experienced in such dealings than this sweet and innocent face would let on." He chucked her under the chin before abruptly reining the big gray onto the trail. Sheridan could hear his laughter as the horse headed through the underbrush.

"Aye," she breathed, following on the Appaloosa. "You'll not be knowin' the half of it, dear sir. Not the half of it."

Eighteen

That night Marcus paced the floor of his room at the Falcon, attempting to analyze Sheridan's words and actions. How could she be so blind to Bainbridge's deceit? He let out an exasperated sigh. Why did she go into the wilderness with him? And why hadn't they gone on to Rainbow's End?

He pulled out his pocket watch. It was two o'clock in the morning. He moved to his window, held back the chintz curtains, and peered out. While Everlasting Diggins residents slept peacefully, a couple of dogs nosed their way down the empty street and in the distance a hoot owl cried out mournfully. A cat yowled, then jumped from a pile of garbage behind a nearby saloon.

The stately Empress stood at the end of the street, barely visible in the pale moonlight. He considered Sheridan and the children sleeping inside. No matter what Sheridan had meant during their encounter on the trail, he couldn't stop caring for any of them.

Sheridan was not naive. She'd told him about her work

with the Underground Railroad. She had risked her life, probably outsmarting the most brutal slave hunters. Beneath her gentle Irish charm was a woman of steely determination. She knew exactly what she was doing. Marcus figured, as much as he disliked Bainbridge, Sheridan must have found something of value in him. Otherwise, why would she believe the scoundrel?

Marcus let out a deep breath as a new thought pierced his heart. What if Sheridan was falling in love with Carter Bainbridge? The thought disturbed Marcus so that he began to pace again. Why else would she have become so blind? But then, Bainbridge was smooth. He was also handsome, urbane, intelligent. Marcus had openly declared his love for Sheridan, but she hadn't actually said she returned that love.

With a sinking feeling, Marcus considered his own faults, his brash nature, his selfish tendency to pursue life's offerings for self-benefit. His thoughts jolted to a standstill. How could Sheridan possibly love him? Forgive him for pretending he was some famous private detective? Yes. It was in her sweet and godly nature. But love him?

He remembered their conversation the day they kissed. Sheridan had said she realized how much she cared for him — how he was an honorable and compassionate man — because he had saved little Evangelia.

He drew in a quick breath. Why hadn't he realized it sooner? He strode to the window again and looked out at the starlit night. He loved Sheridan. He knew it with a certainty. But he also faced two probabilities: Sheridan was falling in love with someone else, and — he clenched his teeth at the thought — what he had mistaken for Sheridan's love was mere gratitude. He also knew his pride had been sorely injured. That alone would keep him distant from Sheridan and the children.

Marcus considered his involvement. His first inclination was to pack up and head back to San Francisco. But he smelled danger and trickery. No matter how Sheridan felt about Carter Bainbridge, Marcus didn't trust him.

Sighing deeply, Marcus finally decided that he couldn't leave Everlasting Diggins. Besides, as a newspaperman, he loved a good mystery. Sheridan might be ready to give up her search for Shamus, but he wasn't. He also wasn't ready to give up protecting Duncan or Evangelia. Or Sheridan.

He would watch them from a distance. If Carter Bainbridge tried anything, he'd have Marcus to deal with first. Marcus might not carry a gun or even know how to shoot. Most of the time he couldn't even get his horse to behave. But as he finally laid down and pulled the woolen blankets over his shoulders, Marcus vowed — wounded pride or not — he'd fight Bainbridge to the death to protect Sheridan and the children.

The next morning at sunrise, Marcus pulled on his pants and wool shirt and headed down back streets toward the Empress. Unable to shake the feeling that the children were in imminent danger, he watched from an alleyway until Duncan and Evangelia skipped out the hotel doorway, lunch pails in hand. Soon joined by several other children, they moved down Main Street and up the hill leading to the schoolhouse.

Marcus followed, slipping among groups of miners heading to their digs. From a thicket of live oaks and buckeyes, he looked on until the children were safely inside the school-house before turning back to the *Herald Star* office.

When the afternoon school bell tolled, Marcus was again in place, silently guarding the children as they walked back to the Empress. He frowned as Duncan immediately clambered down the stairs to join his friends playing with wagon wheel hoops and sticks. Then he relaxed when he saw Sheridan sitting with Evangelia near the balcony, looking through the window as if she too might be concerned about him.

While he was watching over the children on their way to school the next morning, Evangelia, seeming to sense his presence, turned and met his gaze. She made no move to show her brother, who walked beside her. She just tilted her head with a small smile and kept turning to see if Marcus was there. After that, every morning and each afternoon, she looked for Marcus, her smile widening each time she spotted him.

Marcus took Laramie Burkett into his confidence. Laramie immediately expanded Marcus's role as assistant editor, enabling him to cover meetings and activities in which Bainbridge might be involved. Laramie also suggested that Marcus keep meticulous records and write an exposé based on his investigation.

It didn't take long for Marcus to discover that every time he encountered Bainbridge, a smiling, radiant Sheridan was on his arm.

One night, on behalf of the *Herald Star,* Marcus attended an elegant supper at the Empress Hotel. It was hosted by

Carter Bainbridge for Everlasting's six aldermen, their wives, and the elderly, soon-to-retire *alcalde,* or justice of the peace. He also recognized the colorful and rotund Clementine Love, leader of the town's hundreds of women citizens in a movement for temperance, education, religion, and good morals.

"You'd think the man was running for office," Marcus muttered to himself as he watched the evening's affairs: violin music, candlelight dining, and impromptu speeches by the town's leading citizens. *Of course. Alcalde! Maybe he hasn't announced it yet, but Carter Bainbridge is already in the running.* Marcus made a mental note: more fodder for the planned exposé.

But Marcus's eyes were always on Sheridan. Avoiding his gaze, she played the role of hostess with aplomb. Her Irish wit and good-humored charm had never shined brighter. She enchanted and enticed. She laughed at Carter's jokes and listened to his political views. She praised his progressive ideas. Throughout the evening, the man's face was alight with pleasure. A glutton for adulation, Marcus thought. But he couldn't help feeling sick as he watched Sheridan smile into Carter's eyes.

A few nights later, Marcus covered the opening of a new play, *Uncle Tom's Cabin,* at the Falconer Theater. Marcus figured Bainbridge would be in attendance. It was no secret that he had given money to help build the theater and subsidized the salaries of the performers, said to be from New York.

Marcus arrived early and took his seat directly across from the Bainbridge box. He moved his chair slightly behind a heavy velvet curtain to shield himself from view. Within minutes, Carter arrived, dressed in a dark coat and pants, complete with a stovepipe hat. Then Sheridan entered the box, and the whole world seemed to stand still. Marcus had never seen her look so radiant.

She wore an elegant velvet gown the deep red color of bayberries. He tried to dismiss the unpleasant thought that the frock might have been a gift from Bainbridge.

Marcus drank in her stunning beauty. The neckline of the gown fell slightly off her creamy shoulders. Her hair, as blue-black as a raven's wing, swept upward and formed a crown of loose curls, intertwined with ribbon the same color as her gown. She turned, as though searching the crowd for someone. He couldn't pull his gaze away from her porcelain face with its dimpled chin.

Soon the heavy curtain on stage rose and the play began. Marcus, knowing how Sheridan would be affected by a drama exposing the horrors of slavery, studied her profile as the play progressed. Her expression ranged from rage to deep sadness, even sorrow. In the final scene, Sheridan lifted her hands to her face and wept as Uncle Tom received the beating that brought him death. Marcus fought the urge to go to the box where she sat, gather her into his arms, and dry her tears. But he could only watch from a distance, feeling a desperate alienation.

When the final curtain dropped, a subdued audience filed from the theater. Sheridan stood to leave the box, Carter's hand at her elbow. The play had affected her profoundly, and she desperately wanted a time of quiet to allow her emotions to calm. But as they moved down the heavily carpeted stairs, Bainbridge called out to friends and acquaintances about the upcoming election or the celebration for Papeete Pete. His banal chatter seemed a sacrilege, a grating of fingernails on a blackboard, she thought with disdain.

They stepped into the foyer, and Bainbridge guided her to a group of men and women, mostly Everlasting's aldermen and their wives, a few shopkeepers, and the town's only physician. They were speaking of the drama, and Carter launched into a tirade against "that n—— loving Harriet Beecher Stowe."

Sheridan drew in a sharp breath, feeling sick and angry. "I'm going to step outside for a breath of air," she finally said, biting her tongue to keep quiet. Carter had already moved to another topic and barely seemed to notice as she slipped away.

Moments later, drawing her cape onto her shoulders, Sheridan strolled around the corner of the theater. A sliver of moon illuminated her path as she headed along the brick walkway to a terraced garden sheltered by a ring of oaks. At the far end of the garden near some climbing wild roses, she sank into an iron settee.

A crisp breeze rustled the branches above her, and a few leaves fluttered to the ground. Letting out a deep breath, Sheridan closed her eyes, grateful for the moment of peace and quiet. "Father," she whispered. "Give me strength to continue on — for the children, your precious children."

"Sheridan?"

She looked up, surprised she had been followed.

Marcus moved down the walkway toward her, his footsteps sounding in the dry leaves. "Sheridan." He whispered her name again. The sound of it on his lips was musical. She stood to greet him.

"Are you all right?" His voice, with its gentle kindness, made her want to weep and fall into his arms.

"Marcus," she breathed.

He took both her hands in his. "You're trembling."

She nodded. "Aye. And I don't believe it's from the cold."

"What is it, Sheridan? Please — is there something I can do?" His eyes seemed to embrace her with their caring.

Sheridan brought her hand upward, meaning to caress his cheek, when she heard approaching footsteps. Someone had followed them into the garden. Instead of touching his face, she stepped back, pushing Marcus away from her. "Please, Marcus," she said haughtily. "You need not concern yourself with me."

"Darling! There you are." Carter Bainbridge rounded the corner. His voice carried to the place where Sheridan and Marcus stood. "Clementine said she saw you heading this way." Carter's gaze first rested on Sheridan then settled on her companion. "Don't you think we should be getting back to the children?" he asked Sheridan pointedly, his eyes never leaving Marcus's face.

"Aye," Sheridan whispered and took Carter's arm.

Marcus stood near the rose trellis, watching as they moved away from him. He didn't think Sheridan so much as glanced back.

For days Sheridan cherished the memory of her encounter with Marcus. Before she drifted to sleep at night, she prayed for him, remembering the gentle way he'd looked at her in the moonlight. How she longed to brush back his shock of blond hair that always seemed to fall across his forehead, to touch his face with her fingertips, to gaze into his clear eyes for the rest of her life.

She also prayed each night for strength as she kept her promise to Carter Bainbridge, accompanying him, playing the role of a willing and affectionate companion. Realizing immediately his political ambition, she used that weakness, flattering him with her wide-eyed praise.

Sheridan held on to the hope that Bainbridge had lied about Shamus's death. She vowed that she wouldn't rest until she knew exactly what had happened at Rainbow's End the day her twin disappeared. She waited for Carter to let down his guard and trust her implicitly. Then she would begin her search for information about Shamus.

While Sheridan waited to make her move, she cared for the children, helping them with schoolwork. Duncan was a quick learner. He'd already memorized the alphabet and had started reading simple words. More often now, Evangelia's little face was wreathed in smiles, and she stopped sucking her thumb except at bedtime.

After school one day, Duncan ran breathlessly into their rooms at the Empress after school. "Have you heard about Pete?"

Sheridan looked up from where she was helping Evangelia print her name on a small slate. "Pete? No, I haven't heard. Is he a new boy at school?"

Duncan laughed. "No! It's our new hand-pumper fire engine. Comin' all the way from San Francisco. It's comin' into Everlasting Diggins on a big wagon. The whole school's goin' down to meet it."

"Oh, yes. Tomorrow?"

"A few days from now. Seems they don't know how long it'll take to get here from San Francisco. They're having to take the long way, so's to miss goin' through the gorge."

Sheridan laughed, remembering their treacherous trip through. "Aye, 'tis a good thing."

"Folks are already out watchin' for it, though." The little boy's eyes were fairly dancing with the news. "And it's red — bright and shiny red. We're gonna have a parade and everything when it gets here. Music and dancin' and lots to eat. Can we go? Someone said we can even be in the parade if we want. Oh, please, Miss Sheridan, say we can."

Sheridan laughed. She'd never seen Duncan so full of lively hope, exactly the way a child should experience life. She tousled his wiry red hair. "I believe we'll all be there with bells on!"

Duncan gave her a quick hug, then bounded through the door and down the stairs to play hoops with friends.

A few minutes later, Sheridan, with Evangelia's tiny hand in hers, stepped from the Empress to the street. Sheridan breathed in the sunny warmth of the Indian summer afternoon and commented to Evangelia about the beauty of the purple-blue heavens. The child, as daintily as a wood sprite, stepped into a patch of sunlight, lifted her face, and closed her eyes, relishing the warmth on her skin. Sheridan lifted a quick prayer of thanks for Evangelia's discovery of such a simple joy.

"I think I'll start calling you my little sunflower," she said, stooping and giving Evangelia a squeeze. "Though I much prefer your freckles to sunflower seeds." She kissed the little girl's freckled nose. Evangelia's bright eyes opened wide and she giggled softly.

After a moment, they headed down Main Street toward the mercantile where Sheridan planned to buy some yarn for darning the children's worn stockings. There was a hubbub in the air. Along the walkway, small groups of people milled about, speaking excitedly about the fire engine, the parade, and the town-square ball afterward.

Suddenly, Evangelia yanked at Sheridan's arm to stop. The little girl pointed across the street.

There, leaning against a tall post, was Marcus Jade, hat nearly over his eyes. Sheridan had the impression that he'd been watching them. Evangelia let go of her hand and ran as fast as her little legs could churn, dodging horses and carriages as she crossed the street. She raised her arms at the same time that Marcus knelt down and opened his.

Sheridan felt a sting behind her eyes as she watched Marcus scoop Evangelia upward. He lifted her into the sunlight, chuckling softly as they twirled round and round. Then, bringing her close to his heart, he nestled her in his arms. Evangelia's tiny arms circled his neck as if she would never let go.

Stepping from the sidewalk into the street, Sheridan made her way toward them.

"Marcus," she whispered as he met her eyes over the top of the little girl's sun-gold hair. She was surprised by the cool assessment of his gaze.

But before either could speak, Sheridan noticed Carter Bainbridge step from the Goldstrike Mercantile on the other side of the street.

"We really must be going," she said sternly.

Marcus stooped to let Evangelia down from his arms. "I understand," he said without emotion.

But Sheridan didn't answer. She just hurried away from him, pulling Evangelia along with her. Moments later the two disappeared inside the mercantile.

Marcus let out a deep breath and leaned back against the post, his ankles crossed, his hat pulled low. As usual, seeing Sheridan close up had scrambled his thoughts. He wanted nothing worse than to pull her into his arms and hold her there forever — Bainbridge or no Bainbridge. He'd had enough of playing guardian angel from a distance.

Marcus turned his thoughts to Shamus O'Brian. Though he worked his day's activities around keeping an eye on the children and Sheridan, he'd been busy uncovering details involving Rainbow's End. As Laramie Burkett had suggested, he'd asked around the saloons for Jackson Bent, the witness on the grubstake loan. He'd even visited a couple of bear and bull fights and a cock fight, where many of the miners gathered to bet the little gold they pulled from the earth. Though the blood and violence sickened him, he'd found it was a place where miners — their minds on the "sport" — let out tidbits of information they might otherwise have kept to themselves.

Just that morning at a griz and dog fight, he'd finally heard that Jackson Bent now lived in a rough-hewn cabin at a place called Muleskinner Hill. The information was so reliable that Marcus planned to ask a few more questions in town, then head out and pay the old miner a visit.

He waited until Sheridan and Evangelia left the mercantile and moved safely inside the Empress before leaving his post. Then he turned and strode through the open doorway of a nearby stable.

"Help you?" A grizzled old man with long, straggly gray hair looked up.

Marcus hadn't seen him in the place the last time he was by to ask questions. "You new?"

"You don't think I can take care of yer animals as good as the next man?"

"No offense, sir." Marcus held up his hand in a conciliatory manner. "I just hadn't seen you in here before."

"It's my first day."

"You leaving mining?"

The man sighed. "Now how'd you know that?"

Marcus shrugged. "Guess because you look more like a miner than a stable hand." When the man didn't comment, he went on. "Maybe you can help me find someone. Man who used to keep company with an old miner named Bent."

"Lotta old miners around here."

"This one's different. Seems he had only one eye."

"Lotta those around, too."

Marcus let out a long, exasperated sigh. Seemed he was always having to pay for information that ought to be free. He dug into his pocket for a coin, then dropped it in the man's open hand.

"One eye you say."

"You heard of him?"

The man nodded. "Worked a long tom next to a man like that once — some time ago."

Without being asked, Marcus reached in his pocket for another coin. "Is that right?"

"Odd fellow. Surly. Someone you didn't want to cross, that's for sure."

"Go on."

"Liked to fight — knives mostly. That's how he lost his eye."

"Of course we don't know if this is the man I'm looking for. Did he keep company with Bent?"

"You might say so."

"How's that?" Marcus squinted in concentration.

"They's brothers." The man looked smug. "I thought everybody knew that."

Marcus ignored the jibe. "So what's his name? Besides the last name of Bent, of course."

"Alf, Alfred Bent, III." He chuckled. "But I heard tell he liked just plain Alf a whole lot better." He hit the rump of a mule to get him away from a nearby corral fence.

"Do you know where he is now?"

The man shrugged. "I might." Then he spit at a pile of hay.

"Where is he?"

"Dead."

"How'd he die?"

Drawing in a deep breath, the man narrowed his eyes. He cast a nervous glance through the stable doors in the direction of the Goldstrike Mercantile. "Seems he experienced a terrible accident while working for Mister Bainbridge."

"Hmmm." Marcus pulled out his pocket watch, uninterested. He hoped the man would take the bait so he wouldn't have to pull out another coin.

The ploy worked. The man hurried on. "Seems him and his brother were on a job for Mister Bainbridge when one of 'em double-crossed him. Anybody in their right mind knows better than to do that, believe me. But poor ol' Alf never did seem right-minded anyway."

"And?"

"Well, all's I know is that soon after, they buried poor Alf, and his brother Jackson went off to live with the mules."

"Do you have any idea what the double-cross was?"

"Yes, sir. I do." He spit again. "Seems the two Bent brothers were to take some poor miner to San Francisco and see that he ended up as cold as a wagon tire somewhere along the way." He raised his eyebrows. "If you catch my meanin'."

Marcus nodded. "They were supposed to kill him."

"Yes, sir. That's right. But I heard tell they liked this young chap. They'd been workin' fer him right along. Thought he treated them fair-like. But they's too afraid of Bainbridge to go openly against his orders."

"So what'd they do?"

"Shanghaied him."

"What?"

The old man smiled. "I heard tell they sold 'im to a sea captain on a clipper bound for China. Saved the young chap's life." He shook his head slowly. "Though I can only imagine what kinda life that'd be."

"Do you know this young miner's name?"

"Nah. I don't remember that."

Marcus reached for another coin and held it between his fingers in front of the man's face.

The man gave him a toothless grin. "Well, now," he said with another nervous glance toward the stable door. "Let me see what I can recollect."

Nineteen

The old man spit at another pile of straw, scratched his skinny ribs for a moment, then grinned again. "Let me see now," he continued in a raspy whisper. "The mine we've been speakin' of is Rainbow's End. And the young chap?" He glanced nervously toward the stable doors, then dropped his voice even lower. "Seems to me I remember the young fella bein' Irish. But his name?" He frowned and looked toward Marcus's coin pocket.

Marcus pulled out his watch, shrugged, and turned as if to leave.

"Oh, yes. I remember," the man called out. "It was O'Brian. Shamus O'Brian. And a right handsome young man he was, too. It was a shame, what happened to him."

"Do you know why Bainbridge wanted him dead?"

The old man laughed, a deep rattling sound that ended up a cough. "Oh, yes. Folks in these parts all know why Carter Bainbridge does most've what he does."

Marcus raised his eyebrows. "And that is?"

"Greed, Mister. Just plain ol' greed."

It was too late to head out to Muleskinner Hill, some ten miles south of Everlasting Diggins, so Marcus strode to the *Herald Star* in search of Laramie. Minutes later he'd filled in the editor on his latest findings.

"I've got to ride out there tomorrow at first light."

Laramie rubbed his shiny head, frowning in thought. He settled back in his chair and nodded for Marcus to sit down opposite him. "I'd give anything to go with you, but I heard Pete's finally arriving in the morning. One of us should be here to cover the goings-on." He shook his head. "What a day it'll be."

Marcus agreed. "I'll try to get back as soon as I can — though I'll probably miss the parade and barbecue."

"There's still the Fire House Social in the town square. Candlelight. Dancing." He winked. "No matter what's happened, you need to give that little gal a whirl. Bainbridge can't keep her to himself all night."

Marcus nodded slowly, leaned back, and laced his hands behind his head. "I'll need to tell her I've got news about Shamus — maybe the only way I can will be during a waltz." He looked up at the ceiling, briefly lost in the thought of holding her in his arms.

"That'll give you something to dwell on while you're ridin' back from Muleskinner Hill." Laramie chuckled, seeming to read his thoughts. "You heard anything about the place?"

"Not much — only that Jackson Bent lives there."

"Surrounded by mules."

Marcus tried to picture it. "Mules?" It stood to reason with a name like Muleskinner Hill. He grinned. "Wild?"

Laramie laughed. "Most are as tame as you and me, though some have gone feral. I'll say this, though, there're more'n you could ever count in one setting. That's the stopping point for all the packtrains coming in and going out of the mother lode. At any given time there's hundreds — all on that hill. It's the job of the muleskinner in the shack at the top to take care they don't run off while they're grazing."

"Where're the others — the muleteers that brought them there?"

"Oh, that's their time to celebrate. They pay Bent — or whoever's the latest hire — to watch the teams while they go into Jamestown and raise Cain." He chuckled. "Some never come back. Their poor critters turn wild, still living on that blasted hill."

"Sounds like a place to avoid."

"The braying and carrying on is such that you can't hear another person's voice even if he's screaming in your ear. And the smell — whee-oo!" He laughed again. "Young man, mind me. After spending even a few hours with Jackson Bent, you'll need to think about takin' a dip in the nearest creek." Laramie pulled off his spectacles, fogged them with his breath, then proceeded to polish them crystal clear. Then he chuckled again. "Especially before you show up at the Fire House Social. If you don't, I fare-thee-well guarantee everyone there'll know where you've been."

Marcus rose before sunup the following morning. As he headed down Main Street toward the livery stable, dawn had just begun to break over Everlasting Diggins. Word had spread that Pete was nearing town, and children and adults

220

were already hanging banners for the parade. They shivered in the cold and stood around stamping their feet to keep warm.

Desperado waited impatiently by the corral fence as if he had expected Marcus. He let out a long, loud snort and pawed at the ground with one hoof. If Marcus hadn't known better, he'd have thought the horse had missed him during the past several days.

As Marcus opened the corral gate and stepped inside, Desperado reared up, and there was fire in his eyes. Then the horse charged, running right up to Marcus and stopping cold. Terrified, Marcus swallowed hard but stood his ground.

The big black butted at him with his nose. Marcus lost his balance and landed in the most undignified manner on his backside. Scrambling upright and brushing himself off, Marcus glared at the beast. Then after a moment, he reached up and patted the velvet between Desperado's eyes. The horse whinnied softly, though he flared his nostrils just to make a point.

Marcus kept rubbing. He was beginning to understand the stallion. "Okay, big fellow," he said gently. "We know who's boss. It's you. And you don't need to worry. I'll likely not ever forget it."

Desperado twitched his ears and snorted again.

By the time Marcus had the stallion saddled, the sun was slanting over the hills above Everlasting. Just as Marcus stuck his foot in the stirrup and swung his leg over the saddle, the school bell rang. He walked the stallion around the back of the stables and took the back way to the schoolhouse.

Partway up the hill, he halted the black and turned in the saddle to watch Duncan and Evangelia make their way toward school with the rest of the children. Satisfied they were safe inside the school yard, he then nudged Desperado in the flanks and headed down the trail to Muleskinner Hill.

"I saw that newspaper man in here talking with you yesterday," Carter Bainbridge said. "I'd like to know what you were discussing."

For a moment the old stable hand didn't answer, just kept on repairing a bridle, bent over his work. "'Twasn't much," he finally muttered.

"I don't care what you think, old man. I want to hear it anyway."

The old man turned and eyed Bainbridge suspiciously, then swallowed hard. Behind him some mules brayed and a horse snorted. "I don't mind tellin' — I just like bein' paid for my work. That's all."

"I think I can arrange for a reward — if the information's good enough." Bainbridge didn't smile.

"Well, that's a different kettle of fish." He grinned, then spit across the room. "The man said he's lookin' fer some brothers named Bent. Alf and Jackson, I believe it was."

"What else?"

"He said he thought they had somethin' to do with someone's disappearance."

"I want to know every detail of the conversation. The more you tell — the greater your reward. Got that?"

The old man nodded greedily. "I believe I do, sir. Yes, sir. And I'll be happy to comply." And he began to talk, careful to leave out nothing. He even made up some extra details for good measure.

Sheridan looked up and smiled as Carter strode toward her. Before she could speak, he grabbed her arm, pinching her flesh with his fingertips, and drew her inside the Empress.

"I thought I told you to call off the search for your brother." He still pulled her forearm, heading toward the downstairs parlor.

"I don't know what you're talkin' about, Carter." Fear welled inside her. He dropped her arm, and she settled into a nearby settee before her knees gave way. "I haven't even thought about lookin' since you told me the unfortunate news about…" Her voice quavered. "About Shamus's death."

He sat next to her and reached for her hand, squeezing it hard. "I told you what would happen if I heard any hint about an investigation. Your children —" He let the words drop menacingly. "I haven't wanted to worry you," he began pointedly, "but I've made inquiries about their Uncle Sonny. Found out he didn't die in the hanging after all. I heard from a reliable source that he might be on his way to Everlasting."

He smiled, his gaze unrelenting. "Now, wouldn't that be a shame for the children? He's their only living blood relative. I checked with my lawyer on your behalf. Legally, it would be up to Uncle Sonny to raise Duncan and Evangelia." Carter shook his head in mock sympathy. "I can't imagine the kind of upbringing someone like that could provide. Can you, Sherrie?" His eyes threatened to pull her into a gray and empty darkness.

Sheridan felt her long-simmering anger reach a boiling point. She swallowed hard, fighting to keep her emotions in control. Picturing the sweet faces of the children, she drew in a deep breath. "Now, Carter, don't go jumpin' to conclusions," she said, forcing a smile. She pulled her hand away from his. "Aye, I would've told you, if I'd heard anything about an ongoin' search. I know how important it is to you — to us — to keep your name away from, well, from any scandal like this. Now, please. Tell me what you've heard that raised your ire."

The expression on Carter's face relaxed. He seemed to believe her, and Sheridan let out a small sigh of relief.

Carter watched Sheridan carefully as he told her only what he wanted her to know, speaking in general terms about his conversation with the old stable hand. Then he explained that he needed to rid the newsman of his obsession with Carter's business affairs.

Sheridan didn't flinch when he mentioned Marcus Jade by name. But Carter saw a flicker of light behind her eyes and knew for a certainty what he'd suspected all along. The beautiful young woman by his side was in love with Jade. He could have laughed with the delightful news.

Instead, he just smiled and lifted her fingers to his lips for a lingering kiss, holding her gaze as he did so. He had just discovered her other weakness. First, the children. And now, Marcus Jade.

Marcus spotted Muleskinner Hill soon after ferrying across the Stanislaus River. He passed through Jamestown and asked for directions. A short time later, just as the muleskinners in town told him, a wide, trampled trail could be seen winding upward through the evergreen oaks and scrub brush. A crudely lettered sign had been nailed to a scraggly oak at the bottom of the hill stating the daily and weekly prices of leaving a muletrain.

Marcus kicked Desperado in the flanks, and they headed up the trail. Within minutes, he heard the ruckus made by hundreds of mules. As he rounded the final bend before arriving at the Jackson Bent cabin, he suddenly found himself surrounded by a sea of brown and black mule backsides. The din was louder than he had imagined; the smell, worse.

Still astride Desperado, Marcus made his way through the mules to the shack. As he rounded the side and headed for the gate, he saw a man he assumed to be Jackson Bent sitting in a straight-backed rocker on the porch. He appeared to be asleep, a straw hat pulled over his eyes. Across his knees lay a weapon, a buffalo rifle, judging from its size.

Marcus tried shouting "Bent," afraid to ride up and startle him. But his shouts just vanished into the cacophony made by the mules. Marcus let out a deep breath and nudged Desperado toward the gate, keeping his eyes on the man.

"Hey!" he yelled as he drew closer. Still no response. "Hey, there!" he shouted again, much louder this time. He was now within range of the gate latch.

He'd just leaned over Desperado's neck to open the gate, when he sensed, rather than saw, a movement on the porch.

Marcus looked up to see the plains rifle aimed square at the center of his nose.

Jackson Bent, wiry and leather-faced, said something Marcus couldn't make out in the din made by the mules. Marcus reached slowly toward his ear, cupped his hand behind it. "I can't hear you," he mouthed, hoping the man could read lips.

Slowly, Bent took down the gun and nodded for Marcus to continue coming through the gate.

"Name's Jade," he shouted into the man's ear, once he'd dismounted and strode onto the porch. He stuck out his hand in greeting, and Jackson Bent shook it amiably.

Bent motioned for Marcus to follow him inside the shack. He closed the door behind them, shutting out much of the mule noise. Marcus looked around. The place was surprisingly clean. A sturdy table with a gingham tablecloth stood near the only window. An oil lamp was at its center, and a ladder-backed chair was pulled neatly in place beneath the table.

Two small bookcases flanked the table; each was lined with thick, well-worn books. Marcus blinked in amazement as he scanned titles by William Shakespeare, Nathaniel Hawthorne, Charles Dickens, Ralph Waldo Emerson, Washington Irving, W. M. Thackeray, Charlotte Brontë, Henry David Thoreau, and Harriet Beecher Stowe. Perhaps, most surprising of all, open on the table beneath the lamp was the Holy Bible, printed in Latin.

He looked up and met Bent's gaze. The man was watching him as if amused by Marcus's scrutiny. "You're surprised?"

Marcus breathed a sigh of relief. At least inside this thick-walled cabin, the noise of the mules had lessened. He could clearly make out the low timbre of Jackson Bent's voice. He nodded, glancing again at the superb collection of books.

"These are my friends," Bent laughed lightly, gesturing toward the shelves of books. "Sometimes I think, my closest friends."

Marcus shook his head slowly, speechless. The man standing before him was a gentleman. Despite his weathered exterior, Jackson Bent's eyes revealed an intelligence, a sense of inner joy, that fascinated Marcus.

Bent stepped back to the porch to retrieve the spindly rocker. He pulled it up beside the table and nodded toward it for Marcus to sit.

"Now," Bent said with a wry smile. "Tell me, what brings you way out here?" He laughed. "I'm sure it's not just to visit the mules."

"I'm trying to find out what happened to a young Irishman named Shamus O'Brian. A year or two ago, he simply disappeared. Some say he died. Others say he might have...ah, been sent on a voyage halfway around the world."

Bent never blinked, just kept watching Marcus with a discerning expression.

"I was told yesterday that you might help me unravel the mystery."

"Who is this Shamus O'Brian to you?"

"He's the twin brother of the woman I love." The words slipped out unbidden, and they saddened him. He took a deep breath. "It's on her behalf that I'm on this quest."

Jackson Bent nodded slowly, his luminous eyes never leaving Marcus's face. "Love can cause us to do things we ordinarily wouldn't do." He paused, watching Marcus carefully. "Would you have followed this path if it hadn't been for the woman you love?"

Marcus thought about who he was when he first met Sheridan. It seemed a lifetime ago that he planned to deceive her to increase the readership of the *Grizzlyclaw Gazette*. If he'd heard of Shamus O'Brian's disappearance from others besides Sheridan, would he have cared enough to follow the trail? He wondered, and as he did, he saw things inside himself that made him ashamed.

"No," he finally said honestly. "Probably not, though I'm not proud to admit it."

"We've all contemplated ignoble acts. It's part of our nature."

Marcus nodded, sensing Jackson Bent could see into his soul. The odd thing, he realized, was that he didn't mind. After a moment, Bent settled back into his chair and seemed to be applying some sort of measure to Marcus.

"Yes, I knew Shamus O'Brian," Bent finally said in a low voice. "I knew him well. And what you heard is true. My brother Alfred and I shanghaied the young man. And we may have caused his death." There was sadness in his face as he spoke.

"How did it happen?"

"Settle back, son. It's a long story, but one I think it's important to tell you." Bent's eyes seemed to bore right through Marcus. Something in their depths told the younger man that what he was about to hear would change everything.

He nodded. "Tell me," he said simply.

"Many years ago my brother and I left our father's home in the East to seek our fortunes. He was a wealthy man, and we knew our inheritance would someday be immense. So we asked him for an advance, if you will, against what we figured would someday be ours.

"He wasn't pleased with our plan to travel west, but he loved us and gave generously from his heart." Bent swallowed hard and stared through the window at the mules for a moment before turning back to Marcus. "We wasted away our fortunes in no time on those things young men are too often drawn to: women, drink, gambling.

"My brother and I had planned all along to head west, but by the time we got here we didn't have a coin between the two of us." He laughed lightly. "We were flat broke. But we were undaunted. The gold rush had begun, and we soon succumbed to the fever. We figured we would find enough nuggets to more than make up for the fortune we had lost."

Outside, the mules brayed, their voices blending as one. Bent leaned forward across the table, regarding Marcus intently. "We were still filled with hope. Naive hope." He laughed softly, bitterly. "We figured if we could just get someone to grubstake us, our troubles would be over."

"That's when you arrived in Everlasting Diggins and met Carter Bainbridge?"

Bent nodded. "Yes. He seemed to be an honest businessman, scrupulous. Then, more than now, he was highly thought of in the burgeoning community. The miner's friend."

"He grubstaked you and your brother." Marcus could guess the rest.

"Yes, he gave us the mining supplies we needed from his mercantile. We found a likely spot for a mine, started digging. Found nothing. Tried in another area. Again, nothing." He laughed. "Backbreaking work, my friend, for little return. But we were young and filled with ourselves. We figured we'd strike gold any day."

"But it never happened."

He shook his head slowly and lifted his palms as if to show their emptiness. "I don't know that any other miners during the rush for gold ever had such rotten luck." A sad and bitter tone crept into his voice as he went on. "That's about the time Bainbridge called in the loan. We had nothing with which to pay him. He was insistent. At one point, he threatened me with my brother's life. Threatened my brother with mine."

Marcus gave him a look of understanding. "Seems he uses the same tactics today."

"He's had great success with his methods. We gave in. Because we couldn't pay him, we became his hired guns. Not long after, he had us witness Shamus O'Brian's loan, then keep an eye on his takings from the mine by working for the lad.

"When it became clear that O'Brian had struck it rich, Bainbridge had us pocket any gold we took out — to hand over to him, of course." He smiled ironically. "But soon there was too much gold for us to hide. And Bainbridge made the decision that the boy had to go."

"Go?" Marcus frowned, thinking he knew where the story was leading.

"There's a law stating that if a miner leaves his claim for a determined number of days, the mine is considered abandoned. With the loan against O'Brian's claim, it would naturally be Bainbridge's for the taking."

Marcus nodded slowly. "So he wanted Shamus to disappear."

"No, he wanted the lad dead. He devised a plan whereby we would take Shamus to San Francisco to celebrate his fortune." A deep sadness again crossed his worn face. "He trusted us, even planned to pay our expenses in the finest hotels and dining establishments. Ironic, isn't it? We, who were to bring about his demise, were held in high esteem by the only friend we had left in the world."

Bent's eyes brightened as if with unshed tears. "But Alf

and I had never killed a man before. We knew from the beginning that we couldn't go through with Carter's plan. So we came up with another." He paused. "We took him to a clipper ship bound for the Orient under the pretense of meeting the captain, a friend of ours, we said. Once in the captain's quarters, Shamus was overcome by a couple of the deckhands, hogtied, and gagged."

Bent drew in a ragged breath. "I'll never forget the look of betrayal in the lad's eyes when they dragged him away."

Marcus nodded slowly. "And you were paid."

"Some coins, not much. But it might as well as have been thirty pieces of silver." Bent moved his gaze away from Marcus's and stared through the window without speaking.

"Then what happened?"

"I'd never known I could sink so low. And my brother?" He turned back to Marcus and leaned back in his chair. "He hanged himself that night in the hotel room that Shamus had arranged for us."

"What did you do?"

"I fled to the mission. The priests took me in, gave me refuge for as long as I wanted to stay. It was there that I sank into the deepest despair I've ever known in my life." His eyes appeared luminous again as he studied Marcus. "It was also there that I found forgiveness and grace."

"From the priests?"

Bent laughed softly. "Oh, no. They pointed the way. But it was God who did the forgiving. One day I sat in the mission rose garden contemplating my life's ugliness, and Father Benjamin approached me. With a heart of great gentleness, he walked with me and related Jesus' parable of a lost son. Do you know the story?"

Marcus shook his head. "No."

Bent smiled. "Then I shall tell you. It's about a young man who squandered his inheritance far away from the family home. He did everything to disgrace himself and his father, even ended up feeding pigs for a living — the ultimate degradation for a Jew.

"One day he decided he'd rather live as a lowly servant in his father's house than to continue feeding pigs. So he set out for his father's home.

"His father had been watching for him and saw him as he was about to arrive. He ran to his son. It didn't matter what the boy had done, who he'd harmed, the grievous sins he'd committed. All that mattered was that his son had come home.

"He threw his arms around his son and kissed him, clothed him in a princely robe, put a regal ring on his finger, and commanded the entire household to celebrate the homecoming. 'This son of mine was dead and is alive again!' the father declared. 'He was lost and is found!'"

For several minutes, Jackson Bent didn't speak. Then he said, "I finally figured out that I didn't have to be perfect for God to love me. I was that beloved son, no matter what I'd done."

Marcus looked up sharply. How many times had he thought the same thing?

"There are no conditions to God's love, son. None at all. Many think that we need to achieve some kind of impossible perfection to be loved and accepted by him. But Jesus told this story to show us the truth.

"Our heavenly Father waits for us to come to him. He's ready to wrap his arms of forgiveness and everlasting love around us, clothe us in Christ's robe of righteousness. Our own feeble attempts at perfection are like filthy rags in comparison."

Marcus let out a deep breath, again sensing Bent could see things inside him that he had long hidden from everyone else, including himself.

Bent considered him with a kind expression as he continued his story. "God has forgiven me and given me peace. But my remorse is still with me. After I left the mission, I spent weeks in San Francisco, trying to find out more about the captain and ship to whom I sold Shamus."

Bent shook his head sadly. "I received one piece of oft-repeated information — by deckhands, dock workers, sailors, and captains — those who know about shanghaied victims."

"What was that?"

"Without exception, they all said Shamus O'Brian would never make it back alive."

Twenty

"There's a chance Shamus could have gotten away," Marcus said quietly, wanting to believe it.

Jackson Bent nodded slowly. "There's always that hope. I pray hourly for the young man." He frowned. "Now, son. I've done most of the talking, and I don't know that I've helped you."

"You have — more than you realize. You've given me some invaluable details. I plan to write an exposé to be published in the *Herald Star*. Also bring the information before a judge in San Francisco — there may not be an honest lawman in Everlasting who'll listen to the evidence. Everything you've said will help. But do you mind my using your name? You may also be called to testify in court."

"I'm ready. I faced my fear of Carter Bainbridge a long time ago, when I first came back to the mother lode. But you're going down a dangerous road, son. Are you prepared for the cost?"

"The articles won't be published until I see that Sheridan

and the children are safely out of Bainbridge's clutches. Their lives are the only cost I worry about."

"The children?"

Marcus explained about Duncan and Evangelia, including what had happened to them in San Francisco and the sorry news of their Uncle Sonny being an outlaw.

With the mention of Sonny Kelly, Jackson Bent's weathered face took on a strange expression. But he said nothing, just watching Marcus intently, solemnly. After a few minutes, Marcus, realizing the interview had ended, thanked him for his time and rose to leave.

Jackson Bent extended his hand and shook Marcus's warmly. As he walked Marcus to the door, he patted the younger man on the back in a fatherly fashion. He grinned when he spotted the rifle propped next to the jamb. "You know, son, I wasn't planning to shoot you earlier."

Marcus grinned. "I sure wouldn't have known it."

Bent laughed. "I don't keep it loaded."

Marcus was swinging a leg over Desperado's saddle, when Bent shouted at him above the racket of the mules.

"Don't forget the things I told you, Marcus Jade," Bent yelled.

Marcus cupped a hand to his ear. Desperado danced sideways a few steps, and Marcus reined him back toward the porch.

"About the homecoming, son. Don't forget about *your* homecoming."

Somehow Marcus wasn't surprised by Bent's words. He gave the man a quick salute, then dug his heels into Desperado's flanks. As the horse reared up, his nostrils flaring, Bent gave him a wide grin. He lifted his hand in farewell, then mouthed something else.

Marcus nodded, understanding. Bent's final words had been "God's waiting with your robe, son."

"It's comin'! I can see the ol' pumper from here!" Duncan, wiry carrot-colored hair shining in the sunlight, stood on one side of Sheridan, Evangelia on the other. The firehouse celebration parade had just begun, led by Papeete Pete, Everlasting's new fire engine.

"I see it, Dunc! Here it comes." Sheridan craned her neck to look around the crowd. Up and down Main Street children shouted gleefully as the gleaming red engine moved closer, drawn by two high-stepping bays. Audible sighs of admiration rose from the crowd as it neared.

The day couldn't have been better for the celebration. The noon sun shone bright in a cloudless sky. For days people had been talking about the Indian summer warmth, hoping it would hold until Pete arrived. Sheridan couldn't have agreed more, feeling the sun on her shoulders.

"Here it comes, Lia. Look!" She squeezed the child's hand. The bays lifted their necks and pranced down the street, tails high, pulling the ornate, brass-trimmed hand-pumper behind them.

Evangelia's face was a wreath of smiles. She watched the engine with rapt fascination, first looking to Sheridan to see if she was watching, then back to the shiny vehicle. Only once did she pop her thumb into her mouth. That was when one of the firemen walking beside the engine suddenly halted the horses, then wound the siren and let it wail. Children small and large along the parade route squealed with delight.

Evangelia simply watched with a tiny smile, loudly sucking her thumb and clutching Sheridan's hand.

Sheridan did her best to keep up a lighthearted appearance for the sake of the children. But during their encounter earlier, Carter Bainbridge had frightened her terribly.

After school let out, Duncan had pleaded with her to join his friends who were planning to trail along the parade with their hoops and sticks. She finally relented, figuring she would follow along the walkway. But now, as she watched the fire engine pass by, she realized that she dreaded the end of the parade, worried that in weaving among the miners, shopkeepers, merchants, and families along the streets, she might lose sight of the little boy. In fact, she dreaded everything planned for rest of the day: the barbecue and town square social.

"Ah, there you are."

Recognizing the deep voice, Sheridan turned. Carter smiled down at her. "I've been searching everywhere. You've made yourself pretty scarce since this morning."

Evangelia looked up at them, and Sheridan forced a light tone into her voice. "Why, Carter. I guess you just weren't lookin' in the right places. We've been right here, haven't we, Lia?"

In a quick, fluid movement, Bainbridge swept Evangelia onto his broad shoulders. "Now this is the best place to watch a parade," he said jovially, but his eyes were cold as they seemed to examine Sheridan's thoughts.

Papeete Pete headed on down the street. Next in line marched Clementine Love with a group of women carrying placards and tambourines and shouting slogans about bringing everlasting reform to Everlasting Diggins. Behind the women strode a small marching band with drums, cornets, and trombones. A cheer went up from the crowd as they passed.

From her perch on Carter's shoulders, Evangelia kept a solemn gaze on Sheridan's face instead of the parade. Finally, the little girl reached her hands out in a desperate gesture to be released from his grasp.

Sheridan reached up and firmly gathered Evangelia into her arms. For a long time she held the child, unwilling to set her down.

"All you had to do was ask," Bainbridge said pointedly.

Duncan rejoined them and looked up. He stiffened at her expression. "Are you all right, Miss Sheridan?"

Sheridan forced a smile and tousled the boy's wiry hair, touched by his intuitive concern. "Aye, son. I am."

"You are coming with me to the social tonight, aren't you, Sherrie?" Carter gave an obvious tweak to Evangelia's small braid. Thumb in mouth, the little girl turned her head, yanking the plait from his fingers. But Carter's cool gray eyes didn't leave Sheridan's face. Behind him, the parade continued. Yelps of pleasure rose from the crowd as a group of clowns turned cartwheels and backflips down the street. But still Bainbridge stared, almost daring Sheridan to flinch.

She finally nodded. "I am plannin' on it." She let out a deep sigh, finding it more difficult than ever to be civil.

"Good," he said. "I have an important announcement to make tonight, and I want you at my side. Please keep your commitment to me in mind." He smiled at Evangelia and chucked her under the chin before disappearing into the crowd.

"I don't like that man," Duncan said a moment later.

"I don't either, Dunc." Sheridan still held Evangelia firmly in her arms.

Marcus rode Desperado hard along the trail back to Everlasting Diggins, formulating a plan to speak with Sheridan, tell her what he'd learned about Shamus, convince her of Bainbridge's evil nature, and help her get as far away from the man as possible.

On a rise just outside town he halted the stallion and slid from the saddle, letting the horse rest and graze before going on. In the small valley below, Marcus could see Everlasting's celebration in full swing. Music wafted toward him, fiddles and banjos mostly, with the wail of a harmonica joining in now and then. Joyous shouts and peals of children's laughter carried toward him.

The smell of barbecuing meats also rose in the air, reminding Marcus he hadn't eaten since his breakfast of pemmican on the trail to Muleskinner Hill. He smiled. In the hubbub of the barbecue and social at the town square, he would surely find a way to speak with Sheridan privately.

He knew that it would be difficult to find her alone: Carter Bainbridge never seemed to be more than a few steps away. Again, Marcus thought of the danger Sheridan would face if Bainbridge suspected anything. He decided that it would be more prudent to get a message to her, telling her how important it was that they meet.

Nearby, a ground squirrel skittering beneath some sage captured Marcus's attention. It watched him from beneath a clump of lavender and yellow mountain jewels popping up from among their heart-shaped leaves. Marcus slowly smiled, an idea beginning to take form.

All around him, the hillsides were covered with golden grasses and fall wildflowers of every description: ox-eyed daisies, blue violets, and goldenrod were just a few he recognized. Near a shady spring, he spotted a shiny clump of wintergreen with its long strands of sidebell flowers, reminding him of miniature lilies.

The wildflowers could serve a very useful purpose. *Very useful indeed,* he thought. Though many were nearly spent, some still bloomed vigorously under the warm Sierra autumn skies. Marcus began picking only the most beautiful. Soon he had gathered flowers of blue and ivory and gold, and leaves, heart-shaped and verdant.

Minutes later, Marcus rode down the hill and into town. Most of the folks had moved to the town square for the barbecue. Music and laughter and people milling about had transformed the mining town into a carnival, providing the perfect hullabaloo to give Marcus the cover he needed. He rode to the livery and unsaddled Desperado, led him into the corral, then made his way to the Falcon Hotel.

Tearing a page out of his journal, he quickly scribbled a note:

> Sheridan,
>
> It is imperative that we speak. I have found the evidence we have been searching for. I am sending these flowers as a means by which we can communicate. If you agree — and feel it is safe — to speak with me at tonight's social, please carry this nosegay. I will then arrange for a secure meeting place.

Marcus signed his name, folded the paper, and hurried back to the town square. He threaded in and out of the crowds, looking for Duncan. Finally, he spotted the boy playing kick-the-can with his friends. A short distance away, Sheridan, Evangelia by her side, sat talking with Clementine Love, Miss Brown the schoolmarm, and a few other women Marcus didn't recognize.

Marcus waited until the boy kicked the can near him and ran up ahead of the other boys. When Duncan spotted Marcus, he kicked the can back to the others and walked over, a wide grin spreading across his freckled face.

"It's good to see you, Dunc." Marcus moved slowly away from the crowds. Duncan seemed to understand and followed. "I have a job for you. Do you want to help me out? "

Duncan nodded.

"I need you to give this to Sheridan." He held out the nosegay. The boy clutched the flowers with a small, knowing smile. "And this." Marcus placed the folded note in the boy's shirt pocket. "When you give them to her, don't tell her who they're from. At least not right away."

"Yes, sir." He smiled again as if playing Cupid.

"I want you to suggest she go back to the Empress to place them in water. Do you understand?"

He nodded again, vigorously, still grinning ear-to-ear.

"This is serious, Dunc." Marcus's voice was stern. "No one must know about this — no one except you and Sheridan and me. All right?"

"Yes." The smile disappeared.

"Now, when Sheridan leaves for the hotel, I want you to go with her. Wait until you are alone to give her the note that's in your pocket. That's probably the most important part of what I'm asking you to do." Again, he asked Duncan if he understood and the boy nodded solemnly.

Marcus drew a deep breath and looked back into the crowd. As far as he could tell no one had seen them talking, though Sheridan seemed to be looking about nervously.

"Okay, Dunc. You can go back now. Don't forget to do exactly what I've said."

The boy skipped off and headed for Sheridan. Marcus mingled among a group of miners until he saw Duncan hand the flowers to Sheridan. He couldn't help smiling when she held them to her nose. Her cheeks colored prettily, and Marcus wondered who she thought had sent them.

As planned, Sheridan stood to walk down Main Street to the Empress, Evangelia clutching one hand, the nosegay in the other. But Duncan was not in sight. Frowning, Marcus searched the crowd and finally spotted him with his friends.

The boy was supposed to go with Sheridan. Marcus was still deciding what to do, when he saw Duncan glance at his pocket and remember. He cast a frantic look in Marcus's direction, then sprinted across the street toward the Empress.

Shaking his head in relief, Marcus headed back to the Falcon to bathe and dress for the evening.

Duncan hurried along, half hopping, half skipping. At least a block ahead, he could see Sheridan pushing open the Empress door. Then she and Evangelia disappeared inside. He ran faster, worried he'd disappoint Mister Jade if he didn't complete his job. He glanced down to make sure the note was still in his pocket. Breathing a sigh of relief, he saw that it was.

Duncan thought that Mister Jade and Miss Sheridan were sweet on each other. He'd figured that out the first night he met them. Anyone could tell it by the way they gazed at one another all starry-eyed and sweet-faced. Of course, nothing could please him more.

Since Miss Sheridan had taught him to pray, he'd been asking God for a real family. A pa and everything. And a fellow couldn't do better than to get a pa like Mister Jade. He'd like that fine. Real fine.

Puffing as he ran, he thought of Evangelia. God had given him the best little sister in the world, pretty and sugary-sweet and smart as a whip. Why, he just knew once she started to talk again, there'd be no stopping her. Nosiree.

He thought of Miss Sheridan and how her cheeks got red when he handed her the flowers. He'd bragged about her so much at school that the other fellas had finally got sick of it. Told him if he said one more time how she could cipher better than Miss Brown, they were gonna make him prove it. Duncan had no doubt that Miss Sheridan could win the contest, but he didn't want to embarrass Miss Brown.

He had almost reached the Empress when someone stepped out from behind a big elm tree. Duncan had to stop real fast or else he would've run into the man. The boy was looking down and at first didn't see who it was, only the big, fancy shoes.

Then he looked up past the big shoulders to the man's face.

"Good evening, little man," he said, though his voice sounded meaner than the words.

"Evenin', Mister Bainbridge."

It worried Duncan that the man's body, as big and solid as

the nearby elm, blocked him from getting by.

"You sure seem to be in a hurry now, don't you?" Mister Bainbridge still didn't move.

Duncan nodded. "I got somethin' I gotta do."

"And what would that be?"

Mister Jade had told Duncan not to tell anyone about the flowers or the note, and Duncan intended to do his job well. He wasn't about to tell. "I... ah..." He hesitated. "It's a secret, Mister Bainbridge. Just for Miss Sheridan. Please, I gotta go." And he started for the street.

Bainbridge stuck out his arm quicker than Duncan could move. He caught the boy by the shoulder. Before he knew it, Duncan was standing before him as if fixed to the spot, unable to wriggle from his grasp.

"Now, tell me little man, why you're in such a hurry."

Duncan clamped his lips together and gave Mister Bainbridge his meanest stare.

"Well, I guess if you won't tell me, I'll just have to read it for myself, now, won't I?" He reached inside the boy's pocket and pulled out the note.

"No!" Duncan yelled and grabbed for it. "That's mine."

Ignoring him, Bainbridge unfolded the paper. A slow smile crept across his face as he began to read.

Twenty-One

❦

Duncan yelped and grabbed for the note. Chuckling, Bainbridge held it out of the boy's reach, his eyes never leaving the message it held.

Exasperated, Duncan kicked Bainbridge sharply in the shin. When the man doubled over in surprise, Duncan grabbed the note and ran as fast as he could to the Empress entrance.

Breathing hard, he stopped just inside the door, then peered through the window to see if he was being followed. A moment later Bainbridge crossed the street and headed back to the festivities.

"Duncan, child, whatever is the matter?" Sheridan stood at the top of the stairs. "You're as a white as that paper in your hand. What's wrong, son?"

"Miss Sheridan!" he cried, running up the stairs. "I don't like that Mister Bainbridge. Wait till I tell you what he just did."

Bainbridge headed back to his office at the Goldstrike, mulling over the words he'd just read in Marcus Jade's note to Sheridan. He'd figured it was a matter of time before Jade uncovered the evidence about Shamus O'Brian.

But Bainbridge, as usual, was a step ahead. His threats to Sheridan hadn't been idle. Some days ago, he'd sent an agent to San Francisco to look for the owner of the livery who'd paid to get the children out of the orphanage.

The agent had arrived back in Everlasting Diggins just the previous night with news of his success: The livery owner, Titus Roderick, had been delighted to discover the whereabouts of his young wards. He was already on his way to Everlasting, a hired gun at his side, to recover his property. They were scheduled to arrive any day now.

Bainbridge smiled and leaned back in his chair. Jade's note neither surprised nor disturbed him. One mention of Titus Roderick to Miss O'Brian, he was sure, would keep the charming little Irish lass in his control. Bainbridge of course would promise to take care of Roderick — as long as Sheridan continued to openly stand by him. Her final test would be at the ball tonight, when he made his surprise announcement to all in attendance.

If she didn't respond as he expected? He would simply arrange to deliver the children into Roderick's hands. Carter already had the place of transfer in mind. He'd make sure Sheridan accompanied them. He chuckled, picturing the scenario. He knew the woman well enough to realize she would fight Roderick to the death to protect "her" children. Yes, he mused, it would be unfortunate to sacrifice one of such beauty and charm. But in the long run, the choice would be hers.

Marcus Jade was another matter, however. Bainbridge turned in his swivel chair to stare through the window. A crimson sunset had crept across the late afternoon skies, leaving the Everlasting skyline a dark silhouette. He frowned in thought, plotting how to rid himself of the man and his obsession with poking his newsman's nose into Bainbridge's affairs.

Perhaps he could take care of them all — Sheridan, the children, and Jade — at once. The more he considered it, the better he like the idea. He wanted nothing left to chance that might upset his political future in Everlasting or in Sacramento.

Yes, he mused, his eyes lingering on the blood-red sunset, his plan was coming together nicely. He just hoped Titus Roderick arrived in time for the evening's festivities. Carter smiled to himself, anticipating the expression on Sheridan's face when he made the introductions.

Sheridan pulled her pale blue ball gown from the wardrobe, and laid it across her bed, touching its silken folds with her fingers. The frock would go perfectly with the wildflowers, though because Carter had intercepted the note, she couldn't carry them in a nosegay as Marcus had asked.

Standing before the looking glass, she brushed her freshly washed hair until it gleamed, then pulled the sides upward and arranged them in a tumble of cascading waves that fell below her shoulders. Then she fastened the wildflowers, one by one, into a crown of violet, gold, pale blue, and ivory. She wove it into her hair with ribbon the same shade as her gown. After adding a few heart-shaped leaves, she examined the results in the mirror.

Smiling, she patted her hair, pleased with her efforts. Bainbridge would see she was not carrying Marcus's bouquet. And Marcus, she prayed, would see that she was wearing his flowers.

Moments later, Sheridan slipped on the gown, thankful for a waist tiny enough to get by without a corset. As soon as she was ready, she stepped into the children's room to tell them good night.

"You look beautiful, Miss Sheridan." Duncan looked up from the small slate where he was helping Evangelia write her name. Both children were sitting cross-legged on the carpeted floor. His sister poked her thumb into her mouth. Sheridan knew the little girl wasn't comfortable being left.

"Thank you, Dunc." Sheridan sat down on the edge of Evangelia's bed. "Now, I want you to behave for Miss Love. Bedtime is promptly at eight o'clock. Don't you try to talk her out of it. Tomorrow is a school day."

Duncan nodded. "Yes, ma'am."

"And Lia?" The little girl looked up at Sheridan soberly. "When you fall asleep, I want you to think about Jesus and how he holds all the little lambs in his arms." Evangelia nodded, and Sheridan gathered the child onto her lap, holding her close. "I want you to remember how it feels to have strong arms around you — the arms of somebody who loves you." Evangelia looked up, her little face relaxing.

"No matter what happens — from now until you're a grown-up lady — I want you to always know that you are Jesus' lamb and that he loves you." Evangelia smiled softly and nodded again. Sheridan planted a soft kiss on her forehead.

Moments later, Clementine Love knocked at the door.

The woman's round face beamed as she admired Sheridan's gown. Then she said with a knowing wink that Carter Bainbridge awaited Sheridan in the downstairs parlor.

"Aye, I was expectin' him," Sheridan said softly. Then she gave Clementine a grateful hug, glad she had volunteered to watch the children this night. Sheridan was unsure of what lay ahead at the ball. It was better that the children await her return, as far away as possible from the presence of Carter Bainbridge.

"You need a night to yourself," Clementine assured Sheridan, seeming to notice Sheridan's nervousness. "Please — go, enjoy yourself. Don't worry about Duncan and Evangelia. I'll enjoy being with them."

Sheridan descended the Empress staircase, her pale gown seeming to float around her as she stepped toward the parlor. A smiling Carter Bainbridge looked up, dressed in a top hat and black frock coat that emphasized his height and broad shoulders. He seemed to regard her with a shrewd, hard expression on his face, a look different than what she'd seen before. She caught her breath as he reached for her hand.

"My dear, you've never looked lovelier." His voice was smooth, too smooth. He bent to kiss her fingertips.

"Carter," Sheridan said simply, wondering what the night would hold.

Marcus strode toward the town square, hearing the music and the voices of party-goers long before he arrived. Rounding the corner, he took it all in with delight. He'd earlier seen the new gazebo, built just for the occasion right in the middle of Main Street and Central. But now he won-dered if anyone had thought about how they were going to move it once the festivities were over.

The square had been transformed. Lanterns had been hung around the gazebo and from the eaves of shops and businesses up and down both streets. A small orchestra made up of a few horns, several fiddles, a flute, some har-monicas, and even a harpsichord had been set up next to Papeete Pete, with its red paint and brass trim gleaming in the lantern light.

Marcus observed that the occasion appealed mostly to families and husbands and wives. A few roughly dressed miners milled about, looking as if they were itching to cause a ruckus. But mostly they sat on the sidelines, exchanging bottles of whiskey and grumbling that the saloons had been ordered closed until after the ball.

Marcus moved from group to group, searching for Sheridan. He spotted Laramie Burkett and his lively wife, and the three spoke for awhile. Then the orchestra interrupted, striking up a series of Stephen Foster songs. People stopped their talking and, after a few minutes, joined in. Dozens of voices singing "Oh! Susanna," "Camptown Races," "My Old Kentucky Home," and "Jeanie With the Light Brown Hair" rose into the night.

Marcus had just turned to walk to the edge of the crowd to continue his search, when the alcalde climbed the stairs to the center of the gazebo and called for everyone's attention. Silence fell.

Onto the gazebo stepped Carter Bainbridge and the aldermen. Sheridan stood by Carter's side. Her eyes searched the crowd, then finally settled on Marcus.

He met her gaze, his heart sorrowful: She did not carry the nosegay of wildflowers.

"I have an announcement to make." Bainbridge stepped forward. "First of all, I want to say how much this town — this community — means to me. I've lived here for some time now. Together we've been through tragedies and triumphs, fires and times of rebuilding, booms and busts. Yet through it all, we've retained a sense of hope for the future of this great community and for the future of this great state."

Murmurs of agreement rose from the crowd. Carter smiled and went on. "Many of you know that I was instrumental in getting Papeete Pete for this fair community."

Cheers and applause followed. Bainbridge raised his hands humbly. "Any one of us could have done it." He smiled and paused, nodding his head thoughtfully. "But it's on the occasion of this celebration that I thought — at the urging of these standing here beside me — that it would be the perfect time to tell you, the folks who mean the most to me, about my future plans."

Marcus frowned, at first figuring Bainbridge was going to announce his candidacy for alcalde. Though when he'd mentioned the state, Marcus figured he might have set his sights on a higher office.

Bainbridge went on. "So it is at this time," he paused and smiled at Sheridan, "it is at this time that I announce my plans to run for U.S. Senator."

Cheers rose again from the crowd. Marcus looked around, wondering how many knew of the man's corrupt and murderous activities. Bainbridge spoke for a few more minutes about how he would represent the fair state of California.

Marcus moved his gaze back to Sheridan. She still watched him intently.

Then Bainbridge cleared his throat and said he had another announcement to make. All voices hushed as he took Sheridan's hand in his.

"I want to ask the lovely lady standing beside me if she will go to Washington with me — as my wife," he added with a laugh. There was a ripple of soft laughter from the audience. "I think we make a fine team, don't you?" He looked out at the crowd. There was a murmur of approval.

Marcus drew in a deep breath, thinking he would be sick. A heavy silence fell over the crowd. It seemed to last an eternity.

"And, my dearest, what is your answer?" Carter looked intently into Sheridan's eyes.

"Aye," she finally said clearly. "I accept your proposal."

The crowd cheered its approval. The orchestra struck up a waltz, and Bainbridge pulled Sheridan into his arms and began to dance. Other couples joined in, and soon the gazebo and the streets around it were alive with music and laughter and dancing.

Marcus turned to leave.

"Young man," Laramie Burkett had moved to walk beside him, "don't tell me you're givin' up so easy."

Marcus just looked at him, too downhearted to speak.

"There's somethin' more goin' on here than you know."

"What do you mean?"

"I was closer to them than you were. I could see that little Irish lass had her eyes on you the whole time."

He patted the older man's shoulder. "I know you mean well, Laramie. But the truth is, she said she would marry him." Marcus shrugged. "Maybe it's the pull of politics. Maybe it's love. I don't know. And frankly, right now I don't care."

"I don't want to interfere, Marcus. But I think you need to speak with her before you go jumpin' to conclusions."

Marcus considered his words, then shook his head. "I don't know what good it would do —"

"Don't you have news about her brother?"

"Yes."

"And weren't you going to warn her about Bainbridge?"

"Yes — though now I don't know if it'll do any good. I don't know that she'll listen if she fancies herself in love with the man."

"You've got to try, son."

Marcus nodded, knowing Laramie was right. "All right," he said, shaking his head.

After a moment, he headed back to the town square and found a place to wait at the edge of the crowd. The orchestra played on, the waltzes and the two-step. Several young men lined up to dance with Sheridan, and she whirled around the gazebo in their arms, never glancing in his direction.

But Marcus's gaze never left her. He took in her graceful beauty. The pale blue of her gown shimmered in the glow of the lanterns. And her hair. He watched as it flowed around her bare shoulders as she danced. She had pulled it up with flowers and ribbons. It cascaded down her back, soft and flowing. She was lovely, and his heart nearly broke as he watched her.

Then his gaze darted back to the flowers in Sheridan's hair. He frowned in wonder and moved closer to the gazebo. Sheridan again danced by. Marcus spotted the violets, then the daisies, the goldenrod, even the wintergreen with its tiny lily-like sidebells in her hair. And woven into the pale blue ribbon were the heart-shaped leaves of the mountain jewels.

Marcus sprinted up the gazebo stairs, two at a time, and pushed his way through the crowd of dancers. He glanced first to Carter Bainbridge who was deep in conversation with several others.

One of the men was Laramie Burkett who gave Marcus a knowing look. Marcus noticed that the *Herald Star* editor immediately began an animated political tirade of some sort and maneuvered Bainbridge so that his back was to the dance floor. Marcus grinned and winked at his friend.

Moments later, Marcus touched Sheridan's hand. "May I have this dance?"

She turned, her eyes shimmering with unshed tears. "Aye," she breathed. "I thought you'd never ask."

Twenty-Two

Sheridan heard Marcus speak her name, and her pulse quickened. She turned and met his eyes. Around them dancers whirled, a blur of billowing gowns and frock coats and top hats, calico dresses and leather breeches.

He stood before her, his blond hair spilling boyishly onto his forehead, his wide shoulders clothed in a white shirt, open at the throat, and white satin vest. Without speaking, Marcus gathered her into his embrace, gracefully moving to the rhythm of the music.

Sheridan let out a small, contented sigh, relishing the warmth and strength of his arms. "I was afraid you wouldn't see your flowers," she finally said, her voice low.

He pulled her closer, lightly resting his cheek on the top of her head. "I almost didn't," he murmured. "I looked for the nosegay. When I didn't see it, I thought you didn't want to meet me."

She looked nervously about for Bainbridge then tilted her face upward. "Marcus," she whispered hoarsely. "He intercepted the note you sent with Duncan. He read it and scared the child to death. He's threatened us all terribly…." Her words ran together in her hurry to tell him everything. "He's out to harm the children. He's sent for Titus Roderick. In fact, the man may even be here tonight. That's why —" She gulped back her tears. "That's why tonight when he asked me to be his wife —" Her voice broke, and she was unable to go on.

"He's known about the children — their past, the orphanage, the liveryman? He's been threatening you all along?"

Sheridan nodded. "Everything, Marcus. That's why I couldn't come to you. I feared for the children. I thought if I just waited —" Again her voice broke. "I'm so sorry, Marcus. I thought I could outsmart him. But now…" She looked nervously around again. "It's gone too far. I must get the children away. Roderick can legally take them."

Marcus drew in a deep breath. "Sheridan, I've got so much to tell you. I can't possibly get into it all here."

She gazed up at him. Just the sound of his voice was comforting.

"It's mostly about Shamus. I've found a man who knows what happened."

A small gasp escaped Sheridan's lips. She tried to stop dancing, but Marcus urged her to continue. "Don't look upset," he murmured in her ear. "Keep moving to the music. Look like you're having a good time."

She drew in a deep breath and nodded. "What else? Tell me everything, Marcus. Is my brother alive?"

"Bainbridge gave the order for him to be murdered, but the men who were to carry it out, couldn't do it —"

"God be praised!" she whispered.

Marcus nodded, hating to tell her the rest. "He was

shanghaied," he said quietly, then pulled her close, hoping the strength of his arms would somehow help her pain.

"Put on a ship against his will?" She gazed up at him, her face pale. "That's like being sold into slavery."

He nodded again.

"But is he still alive?"

"No one knows." He saw the tears glisten in her eyes. She quickly blinked them away. "God is with him," she said, her voice low. "No matter where he is in the world, God is by his side."

Marcus gently turned with her to the music, attempting to make their dancing appear lighthearted and normal. She sighed, closed her eyes, and moved with him.

After a moment, he continued. "I will come to you tonight after the ball. Wait for me on your balcony. Will you do that?"

"Aye," she whispered. "I will be waitin'."

Marcus pulled her into a gentle embrace. "Sheridan, I've missed you so. I thought —" His voice was low and husky. "I thought that you…and Bainbridge…."

Around them, couples laughed as they danced. The soft music played on. But Sheridan heard only the low timbre of Marcus's comforting voice and felt only the rhythm of his heartbeat. She didn't want the music to end, and when it did, she again gazed up into his face. "These long days and nights, Marcus, I've had time to think. To consider all you've said to me before —"

He nodded. "I've done the same, Sheridan."

Suddenly, Carter Bainbridge was beside them. His smile was forced, cold. "I've come to claim my betrothed, Mister Jade. It seems that she's dancing with everyone but me.

Surely you don't mind if I take the future Mrs. Bainbridge away from you."

Marcus stepped back, and Bainbridge swept Sheridan into his arms, moving slightly too fast as they whirled among the other dancers.

Over the big man's shoulder, Sheridan met Marcus's gaze. She smiled into his eyes before looking back up into Bainbridge's face, laughing lightly at some banal witticism he'd just uttered.

It was past midnight when Marcus made his way down Main Street to the Empress Hotel. The party-goers had long since left for their homes, and the streets were empty and quiet.

A harvest moon hung full and bright in the deep night sky, lighting his way. When he reached the Empress he tried both door handles. They were locked. But he'd already figured he might need to reach Sheridan's balcony by other means.

Marcus moved back into the street, assessing the elms that lined the front of the hotel and the easy reach from their stalwart branches to Sheridan's balcony. He drew a deep breath. He hadn't even climbed trees when he was a child. And now? Tree climbing was lower on his list than riding a horse.

He stepped closer to the massive elm, considering the romantic heroes who had spoken to their loves beneath balconies. They were more fortunate than he, Marcus decided, measuring the height to the bottom branch. As far as he knew, Cyrano and Romeo hadn't had to climb trees.

Marcus was still thinking about his plight when he

looked up and saw Sheridan standing on the balcony. She was gazing down at him, her expression tender and loving. He quickly found a foothold and pulled himself upward with an agility that surprised him. The task was less difficult than he imagined, and within minutes he swung a leg over the fancy ironwork outside Sheridan's room.

The balcony was dark except for the moon's soft glow and the flickering of candles behind the glass-paned doors. For a moment, Marcus stood as if rooted to the place, stunned nearly speechless by the woman before him. She had never looked more beautiful.

Sheridan still wore her ball gown; its pale folds fell in gossamer clouds around her. Her raven hair held the wildflowers he'd picked, and it tumbled past her shoulders in a way that made him want to run his fingers through its silken strands.

She tilted her face toward him as if in wonder at his presence. Marcus noticed her eyes were the color of sapphires in the moonlight.

"Marcus," she cried softly, reaching out to him. "Oh, Marcus!"

He hurried toward her and pulled her into his embrace. Sheridan circled his neck with her arms. His chin rested on the top of her head. For a long time they stood without moving, holding each other as if they could never let go. Sheridan felt his heart thudding, and the strength of it made her think that it was surely her own.

She pulled back slightly and looked up into his face. A lock of his hair had drooped down over his forehead, and she brushed it back with her fingertips. He smiled, and the way his eyes crinkled at the edges nearly stopped her heart.

She gazed into his face and considered all she saw there. He was brave, kindhearted, strong, and proud. Yet there was also a vulnerability about him that touched her.

In the moonlight his eyes again reminded her of the stormy seas off the heather-covered cliffs of her beloved Ireland. She let out a small sigh, thinking of the times she'd seen those same eyes almost dance with hidden merriment.

Now, though, his gaze reflected an unfathomable compassion. He gently took her face in his hands and held it as he spoke.

"I love you, Sheridan. I think I have since the first moment I saw you — that day at the wharf." Marcus laughed softly, his voice husky with emotion. "You had written that you'd be wearing a blue hat. I'll never forget when I spotted that hat — then moved my gaze down to your face, expecting *Mister* Sheridan O'Brian." He lightly brushed her cheek with the backs of his fingers, then touched the dimple in her chin. "Your smile, the lilt of your voice, captured my heart before I spoke my first words to you."

Sheridan smiled into his eyes, placed her hands on his, then lifted them to her lips and kissed his fingertips. "Aye," she breathed. "And you have no idea how you affected me, Marcus. I think the first time I knew my heart belonged to you was that night at the California Palace when you rescued poor Duncan from the viper in the kitchen."

Marcus suddenly stepped back, his expression changed.

"What is it?" Sheridan tilted her head, frowning in concern. "What did I say?"

He took her hand in his and held it gently as he spoke. "That day we kissed, you said you'd realized how much you cared for me — that I was an honorable and compassionate man — because I saved Evangelia. During the past weeks, seeing you with Carter Bainbridge, I'd concluded that what you felt for me was gratitude, not love."

Then Marcus let out a deep sigh and turned away, looking out at the moon, the thin clouds floating across it. "Just now," he continued. "you said my saving Duncan had the same effect on you. I can't help wondering if, because of your deep love for Duncan and Evangelia, you might have confused your feelings for me."

Sheridan considered her words for a moment before speaking. "Marcus," she said quietly to his back. "It wasn't gratitude I felt — ever. It was what I saw in you that touched my heart."

He turned, though he didn't move toward her. She went on. "I saw compassion in you, a depth of caring for those less fortunate, the courage to act swiftly, decisively. Your actions toward Duncan and little Lia showed me a bit of your soul. And that's what captured my heart." She bit her lip, frowning in concentration. "Gratitude?" She let out a small, exasperated sigh. "Of course I was thankful for what you did for the children. But perhaps, Mr. Jade, you're not givin' me enough credit to know my own mind now, are you?" She purposely thickened her brogue at the end and gave him a tremulous smile, challenging him with her words.

A slow grin spread across his face. "You still haven't said exactly how you feel — besides, of course, that your heart has been taken captive." He moved toward her again, lifted her chin slightly with his fingertips. "Maybe this will help." He covered her mouth with his. His lips embraced hers with a softness, a tenderness, that caused her heart to pound and her breath to catch in her throat.

He finally released her, and she looked up. He was watching her with eyes filled with deep affection…and the secret merriment she loved.

When Sheridan could breathe again, she touched Marcus's face, marveling at the feel of his strong jaw. He closed his eyes, and she stood on tiptoe to kiss his eyelids, his cheeks, his temples, his brow. When he opened his eyes, they were dusky with passion.

"Aye," she teased. "I'm aware that I've not told you exactly — in plain words, that is — how I feel about you, Mister Jade."

He watched her expectantly, a smile playing at his lips.

"We Irish don't speak our words loosely, you know. And when certain words are uttered, they're meant to be forever."

His gaze held hers. She thought his eyes shimmered in the moonlight, just like the Irish seas under the light of a full moon, deep and mysterious.

"I love you, Marcus Jade. Haven't you figured that out by now? I love you with all my heart and soul and every wee bit of my being —"

But before she could go on, he had gathered her into his arms and, with a soft groan, had captured her lips once more.

When Marcus released her, Sheridan let out a small sigh and circled her arms around his back. Then she tucked her head back under his chin and settled into his embrace. For a long time, they stood holding each other, looking out at the moon.

"I want to marry you, Sheridan." Marcus whispered. She looked up at him and smiled. "Will you — I mean, when all this is over — will you marry me?"

She frowned and stepped back just slightly. "It's not that simple, Marcus. I come to you with a ready-made family. Duncan and Evangelia's lives are part of mine now. I can't explain. I don't even know what will happen to us all tomorrow, but I feel God has given them to me —"

Marcus touched her cheek tenderly. "I already knew that, Sheridan. I care for them, too. I want us to be a family. I want to be your husband." He smiled hesitantly. "I don't know that I'll be very good at it, but I want to be their father."

Her face was radiant. "Oh, Marcus —" But she couldn't go on because of the tears pooling in her eyes and spilling down her cheeks. She quickly brushed them away with her fingertips. "God will help us get through this. I know he will. Then we'll be a family. He'll have gathered us all into his everlasting arms to be together with him forever!"

Marcus grinned. "Does that mean you'll marry me, Sheridan?"

She nodded vigorously. "Aye, Mister Jade. That it does. I'll marry you. I will!" And she reached up, pulled his face toward hers, and kissed him on the lips, tenderly, joyously. "Oh, Marcus," she breathed. "How I adore you!"

After a few minutes, Marcus gathered Sheridan close, his arms around her waist. She leaned back against him. They looked out over Everlasting, quietly sleeping in the moonlight. "We've got to get away before daylight, Sheridan. All four of us."

Sheridan rested her head on his chest. "I know," she whispered.

"I told you earlier about the man who knows about Shamus." She nodded, watching him seriously. "I want you to meet him. He'll be able to fill in many of the details."

She drew in a shaky breath, thinking of what the man had done to her brother. "Aye," she said simply.

But Marcus noticed her discomfort. "I think it's important that you meet him, darling. He's a different man now than when he was hired by Bainbridge to kill Shamus."

Sheridan shuddered. "Maybe he didn't kill Shamus, but he still caused him great harm. I don't know if I can speak with him, Marcus. It would be painful —"

"I know, darling." Marcus drew her closer into his arms. "I know." He took a deep breath. "But the man — his name is Jackson Bent — has agreed to testify against Bainbridge. My plan is to go straight to Jackson Bent and take him with us to San Francisco. We'll go immediately before a judge and convince him of Carter's complicity and guilt. He'll be arrested."

Sheridan turned again to look up into Marcus's face. "The children consider Everlasting their home. I wanted so much to make it a secure place to live."

"By carrying through with our plan, it will be that safe place, Sheridan."

She regarded him, the soft way he looked at her in the moonlight, the compassion deep in his eyes. She nodded, realizing what he'd just said. "If we're set on making it a secure place for Duncan and Evangelia — does that mean we'll be comin' back, Marcus?"

"Would you like that?"

"Aye, that I would, Marcus."

"I'll build a little house," he said with a twinkle in his eye. He'd never built anything in his life, but when had that ever stopped him? "With plenty of room for a growing family," he added. "I want more than two children, you know — of course, only if you do."

"Aye, a quiver full of them," she whispered, immensely pleased. "But what about the *Grizzlyclaw Gazette?* Wouldn't you miss it?"

"I could speak with Laramie about continuing on with him. Everlasting Diggins is growing. Perhaps someday the *Gazette* and the *Star* could join forces, be a larger newspaper for a larger town. Then we could move my father here from San Francisco to have him closer to his grandchildren."

He laughed softly, hugging Sheridan closer. "I think he'd like that."

"So would I," she said, her smile even wider. She walked to the edge of the balcony and looked out over the town. "It won't be as difficult to leave, if I know we're comin' back."

"Give me two hours, darling." His voice now held a serious tone. "I need to write out instructions to Laramie."

"In case something happens." It wasn't a question.

Marcus nodded. "He needs to have concrete details to complete the Bainbridge exposé I've been working on."

"I'll have the children ready."

Marcus walked toward the elm. "We'll meet at the livery. Have the children wear heavy traveling clothes and their sturdy boots. I hear our Indian summer is about over. Laramie tells me that a northern storm is headed our way."

He gathered her close once again. "Leave everything in your rooms just as it is. If Bainbridge comes looking for you and the children, make it appear you've not left for any length of time."

She nodded.

"If you get to the stables before me, saddle the horses and be ready to leave." He hesitated, looking tenderly into her eyes. "And Sheridan, if for some reason I don't make it in time, you must leave without me. Just ride straight to San Francisco. Go to my father. Tell him everything. He'll guide you to the right authorities. And remember Jackson Bent's name. He's the key witness to getting Carter Bainbridge behind bars. He lives at a place called Muleskinner Hill."

"Don't say you'll not come with us, Marcus —"

He interrupted. "We don't know what Bainbridge may try. Just promise you'll leave without me if you have to."

"Aye," she sighed.

With his fingers resting lightly under her chin, Marcus lifted her face and looked deep into her sapphire eyes. "No matter what happens, don't ever forget that I love you," he murmured. He kissed her softly once more. "And I will forever."

Then he swung a long leg over the iron railing, looking back once more before making his way down the tree. He drank in Sheridan's beauty as if for the last time: her wisps of hair lifting in the breeze, her delicate frame seeming to be caressed by her gown's satin folds, her loving expression as she met his gaze…a look that equaled the full moon's glow and made his heart tumble.

Moments later as he stepped from the elm to the street, Marcus couldn't shake the feeling that they had just said farewell. Telling himself it was his overactive imagination, he briskly made his way to the Falcon.

Behind the corner of the Empress, Carter Bainbridge waited until Marcus Jade had moved down Main Street and rounded the corner to the Falcon, then stepped from his hiding place to the center of the street.

In the candlelit room above, he made out Sheridan's slight figure moving about. As if she sensed someone watching, Sheridan suddenly stepped to the glass-paned doors and drew the heavy drapes.

Bainbridge smiled smugly. No matter, he'd seen and heard enough. After a moment, he hurried to the mercantile, where two of his men awaited their instructions.

Twenty-Three

Sheridan led the sleepy children down the stairs from their rooms at the Empress, through the doors, and into the night. The air was damp, colder than it had been in weeks. She noticed the full moon was now shrouded with clouds. Shivering, she lifted Evangelia into her arms, so they could move more quickly to the livery.

"Miss Sheridan, tell me again where we're headin'." Duncan's voice carried in the night, and Sheridan shushed him.

"Please, don't speak," she whispered gently. "It's important that we not be heard."

They had almost reached the stables when she decided that if anything went wrong, the children needed to know what they were up against. Setting Evangelia down beside her, she reached for Duncan's hand and pulled him closer.

"Remember yesterday, Mr. Bainbridge grabbed the note — the message from Mister Jade?"

Duncan nodded vigorously. "I don't like that man."

"I know, Dunc." She sighed, hating to confirm to them that there was a reason to distrust anyone. "And we have reason to believe he might be out to harm us all."

"What do you mean?"

"He's the one who's behind my brother's disappearance." She didn't want to tell them yet about Titus Roderick. "He's done some bad things to people."

"And now he wants to hurt us? Why?"

"He knows we've found out about what he did to Shamus."

"What's he want to do to us?"

"He doesn't want us to tell what we know." Beside her, Evangelia noisily smacked her thumb and twisted a strand of hair.

"How can he stop us?" The boy lifted his chin defiantly. His fists were clenched at his side. "I won't let him."

Sheridan nodded solemnly. "That's why we're leavin', son. So he can't stop us. We're headin' to a place to pick up the witness to what Mister Bainbridge did, then goin' to San Francisco. We'll contact the law there."

"Why can't we go to the sheriff here?"

"He's a friend of Mister Bainbridge's. I don't think that he'd…" She hesitated, wondering how much the boy could understand. "That he'd believe us."

"Well, I'm ready. I'll take care of you and Lia, Miss Sheridan. You'll see." He stuck out his skinny chest and opened the squeaky livery door.

The trio let themselves into the dark stables. Sheridan had brought a candle. She quickly lit it and directed Duncan to help find their riding gear. Their horses were in the back corral with Desperado. One by one, Duncan brought in the animals and saddled them, including Marcus's stallion.

Sheridan lifted the sleepy Evangelia onto her saddle. Then as Duncan stuck a foot into his stirrup and swung a leg over the saddle, she extinguished the candle. After a moment, she too awaited Marcus from atop her horse situated between the two children.

Just as she expected, the livery door opened, its rusty hinges squeaking. As the shuffling footsteps neared them, Sheridan frowned. It sounded like more than one man.

"Marcus?" she whispered into the darkness.

A low, raspy laugh sounded from across the room. It was joined by a lower voice.

"Shut up, you two," demanded a third voice. Sheridan recognized it as belonging to Carter Bainbridge.

"Miss Sheridan?" Duncan moved the sorrel nearer, and Sheridan reached out for Evangelia's little hand.

"It'll be all right," she murmured, trying to reassure the children and at the same time reaching for the pistol inside her boot. But she didn't move quickly enough.

A match was struck before she could unfasten the binding. Seconds later, a lantern cast a glaring light across the room. Sheridan moved her hand back to her lap.

Bainbridge stood facing the trio, flanked by two beefy miners. Sheridan glanced to the door, wondering frantically if they could escape before Carter or his thugs made a move.

"Don't even think about it." Carter jerked his head to the door. Grinning, one of the miners sauntered over to stand guard, rifle in hand.

Sheridan sighed. "Don't harm the children, Carter. Our issues don't concern them. Let them go."

He laughed. "We had a deal, Sherrie. Or don't you

remember? The children were — make that, are — at the center of our pact. You should have considered them earlier, before you made getaway plans with your Mister Jade."

At the mention of Marcus, Sheridan's hands turned to ice. She had hoped he would come to the door, hear what was going on, and go for help.

She swallowed, fighting to keep calm as Bainbridge went on. "You seem to have forgotten my threats." He stepped closer, and Sheridan could see the gunmetal glint of his eyes. "I never go back on my word, Sherrie. Never." He glanced pointedly at Duncan, then to Evangelia. His expression reflected a cold and calculating triumph when his eyes again met Sheridan's.

"You animal," she muttered.

"Miss Sheridan, what's goin' on?" Duncan whispered hoarsely.

"You'll soon get your answer, little man," Bainbridge laughed.

Suddenly, Duncan scrambled from his horse and headed straight for Carter's stomach, fists flying.

"Whoa, little man." Bainbridge jumped back. The ruffian standing near Carter shot a hand out and grabbed Duncan by the collar. In one swift movement, he'd landed the boy back atop the sorrel.

"And quit callin' me 'little man,'" Duncan muttered under his breath, though Bainbridge didn't hear him.

"Now you boys go ahead and get on your horses," Bainbridge said to the miners. "I'll keep watch while you do." Carter pulled back his jacket to reveal a two-holster gun belt. He slowly pulled out a big revolver and cocked it, his eyes never leaving Sheridan's. Unflinching, she met his gaze.

"It's a Navy Colt," Duncan said in awe. "I've never seen one close up." He seemed more curious than afraid.

Evangelia solemnly watched the proceedings, thumb in mouth, clinging tightly to Sheridan's hand.

When the men had mounted, Bainbridge opened the stable door and slapped the rump of Duncan's sorrel. The horse bolted through the doorway and into the corral. Sheridan followed on Shadrach, leading the palomino.

Soon the two thugs were beside them, each with a rifle crossways on his saddle. It would be useless to try to protect the children with her small pistol, she realized.

The horses skittered sideways, whinnying softly in the cold of the frigid early morning. Bainbridge strode over to them. In the east, a pale dawn was just beginning to creep across the sky.

"You men know the plan," Bainbridge said as he walked closer. "If you fail to carry out my orders, you'll pay with your lives. Understood?"

One man grinned; the other simply grunted.

Bainbridge stared angrily at Sheridan for a moment. "It didn't have to end this way, you know. You had a choice. Any blood that's shed will be on your hands. None of this is my doing. I'm simply upholding my end of our bargain. Remember that, Sherrie, and try to sleep well tonight."

He smiled coldly, then again whacked the rump of Duncan's sorrel. The horse reared and neighed before galloping through the corral gate onto Main Street ahead of the others. Within minutes the group of riders were heading out of town, onto the trail leading south.

Sheridan attempted to collect her thoughts as they rode. She managed to make sure that the children rode close beside her. She and Duncan exchanged looks. He seemed to understand that they needed a place to talk privately.

A thin sun had barely risen, when Duncan doubled over in pain. He groaned loud and long. One of the ruffians glanced over at him, frowning. "What's the matter, boy?"

Duncan merely answered with another moan.

"What's wrong with 'im?"

Sheridan frowned with worry. "I don't know."

"I…I'm sick." He bent over the saddle again. "Oh, Miss Sheridan! I'm so sick I think I'm gonna puke." He groaned again.

Sheridan nudged Shadrach closer to Duncan. All the horses had slowed to a walk by now. "Dunc?"

"Ooooh." He covered his mouth. "Help me…please."

Sheridan looked at the miners. "Can we stop? He needs to get down."

The thugs exchanged looks. One shrugged. "Okay, but don't try anything," the other muttered.

Sheridan slid from the saddle and placed her arm around the ailing boy to help him down. Duncan leaned against her shoulder as Sheridan helped him to the side of the road.

"I got my rifle aimed right at the little squirt," one of the miners growled. "So don't be trying anything."

Sheridan glanced back at Evangelia. The little girl met her gaze solemnly, but she didn't look afraid. Sheridan nodded, her eyes never leaving the little girl's face. "I'll be right back, Lia."

Duncan moaned again, ran to some nearby sagebrush, then made some impressive vomiting sounds. Sheridan stooped over him, whispering in his ear as he continued his act.

"You must try to get away, Dunc. Do you understand?"

He nodded and made some more sick sounds as she continued. "I want you to head back to Everlasting. Try first to find Marcus. If something has happened to him…" She felt the sting of tears at the thought. "If something's happened, go to Laramie Burkett at the *Herald Star.* He'll know what to do."

She glanced back toward the trail. The miners looked nervous. "He'll be all right in a minute," she called out.

Duncan moaned again, loudly. "Now, son," Sheridan continued, "it's goin' to be up to you to figure out when to leave." She patted his back as if comforting a sick child. "Look for a thick stand of trees — a place where you can get away without anyone being able to squeeze off a shot. Then stay off the trail. Follow it, but ride to the side, in case Bainbridge decides to follow us."

He groaned pitifully.

"You do this well," Sheridan whispered.

He grinned. "I learned it from you."

Sheridan remembered the time and, with a small smile, patted his shoulder again. "Son, you've got to wait to see where they're takin' us before you leave. Can you do that?"

He nodded again and moaned loudly.

"Hurry it up," one of the thugs yelled out. "What's taking so long?"

"We'll be right there," Sheridan called lightly. "I think he's gettin' better."

Duncan coughed a couple times, then groaned once more for good measure.

"Dunc," Sheridan whispered. "I love you, son. I could never be more proud of you than right now."

He gave her a grateful smile, then stood and brushed himself off.

"He said it was the barbecue food from last night," Sheridan said solemnly to the miners as they remounted.

"That right?" said one. "What'd he eat?"

"The beef."

"That right?" he repeated, sounding worried. "That's what I had."

"Me, too," said the other. "And I don't think I'm feelin' so well, either." He rubbed his stomach and his face paled.

Sheridan exchanged glances with both children as they dug their heels into the flanks of their horses. All three smiled as they headed down the trail again.

By midmorning, they had reached the Stanislaus River. The small band made its way to the bottom of the steep gorge.

"We'll cross here." The ruffian who now had given his name as Lute squinted across the water.

"I still say we oughta take the ferry," said the other, a pudgy man Lute called Candy.

"Mister Bainbridge said not to."

"He won't know." Candy seemed to be measuring the distance across with his eyes.

"Nah. He said he don't want no trace left of what we're doin' — for our sakes as well as his."

"We're gonna have to swim the horses."

"So?" Lute looked irritated with Candy's reluctance.

"I don't like it. The water looks too fast."

"We'll make them go first. If they make it, then we'll go. How's that?" Lute laughed. "That'll work for you, Candy."

The pudgy miner sighed. "I reckon." Then he looked over

at Evangelia. "Nah," he said. "That ain't right."

Lute shrugged. "Let's go then." He waved his rifle at Sheridan and the children. "Get goin'," he demanded.

Sheridan put up her hand in protest. "I want her to ride with me." She nodded to Evangelia. "We'll tether the horse."

"Go ahead," Candy said with a nod.

Sheridan reached over and pulled the little girl onto the saddle with her. Evangelia nestled into her arms. "We're ready," she said, after tethering the palomino.

The riders moved their horses into the water. The current was swift, but Sheridan appreciated the strength of the Appaloosa's legs as he swam. The palomino snorted nervously, and Sheridan was glad she'd moved Evangelia to her saddle. Beside her, Duncan seemed to be enjoying the adventure with no thought of the danger.

He kept making sounds of awe and appreciation for the movement of the horse in the water. Before they'd reached halfway, he was riding beside Candy and Lute, asking them about their horses and how many rivers they'd crossed and how to best get through the currents. The men seemed flattered by the boy's questions. By the time the horses, dripping wet, scrambled up the bank on the far side of the river, Candy was talking a blue streak about his experience fording rivers by horse and, years earlier, by wagon.

When they headed the horses back onto the trail, Duncan rode beside the two men, asking them questions about everything from mining to where they'd been born. Evangelia was back on the palomino and sat solemnly in her saddle, thumb in mouth.

They'd just ridden past the outskirts of Jamestown, when Duncan asked where the group was headed.

"Ever heard of Muleskinner Hill, boy?" Candy asked.

Duncan shook his head.

"Well, that's the place."

"What's there?" The boy looked intently at Candy.

The man shrugged. "I dunno. It's just where Mister Bainbridge said to take you. Said somethin' about the racket from the mules coverin' any chance of you all yellin' fer help."

Rather than being afraid, Sheridan felt the first glimmer of hope since they had left the livery. Marcus had told her all about Muleskinner Hill and its resident, Jackson Bent, the man who'd double-crossed her brother. No matter what she thought of him, maybe he would help them escape.

"We got some business to do there first, though," Lute laughed. "Some crazy ol' coot we gotta get rid of."

Sheridan's heart sank. Jackson Bent was the only witness who could testify against Bainbridge. "No," she said. "Don't hurt anyone on our account. Please."

Lute laughed again. "Now don't you go worryin' none about what's ahead. You heard Mister Bainbridge. We gotta do what we gotta do."

They rode on in silence. It was now nearly noon. Sheridan knew the children were hungry. "We need to rest and eat," she called to the men, now riding slightly ahead.

"It won't be long now, missy," Lute called back.

"Just a ways," Candy agreed.

They rounded a curve on the trail. To the right, they could see a sign nailed to a tree at the bottom of a steep hill. It was a roughly written message about the costs of boarding mules.

Lute halted his horse. "You go on ahead and take care of

the ol' coot," he said. "I'll stand watch till I hear your signal."

Candy nodded. "One shot for the coot. Two more for all's clear." He rode off.

Overhead, the gray skies seemed to be darkening. They'd stopped near a grove of live oaks and buckeye brush. Sheridan glanced at Duncan. He looked scared, his freckles showing dark on his pale face. She smiled, silently communicating that they'd reached the place for him to leave them. He swallowed hard and blinked. The horses danced nervously sideways as they waited.

"Should be any minute now," Lute said. "That ol' man won't put up much of a fight."

He was right. A single shot echoed from the top of the mountain. Sheridan bit her lip at the sound, tears welling in her eyes. No matter what Bent had done to Shamus, Marcus had spoken highly of the man. She was sorry for what had befallen him.

The rifle report was followed by two others.

"Let's go!" Lute yelled nudging his horse hard in the flanks.

Sheridan nodded again at Duncan. He gave her a brave grin, kicked his horse, and headed into the thicket of trees.

Twenty-Four

Sheridan and Evangelia followed Lute up the hill. Sheridan prayed the man wouldn't turn and see that Duncan had ridden off.

He didn't. As they approached the top of Muleskinner Hill, hundreds of mules held his full attention. And the ruckus surrounding them covered any noise made by Duncan's departure. The animals, long ears twitching this way and that, brayed and kicked and snorted, a noisy sea of gray-brown backs and swishing tails.

Beside Sheridan, Evangelia gave a happy little smile, reaching out to pat the beasts' heads as the group wound its way to the cabin.

Candy stood on the porch, waving them forward. He suddenly yelled something and waved his hands to Lute. Sheridan caught her breath, figuring he'd noticed Duncan was missing. But Lute just shrugged and kept moving forward through the mules, unable to hear a word Candy called out.

It took longer than Sheridan expected to reach the fence

that surrounded the small cabin. With each minute that passed, Duncan covered more ground. Sheridan breathed a prayer of thanks.

Lute reached down from his horse and unlatched the gate. All three horses moved through, Sheridan and Evangelia following Lute's lead. Then Candy ran down the porch steps and yelled something into Lute's ear, gesturing wildly toward Sheridan.

"Where is he? Where's the boy?" Lute's eyes were wild.

Sheridan couldn't hear him, but she knew what he was asking. She looked worried and pointed toward the mules as if the boy was lost among them.

For a moment, the expression on Lute's face told her he believed her. He squinted out at the noisy sea of animals, then back to her. A flicker of anger showed in his eyes as he realized Duncan had escaped. He jerked his thumb toward the cabin door.

"Get in there," he growled into Sheridan's ear as she dismounted. She nodded solemnly and helped Evangelia from her saddle. They moved up the porch stairs, then turned as Candy remounted and headed out the gate, rifle in hand.

Sheridan squeezed Evangelia's hand, whispering another prayer for Duncan as Lute swung open the door.

As soon as they entered the room, a wooden bar dropped on the outside, locking them in. She sighed, pulling Evangelia close and letting her eyes adjust to the dim light.

She had expected anything but what she saw. The place was clean, immaculately scrubbed from the bare wood floor to the one small window to the pantry shelf filled with canned foods. The table beneath the window was covered with a bright tablecloth, a lamp at its center. Beside the lamp a loaf of hard-crust bread had been left on a blue-willow plate, flanked by a table knife on a folded napkin, and a small dish of honey. A pewter pitcher filled with water stood off to one side.

Sheridan's eyes next focused on a large Bible, open beside the bread loaf. She moved toward it and reverently touched its pages, realizing that Jackson Bent had probably been reading it before partaking of his meal. Before he was interrupted by Candy, she thought sadly. She prayed he'd been frightened off, not killed, with the shot she'd heard Candy fire.

In the corner of the room was a small iron bed. Worn but clean blankets and quilts covered it, and a pillow with a clean, ironed cover had been plumped against the headboard.

Sheridan felt a sense of peace and hope as she considered this warm little room. God was with them. He was providing for their needs even in this, the worst of circumstances.

She cut two thick slices of bread and spread them with honey. She gave one to Evangelia, then poured two cups of water from the pitcher.

The little girl started yawning as soon as she had eaten. It was no wonder. She had been awake half the night. Sheridan carried her to the bed. Evangelia curled up, popped in her thumb, and closed her eyes as Sheridan sat beside her. The tiny child was fast asleep before Sheridan finished unlacing her boots.

Sheridan reached for the small pistol she kept bound to her ankle and slipped it into her pocket, hoping she didn't have to use it. Then, still sitting beside the sleeping child, she leaned against the iron bedframe facing the door with her hand on the pearl-handled gun. Outside, she could hear the brawling mules.

Sheridan glanced around the room again, this time noticing a hand-carved wooden cross on the wall above the door. She wondered about Jackson Bent. The same man who'd hung it there — perhaps had even carved it himself — had shanghaied her brother, had even contemplated murder.

Her eyes rested on the cross. It was the symbol of God's resurrection power, his grace, his forgiveness. If God could raise Jesus Christ from the grave, he could also create life in a heart long shriveled and dead because of sin. He could change even a man such as Bent.

She let out a deep sigh. Her God was mighty to save... and to forgive. She wondered, though, if she were asked to forgive Bent for what he'd done, whether she would find the strength within to do so.

Sheridan considered the cross and her God's might and power once more. "Be with Duncan," she prayed, her eyes never leaving the cross. "Give him courage and wisdom. Keep him from harm as he rides for help." Then she lifted Marcus before him. "Oh, dear Father," she breathed. "I love him so. Keep him — keep us all — surrounded by your angels."

She thought about her beloved grandma'am's words about God's care, about how he sometimes brings trying and confusing times just so we'll look to him.

"It's hard to thank you for times so filled with troubles," Sheridan whispered. "But if they're here to draw me closer to you, I'll try hard to be grateful for your tender mercies."

Sheridan gazed up at the cross again. "And dear Father," she prayed, "help me remember, no matter what happens, that in everything you are the same today — faithful, kind, holy, powerful, wise — as you have always been. Even your compassion is eternal. You watch over little Lia, Duncan, Marcus and me with an everlasting love," she murmured, her eyes closing with a sense of sweet peace invading her soul. "If it takes these troubles to remind me of who you are, then, aye, Father, I can be thankful," she added with a small smile. "Aye, that I can."

Unable to fight her deep-bone weariness, Sheridan slipped into a dreamless sleep.

In the stupor of her fatigue and deep sleep, Sheridan thought she was dreaming when she heard the small, soft voice next to her.

"Mama," the little voice said.

Sheridan sighed, murmured a response, then slipped back into a deep sleep.

"Mama," the voice said again.

This time, the sound jarred Sheridan to consciousness. It was Evangelia.

She was frantically tapping Sheridan's arm. "Mama," she cried, now whimpering.

Sheridan's eyes opened sleepily. She looked first to her the child, then to the place Evangelia pointed.

The door had been pried open. The gray light outside created the faceless silhouette of a man. He was tall. His head practically reached the top of the doorjamb, and he had a thin torso and long, lean legs. She could see the outline of his wild, long hair against the outside light.

Sheridan swallowed hard and sat up. Evangelia scooted

closer, tucking her little body under Sheridan's arm.

Sheridan reached under the pillow and fished about for the pistol, pulled it out, cocked it, and aimed.

"I'd put that away if I were you, ma'am," drawled a deep voice. And he sauntered through the doorway. Another man appeared behind him, hesitated a moment, then followed the first into the room.

"I'm sure he's got them," Marcus said to Laramie. He'd been at the *Herald Star* most of the night and into the morning. "I've tried to find out where —" He put his head into his hands, rubbing his eyes. "I've looked everywhere, asked questions. No one saw them leave. The man owns the town, and no one will speak out against him."

"Son, you said you told Sheridan not to wait, to go on without you if you didn't show up on time?"

Marcus nodded. "That was the plan. I worried that Bainbridge might try something. I wanted her to get away, even if I didn't." He let out an exasperated sigh. "But I got there on time." He shook his head slowly.

"You've seen if Bainbridge is still in town?" Laramie took off his spectacles and set them on his desk.

Marcus nodded. "That was the first place I checked. I watched the mercantile from across the street. He was inside taking care of business as usual."

"She still may have gotten the time wrong — thought you were late and went on to San Francisco."

"Sheridan's not like that. She's exact in her timing when it comes to something like this."

Laramie settled back in his chair, thoughtfully rubbing

284

his forehead. "Bainbridge threatened her by saying he'd sent for the liveryman — what was his name again?"

"Titus Roderick."

Laramie nodded slowly. "If he found out that she was leaving with you — say he saw the two of you on the balcony last night — wouldn't he carry through with the threat?"

"I thought he'd come after me. In the note he intercepted, I told Sheridan I had evidence against him." Marcus groaned into his hand. "I thought it would be me he'd want to get at — not a woman and two defenseless children." He looked up and drew a ragged breath. "I should never have left them. Why didn't I insist that we all leave then?"

Laramie reached across the desk and patted Marcus's hand. "Don't blame yourself, son. You don't know for sure what happened."

Marcus swallowed. "If he's got them, I'll never understand why he didn't come after me instead."

"Where did you go after leaving Sheridan?"

"First to the Falcon, then here. I was here all night, working on the article downstairs."

"Did you leave any lights on up here?"

Marcus shook his head.

"Maybe he did go after you, son. He just couldn't find you. Even the brightest lamplight downstairs doesn't show up here — especially from the street. No one would know you're here."

"He came — or sent one of his thugs — for me, then went after Sheridan and the children, didn't he?"

Laramie didn't answer, just picked up his glasses and started slowly polishing them. After a moment, he sighed.

"Perhaps there's a way you could turn the tables."

Marcus looked up.

"Confront Bainbridge with your accusations. Tell him you want to see Sheridan and the children returned unharmed. If he doesn't comply, you'll see that the exposé is published immediately."

"Then he'll come after you."

"Not if you tell him that it's also been sent to San Francisco for joint publication — which is not far from the truth. I plan to send off your story as soon as you give me the word."

"There's only one problem I see with the plan. What if Sheridan *did* leave for San Francisco? I wouldn't want to put him onto her trail."

Laramie lifted an eyebrow. "Maybe if you just show yourself to Bainbridge, his reaction will tell you what — and how much — you should say."

Moments later, Marcus left the *Herald* for the mercantile. Before he crossed the street, however, three men emerged from the building: Carter Bainbridge and two others Marcus didn't recognize. They walked down Main Street toward the livery.

Marcus followed a distance behind. When the men entered the stables, he slipped around to the side of the building. Moments later the men reappeared, the two strangers leading their horses.

They spoke briefly, in low voices with Bainbridge before mounting their horses. Marcus strained to hear, but could only make out bits and pieces of the conversation. Muleskinner Hill was mentioned a couple times, then a few words about the ferry across the Stanislaus.

Marcus was still trying to figure out the men's signifi-cance, when he heard Bainbridge say the name Roderick. Then, clearly, Carter told the men he was glad they'd come so promptly.

Titus Roderick. Marcus drew in a sharp breath. Of course. Bainbridge was carrying out his threat. He'd sent Sheridan and the children to Muleskinner Hill to await capture. And now he was sending Roderick to claim his wards. A few more words were exchanged, then Bainbridge said he expected Sheridan to defend the children. "And let her," he laughed, loud enough for Marcus to hear clearly.

Incensed, Marcus fought to control his emotions. After a few more minutes, the men rode from the livery and Bainbridge walked back down Main Street toward his mer-cantile. Marcus headed to the rear of the stable where Desperado was corralled. He whistled for the horse. For once, Desperado didn't pull any shenanigans.

Marcus followed Roderick and his sidekick down the trail, keeping a respectable distance behind as they headed south. He knew the way to Muleskinner Hill, but he wanted to keep his eye on the men. Besides, he needed time to devise a plan. He wished he'd listened to his father years ago and learned how to shoot.

How was he going to overcome the thugs who were surely guarding Sheridan and the children, plus take care of the two ruffians in front of him? At least four against one, he thought grimly, perhaps more. And the one without a firearm.

They reached the cliffs above the Stanislaus gorge just

after midday. Roderick and the other man clambered down the rocky trail to the ferry landing. The raft was on the far side of the river, just beginning to move back across.

Marcus left the trail and climbed to an overlook. Heavy clouds had settled close to the ground; Marcus could feel a light mist hitting his face as he got down on his belly and crept to the edge. He pulled out his telescope to its full length and had just put it up to his eye when he heard a rustling in the brush.

He turned to look. A squirrel skittered beneath a clump of fragrant sage and disappeared. Marcus put up the telescope again.

A twig snapped. Marcus felt the hair rise on the back of his neck. He desperately hoped it was Desperado sneaking up behind him from the place where he'd left him grazing.

But it wasn't.

First he saw a flash of wiry red hair above a scared freckled face. Then Duncan let out a small cry and flung himself into Marcus's arms.

Twenty-Five

"Duncan!" Marcus shouted, squeezing the boy with gruff affection. "What are you doing here? Where are the others?"

Duncan raised his dirt-streaked face. "It was that Mister Bainbridge. He stole us away out of the stables this mornin'."

"I figured that's what happened." He hugged the boy's shoulders. "You look tired and scared. Have you ridden a long way?"

Duncan nodded vigorously, seeming to regain his courage. He stuck out his jaw and took a deep breath. "I got away from 'em up at Muleskinner Hill —"

"I know the place," Marcus interrupted. "Go on."

"It was Miss Sheridan's idea. I faked sick — just like she did that other time inside the tent. You remember?"

Marcus couldn't help smiling. "I remember, son. Then what?"

"She told me to wait till I saw where they were takin' us, then to ride as fast as I could to find you back in Everlasting. I didn't know I'd run into you here. Way back, I saw three riders — those two down there and you followin', only I didn't know it was you." He looked back down the hill at Desperado. "I saw the big black and hoped and prayed it was you. But I thought it was surely too good to be true, after everything that'd happened."

"What about Miss Sheridan and your sister?"

"They were headin' up Muleskinner Hill last I saw." He shrugged his thin shoulders. "That's all I know."

"There's a man up there who's maybe helping them," Marcus said to comfort the boy. He hoped it was true. "His name is Jackson Bent."

But Duncan shook his head. "They were plannin' on shootin' him."

Marcus frowned. "They told you that?"

He nodded. "They said that's what Mister Bainbridge told them to do. Said they were to get rid of him."

Marcus took a deep breath. "He was a friend of mine," he said simply. "He was a good man."

"Are they still down there?" Duncan got down on his belly and scooted to the edge of the cliff. "Why are you followin' 'em?"

"See for yourself." Marcus handed Duncan the telescope.

Duncan gasped. "It's Mister Roderick. He's the one who bought us out of the orphanage." There was terror in his voice. He turned to look frantically at Marcus.

"I know, son."

"Is he —" The boy frowned, trying to put the pieces of the puzzle together in his mind. "Is he on his way to Muleskinner Hill? How did he know we'd be there?"

Marcus nodded. "Bainbridge found out about your past."

Duncan looked stricken. "I told him that night we ate

supper together. I didn't know he was bad —" He sniffled and rubbed the back of his hand under his nose. Marcus handed him a handkerchief.

"You couldn't have known, Dunc. It's not your fault. Bainbridge is the kind of man who would have found out another way — even if you hadn't told him." He looked the boy in the eyes. "Don't blame yourself."

Duncan looked away, embarrassed about his tears. He drew in a shaky breath, looking down at the river. "What can we do?"

"We're going to get there before them." But they saw the ferry now pulling up to the landing and Roderick and his sidekick boarding. By the time they awaited the next crossing, the two men would have at least an hour's head start. Because Marcus was unarmed, he was counting heavily on the element of surprise to overcome the odds.

Marcus took a deep breath. "We need to get to Muleskinner Hill first, though it's going to be difficult to overtake them."

"I know how we can beat 'em across the river," Duncan said. He looked up at Marcus with shining eyes.

"How's that?"

"We'll swim the horses across. I've done it twice now."

Marcus swallowed hard. "You have?"

The boy nodded energetically. "It's easy. You should see that ol' sorrel swim. He's a caution."

"I'll bet he is." Marcus glanced down at Desperado, still grazing in a patch of dried grass. As if he'd heard them, the stallion lifted his head and flared his nostrils slightly. Marcus turned back to Duncan. "You know the best place for fording, do you?"

"Yes, sir!" He stuck out his thin chest proudly.

"All right, then. I say let's do it."

A few minutes later, Marcus and Duncan sat atop their horses by the river's edge, measuring the distance across the stormy gray waters with their eyes.

"Mmm," Marcus breathed. "It's a ways."

"We'll be on the other shore in no time," Duncan said, digging his heels into the sorrel's flanks and plunging into the water. He yelled "Wah-hoo," let go of reins and saddle and waved both his hands in the air.

Marcus waded his horse into the river, following in the boy's wake. Desperado snorted his displeasure, long and loud, shaking his massive head and sputtering.

"Easy now," Marcus mumbled, patting the stallion's gleaming black neck. "I sure hope you know how to swim, big fellow, because I don't."

A half hour later, as Desperado and Duncan's sorrel scrambled from the river, water splashing and streaming to the rocky shore, Marcus felt like kissing the ground. Instead he pulled the stallion up by Duncan and said calmly, "You all right?"

"Of course. You?"

Marcus gave him a quick nod, then nudged Desperado forward. They rode hard for more than an hour. From time to time, they could see Roderick and his partner on the trail behind them.

Dusk was now falling quickly. The mists had turned to a drizzle and the horses' hooves were covered with mud. By the time they reached Muleskinner Hill, Duncan was shivering with cold. They dismounted by the sign at the bottom of the trail that led to the cabin. Marcus removed his coat and wrapped it around the boy's shoulders. Duncan smiled gratefully.

"Let's go up to the cabin." His teeth chattered with the cold. "We've got to see about Miss Sheridan and Lia."

"Dunc, we need to wait here for Roderick." Marcus wanted desperately to go to Sheridan himself. But he had figured out Bainbridge's plan. The exchange of children was supposed to take place in the cabin. Bainbridge wanted Sheridan out of the way, so he'd purposely sent her to fight for the children. From what he'd overheard at the livery, Titus Roderick had received instructions to do just that. Sheridan was expected to defend the children, and a bullet from the resulting gunfire was meant for her. Marcus knew he had to stop Roderick from reaching the cabin.

"Why?"

"By waiting here, we'll outsmart them."

"How?" Duncan wrinkled his nose. Marcus could see he didn't like the idea.

"First of all, I'm going to mix our horses in with the mules. I'm afraid they might give us away otherwise." He remounted Desperado, nudged him forward, then led the sorrel to the top of the trail.

As he neared the cabin, Marcus rode toward the single window. He saw Sheridan sitting in the rocker, holding Evangelia. She appeared unharmed, and he breathed a prayer of thanks. He walked Desperado back into the sea of braying mules, dismounted, and headed back down the trail to the boy.

Duncan had settled into a copse of manzanita trees. It was sheltered enough to provide dry ground. Exhausted, he had curled up against a large boulder. Marcus sat down beside him.

"It's been forever since last night," Duncan yawned.

"You didn't get much sleep," Marcus agreed. "And it's been a long day."

"How much longer till Roderick and his partner get here?"

"I think they're about an hour behind us. Why don't you rest until then?"

Duncan yawned again, stretched his arms, then leaned his head against Marcus's shoulder. Looking down at him with affection, Marcus thought he'd never seen anything like the courage the boy had displayed that day. He smiled with pride. Someday soon he hoped to be the boy's father.

Seeming to sense he was being watched, Duncan opened his eyes and grinned sleepily. "You know," he said as if he knew what Marcus was thinking, "if I could have a pa, he'd be just like you."

Before Marcus could answer, Duncan was snoring softly. Marcus pulled the big coat closer around the child's shoulders, tucking it under his chin. As he did so, he remembered the story that Jackson Bent had told about the lost son. The father had forgiven him, wrapped him in a regal robe, and celebrated his homecoming.

He looked down at the thin boy beside him, wrapped in his big coat. Fatherly love welled up in his heart. He'd give his life for Duncan as readily as he'd given him his coat. He couldn't love him more if he were his biological son.

Sheridan had once told the children that each person on earth is adopted by God and has the right to call him Abba, Father. She had explained to them that Abba meant something special and intimate, like papa.

Marcus considered that kind of compassion for an adopted child. Now that Duncan and Evangelia had come into his life, he could better understand such love.

Did God care for him in such a way? Enough to wrap him in the regal robe of Christ's righteousness — with all that implied about forgiveness and grace and healing? Enough to adopt him into his family forever?

Somehow Marcus knew it was true. God loved him with an everlasting love. Marcus stared into the night, aware that he was no longer alone. No matter what happened, God was with him, with them all.

A short while later, the distant sound of horses' hooves carried through the damp night. Marcus waited motionlessly, watching for the first signs of the men. Soon he could see a glow of lantern light through the trees, coming closer and closer.

Marcus bent over Duncan, careful not to disturb him, and gently pulled the big coat from his shoulders. He slipped it on, then took a deep breath and stepped out onto the trail.

Marcus stuck his fist in his pocket where a pistol would rest in a holster — if he had one. He drew in a shaky breath, hoping that the way his coat folded back would conceal the fact that he was unarmed. Frowning, he adopted the stance of a gunfighter, rolled his shoulders, and swaggered a bit as he spread his legs to stand facing the approaching men.

He'd decided he was as ready as he'd ever be when Roderick, still on horseback, rounded the corner, holding a lantern. His companion was riding directly behind him.

"That's far enough," he yelled out, his voice low and mean. "Drop your weapons."

The men stood still as statues.

"I said drop 'em. Now!"

Just then, Marcus heard voices approaching from the trail above, from the direction of the Muleskinner Hill cabin. He groaned inwardly, though he kept his viper-eyed stare hard on the men in front of him.

They still hadn't dropped their weapons.

Then Marcus heard Sheridan's lilting voice and his heart stood still. He didn't dare turn, or he would lose his advantage. In his mind, he willed her to take cover.

But the sounds of voices and footsteps continued drawing nearer.

The exchange! The hired thugs who'd captured Sheridan and the children had come to make their trade with Roderick. Too much was at stake. Marcus could feel his heart pounding beneath his ribs.

He slowly widened his stance and rolled his shoulders again, hardening his stare at Roderick. "Maybe you didn't hear me before," he growled, moving his arm slightly as if itching to draw. "I said," he drawled, "drop your weapons. I'll give you to the count of three."

Roderick swallowed hard, and the man behind him looked pale.

"One."

Again he heard Sheridan's voice, then an audible gasp, as she obviously saw the standoff. Heavy footsteps behind him moved closer. Still, he didn't turn.

"Two." He prayed he wouldn't get to three.

Now the men glanced up the trail behind him. Marcus couldn't wait to see what they were looking at.

"Three!" He shouted, preparing for them to raise their weapons and call his bluff.

But they dropped their rifles and put up their hands.

"Now, get down — and I mean right now!"

But the men seemed dumbfounded and unable to move.

"You heard the man," a voice beside Marcus drawled. Marcus looked over, a wide grin spreading across his face. It was Jackson Bent. Alive! Aiming his buffalo gun straight at Roderick's nose. It was probably as empty as the day he'd aimed at Marcus.

"He said git down, and I believe the man means it," another voice growled, this time from Marcus's other side.

Marcus turned to see a wild and wiry-haired man, holding a Hawken twice the width of his thin arm. "Name's Sonny Kelly, Jade. And I'm pleased to make your acquaintance." He lifted an eyebrow in Marcus's direction, but his rifle was aimed at the center of the sidekick's head.

"Marcus!" Sheridan called out joyously from behind him.

He turned and looked up the hill. She held a lantern in one hand. Evangelia stood by her side.

She set down the lantern and ran toward him. Marcus met her halfway up and pulled her into his arms. A small cry escaped her lips as she gazed at him.

"Sweetheart," he murmured, holding her close enough to feel her heartbeat. "Oh, my sweetheart." He pulled back slightly and looked into her eyes. They shimmered with tears. "Are you all right? You're not hurt?"

She shook her head, her tears now spilling down her cheeks. "I'm all right now," she whispered in a tremulous voice. "Now that I'm again in your arms." Then she frowned. "But what's happened to Duncan? He's with you?"

Marcus told her about the exhausted little boy sleeping nearby.

"Papa," a little voice interrupted by Marcus's side. He felt a tug at his pant leg and looked down.

Evangelia's sweet face gazed up at him. She smiled and lifted her arms. He swept her up and twirled her around with a joyful shout, then pulled her close for a hug. She buried her face in his neck. "My little champ," he whispered to her and pulled Sheridan close with his other arm.

Evangelia reached for Sheridan's hand and squeezed it. "Mama," she murmured. Sheridan met Marcus's proud gaze over the tiny girl's head.

"Hey, what's goin' on?" Duncan stumbled out from the manzanita shelter. He rubbed his eyes, glancing quizzically at Jackson Bent and Sonny Kelly, who were marching Roderick and his hired gun back up to the cabin.

Then Duncan looked at Marcus, Evangelia, and Sheridan with amazement. With a small shout, he headed for Sheridan's arms. "Ma!" he cried. "Ma! I'm back."

"Aye, and glad I am to see you, son." Sheridan gave him a fierce hug. "We're all here together now and safe."

The light rain had stopped, though the pines and evergreen oaks still dripped noisily. Above them, the clouds had parted, and a round silver moon hung in a sapphire sky. Behind them, from Muleskinner Hill, the soft sounds of the braying animals floated toward them. And from a nearby oak an owl called out softly, adding to the haunting night music.

Marcus, still holding Evangelia, gathered Duncan and Sheridan close. His eyes met Sheridan's. "How did this happen? I thought you were being held in the cabin."

Sheridan smiled, though a bit sadly. "It seems that Lute and Candy — the men who were holding us captive — instead of shooting Jackson Bent as they'd been told, ran him off with a few rifle shots. They'd been told he was a crazy ol' coot, and they thought he'd simply hide in the woods."

She ruffled Duncan's hair, aware that Marcus's and the children's eyes were on her. What she had to tell them wouldn't be easy. She swallowed hard and continued.

"But instead, Jackson Bent went to Jamestown for help. He brought Sonny back to help him capture Lute and Candy. They are tied up in the chicken coop waiting to go to Jamestown tomorrow." She paused, "Sonny Kelly is a friend of his — and Jackson knew that he's the children's uncle."

Marcus drew in a deep breath. "I told him. I had no idea they knew each other."

Sheridan touched his arm. "It's all right," she said softly. "He's a good man."

"I thought he was an outlaw."

"No. That accusation couldn't be further from the truth."

"He's not?" Duncan tilted his head and watched her expectantly.

"He was falsely accused of murdering a man some years ago," Sheridan continued. "Almost hanged — until the real outlaw came forward."

She laughed lightly. "Actually, your Uncle Sonny's a circuit preacher."

"A what?" Duncan squinted, trying to understand.

"He travels around from town to town, preaching at churches, performing funerals and weddings — that sort of thing."

Duncan's eyes were shining. "He's a good man, then?"

Sheridan nodded. "The best." She drew in a deep breath. "But let me finish tellin' about our rescue."

As she spoke, the little group started walking slowly back up Muleskinner Hill to the cabin. "When they came ridin' up, they surprised Lute, who'd fallen asleep on the porch.

Candy was off lookin' for Duncan. When he came back, Sonny stepped out of the shadows and nearly scared the man off his horse."

Sheridan stopped walking and gazed at Marcus. "Before we came out to investigate the lantern light we saw movin' up the trail, the three of us — Jackson, Sonny, and myself — spoke of many things." For a moment she looked off in the distance. "Jackson told me what he'd done to my brother, Shamus." She turned again to Marcus, who had stooped to pick up the lantern. "He asked my forgiveness."

"And you gave it?" Marcus's tone was gentle.

She nodded. "Aye," she whispered. "Though it wasn't easy, and I still grieve for my brother."

They started walking again, Duncan next to Sheridan, Evangelia still in Marcus's arms, her head lying on his shoulder.

"Then Sonny Kelly and I spoke about the children." Sheridan felt the heat of unshed tears behind her eyes.

Marcus stopped and faced her. His solemn expression told her he had guessed her next words.

"What did he say?" Duncan asked.

Evangelia raised her head, watching Sheridan intently.

"He said that he wants to be part of your lives — get to know you better. Spend some time with you."

"Sonny's not gonna make us live with him, is he?"

Sheridan placed her fingers on Duncan lips. "He's your only living relative."

Duncan had guessed the truth. Sonny had said that he wanted to give the children a real home after they had time to get used to the idea. It broke her heart to say it. "Not right now, Dunc, but someday he'd like you and Evangelia to —"

Duncan interrupted Sheridan with a cry and threw himself into her arms.

Twenty-Six

&

I was wrong," Sonny Kelly said, his voice booming as he strode down Muleskinner Hill.

He was greeted by a tearful silence.

"I spoke earlier from a caring heart and a sense of responsibility for my brother's family." His eyes met Sheridan's as he approached. "You told me in the cabin that you loved these children, that you and Marcus Jade plan to marry and to raise Duncan and Evangelia as your own. But your words were no match for what I saw happen out there a while ago."

Sonny looked to Marcus. "I saw you stand up to two armed men without a gun, even an unloaded gun," he smiled wryly, "and try to protect Sheridan and little Lia."

Then he turned to Duncan. "And son, I saw how you ran to Sheridan and called her 'Ma.'" He tousled the boy's hair, then gently tugged on a wiry curl. "And even though you and I have a certain family resemblance," he gave Duncan a lopsided smile, "the love I see here is binding and strong."

He touched Evangelia's face. "You know, sweetie? You look just like my mother — your grandmother. You've got her coloring, her eyes, her pretty face. You're a Kelly, all right. And as much as I'd be delighted to raise you as my own, I can see that you belong here. Here with your mama."

Evangelia gave him a shy smile, then buried her face in Marcus's big coat.

"God's brought you together," he continued softly. "Your love is strong enough to get you through whatever's ahead."

Sheridan was too moved to speak. Marcus finally stuck out his hand. "You're a good man, Sonny. I promise we'll take good care of Duncan and Lia."

"I ask only one thing."

"Anything." Marcus answered.

"I'd like to be part of this family — spend time with you and the children." His voice dropped off expectantly.

"Aye, Sunday dinners, perhaps?" Sheridan asked with a soft laugh. "I hear preachers have legendary appetites."

Sonny laughed. "You've heard right. You just name the time, though it may take me a while to get to your place from wherever I'm preaching."

He turned to leave, then looked back with a half-smile. "There's one more thing." He smiled gently at Sheridan, and she knew that the question was for her; that it had more to do with forgiveness than hospitality. "I usually take my Sunday dinners with Jackson Bent. Would it be all right —"

"Aye," Sheridan interrupted. "He will also be invited."

"You're kind," Sonny said simply, seeming to understand Sheridan's heart. Then he laughed lightly. "Besides, I don't think I could do without his Sunday-go-to-meetin' bakin' powder biscuits."

The following morning, after seeing Sheridan and the children safely back to the Empress Hotel, Marcus headed for the *Herald Star*. He explained to Laramie what had happened on Muleskinner Hill.

"It's time to go to print," Laramie said solemnly.

Marcus nodded. "It may be weeks before Bainbridge is arrested for his crimes."

"I'm not afraid of the man. I've waited a long time for a story such as this."

"It's all yours. I'm heading out in a few days with Jackson Bent and Sonny Kelly for San Francisco. Bent's prepared to testify against Bainbridge. It's not a lot, compared to all that Carter's done, but it's a beginning."

Laramie sighed. "Then you'll give another copy to your father to print in the *Grizzlyclaw Gazette*?"

Marcus nodded. "As soon as I get to San Francisco."

"Good luck, son," Laramie said a few minutes later as he walked Marcus to the door. "By the way, how're things with you and Sheridan?"

"Couldn't be better. We'll be married by Christmas." Marcus couldn't stop his grin from overtaking his face.

"Here in Everlasting?"

"Couldn't be anywhere else."

"Does that mean you're plannin' to settle here?" Laramie's smile was also widening.

"It sure does."

"That mean you can stay on with the *Herald Star*?"

"If you'll have me."

"I can't pay you the big city money you're used to." The older man winked, aware of the bare-bones subsistence

303

Marcus eked out at the *Grizzlyclaw Gazette*. "Though with your stories increasin' our sales…" Laramie pulled off his spectacles and gave them a rub with his handkerchief. He stuck them back on his nose and continued in a droll tone, "I figure the *Star* will soon make us both a better livin'. We won't get rich, but we'll surely turn this town upside down." Laramie's eyes twinkled as he slapped Marcus on the back. "I couldn't be more delighted, son. Welcome aboard."

The *Herald Star* hit the newsstands the following morning, and within hours Everlasting was abuzz with the news of Carter Bainbridge and his illegal activities. Within the week, Bainbridge closed up the Goldstrike Mercantile and Mining Supply and left town.

Three days later, Marcus kissed Sheridan and the children good-bye. "I'm sorry we've got to be parted," he said as he swung onto Desperado. "But remember…" His eyes caressed her once more. "Remember, I'll be back in Everlasting Diggins before Christmas." Marcus planned to investigate Bainbridge's whereabouts, suspecting he was in San Francisco, and to contact officials to begin the legal proceedings.

"Hurry home, darling," Sheridan said softly, missing him already. However, with the wedding to plan, she and the children would have plenty to do while he was gone.

Christmas Eve morning dawned gray and chilly. A light snow began at noon.

"Mama," Evangelia said, standing at the Empress window

and watching the thick snowflakes fall from the sky. "How will Papa get here in time? What if Desperado can't make it through the snow?"

Sheridan never tired of hearing the little girl's voice. "He'll be here. I know your papa very well. He won't let anything keep him away from Everlasting today. After all, it's our wedding day!"

She picked up a giggling Evangelia and swung her around the room. A cheery fire crackled and popped in the corner fireplace. "God will bring him safely to us — on time. You wait and see," she said, setting Evangelia down. "Now, we need to see about getting you dressed, my wee one."

Evangelia nodded and trotted to her room. Moments later, she reappeared, carrying her rose velvet and lace gown. "You're prettier than a princess," Sheridan whispered, slipping it over the child's head.

Evangelia danced a little jig. Since she had started talking that day at Muleskinner Hill, she hadn't stopped. And as the wedding day drew nearer, the little girl's excitement knew no bounds.

"Now it's your turn, Mama," she said, running to the wardrobe, flinging open the door, and pulling out Sheridan's gown. She'd tried to get Sheridan to wear her wedding gown every day since they'd brought it home from the seamstress that Clementine Love had suggested.

"Aye, and you're goin' to help me now?" Sheridan laughed, stepping into her lacy petticoats.

Evangelia nodded vigorously.

It was a bit early, and after all, Marcus had not yet arrived from San Francisco. But Sheridan, her own excitement building, smiled at the child. "All right, Lia. I'll need your help, though, fastening the buttons."

Evangelia nodded again, her eyes bright and cheeks glowing.

Several minutes later, Sheridan stood in front of the mirrored wardrobe door while Evangelia labored over the tiny, silk-covered buttons that lined the gown's back.

Sheridan ran her fingertips lightly over the soft folds of silk at the skirt, then touched the pale Irish lace trim, her eyes misting as she regarded her reflection. "Aye, Grandma'am," she breathed. "If you could only see what God has brought about."

Then she sat at the dressing table and let Evangelia help adjust her silk-floral and ribbon headpiece. Later, a long net veil would be attached.

"You're beautiful, Mama," the little girl cried. "We're beautiful together." And she put her little face next to Sheridan's and gave an impish smile to the mirror.

Duncan came into the room a few minutes later dressed in dark trousers and a matching coat. Sheridan's eyes were moist as she watched the happy children play bride and groom, humming the music they'd helped Sheridan pick for the ceremony. They already considered this wedding day as much theirs as it was Sheridan and Marcus's.

Sheridan moved to the glass-paned doors at the balcony, pulled back the lace curtain, and peered out. She tried not to worry about Marcus, now making his way to Everlasting. He'd written almost daily since he left her almost two months before, and in his last letter, sent as usual by Wells Fargo, he wrote that Carter Bainbridge had been arrested. The trial was to begin in ninety days. Meantime, he planned to head back to Everlasting, promising to be there by

Christmas Eve — in plenty of time to prepare for the wedding ceremony.

Outside her window, soft flakes of snow fell on the balcony. She remembered the night just weeks earlier when she and Marcus had held each other and declared their love. Now, looking back, it seemed that she had always known him, always loved him.

There were so many things to remember, to treasure, about Marcus Jade. She thought about the way he considered her with a secret merriment and joy, his eyes alight with an inner fire that made her cheeks flush and her heart pound.

But it was his compassion for others that touched Sheridan's soul and brought quick tears to her eyes. In his letters, Marcus spoke of a new awareness of God's love and guidance. Their Lord had blessed them by bringing Duncan and Lia into their lives.

While in San Francisco, Marcus wrote, his eyes had been opened to the needs of other children in similar circumstances. He knew they couldn't adopt them all, he assured her, but maybe by using his pen as a weapon, he could do something to help. He planned to write about children being bought from orphanages only to work from dawn to dusk in slave-like conditions. He also planned to work to see that laws were passed to protect them.

He wrote his thoughts about Luke 9:48: "And whosoever shall receive this child in my name receiveth me."

"I have a growing understanding," Marcus went on, "that each act of kindness toward another — each act of love — especially toward a child, is an act of love toward God himself."

Sheridan sighed as she listened to the happy voices of the children in the room behind her. She thought about how clearly Marcus's words reflected her own thoughts, her own desires.

A light knock interrupted her thoughts.

"It's Papa!" yelled Evangelia. "I hope it's Papa!" She scrambled to beat Duncan to the door.

But it wasn't Marcus who greeted them.

A dusting of snow covered Marcus's hat and coat. It was just past midday, and he'd been riding hard since before dawn. He spotted the outcropping of boulders where he'd first kissed Sheridan. Nudging Desperado to the point where he could look down at Everlasting, he dismounted to give the horse a rest.

He gazed down at the town, the windows of its houses and shops glowing with candlelight and kerosene lamps through the falling snow. Sheridan was awaiting him; his heart leapt with the knowledge that she would soon be in his arms. He thought of the gift he had for her. Checking his pocket to make sure of its presence, he sighed deeply. Nothing he could give her would bring her greater joy.

The small white church at the east of the town caught his attention. Its tall windows were already aglow with light and warmth. Within hours he would stand at the altar and watch Sheridan walk toward him down the aisle, her eyes holding his.

He considered the commitment he and Sheridan were making to each other — and to the children. He had never been more certain of anything in his life.

As he remounted, Marcus spotted a clump of crimson snow flowers nearly hidden in a small grove of pines. He nudged Desperado closer and picked some for Sheridan's wedding bouquet. Then, smiling with anticipation, he headed down the trail and into Everlasting Diggins.

The children swung open the door.

"Uncle Sonny!" Duncan shouted in delight. Evangelia crowded in front of her brother to be first in line for a hug.

The tall, red-haired man laughed, his voice booming into the room. He was dressed in a silk shirt, blue waistcoat, and long dark frock coat. "Sheridan, I've got a gift for the bride."

"From Marcus?"

Sonny nodded. "No other."

She smiled, her eyes misting, as he handed her the bouquet of winter wildflowers. "He's here," she breathed. "He's here at last?"

Sonny nodded. "He rode in about an hour ago. He's over at the Falcon, dressing in his finest duds as we speak."

"But I want him here," Evangelia pouted.

"Why didn't he come see us first?" Duncan added, frowning.

Sonny threw back his head and laughed. "Ah, a little patience is in order. To see the bride before the wedding is simply not done. Besides, it's not long until I'll drive you and your sweet mama to the church." He smiled grandly. "Your carriage awaits downstairs."

After the ride to the church, Sonny held open the carriage door, and Sheridan stepped to the snow-dusted ground.

Large, graceful flakes still floated to earth. The children hurried behind Sheridan to the entrance doors, though Evangelia stopped twice to catch snowflakes on her tongue.

Sheridan caught her breath as she stepped into the warm room. Even Evangelia and Duncan stopped their excited chatter.

"Do you like it?" Sonny asked expectantly.

Speechless, Sheridan nodded. Kerosene lamps had been placed outside the stained-glass windows, casting warm rainbow colors of light throughout the small sanctuary. Inside, dozens of candles glowed from tables and altar, and garlands fashioned of pine and holly lined the center aisle. Miniature pinecones and holly berries had been woven into the garlands, tied with ribbon bows of ivory velvet. A fragrance of pine, cedar, and candles — the scent of Christmas — wafted through the room.

"Clementine Love, Miss Brown, and the school children have been here all day decorating," Sonny explained.

"Aye," Sheridan whispered in awe. "A gift of love."

Sonny ushered Sheridan and the children into a small chamber just off the foyer. The curtained room kept them from being seen by the arriving wedding guests.

A short time later, the organist began playing the soft strains of "Jesu, Joy of Man's Desiring." The sound was wheezy as the older woman pumped the foot pedals, but Sheridan thought she'd never heard more heavenly tones. When the violin and flute joined in, Sonny squeezed Sheridan's hand, then, with Duncan at his side, slipped out to join the groom at the front of the church.

As the music dropped, Sheridan and Evangelia moved to the back of the sanctuary. Marcus turned toward them, a look of adoration on his face.

Sheridan gave him a tremulous smile, her gaze never leaving his. The music played softly, and Evangelia started down the aisle, her little chin held high. She smiled at school friends and Miss Brown, her teacher. Then she spotted Clementine Love and waved.

Sheridan marveled at the change in the little girl. From Marcus's expression, she knew he was thinking the same thing.

Evangelia had nearly reached the front of the church, when she forgot all about the wedding. With a small, happy cry, she ran the rest of the way to Marcus. With a wide grin, he stooped down and swung her into his arms. She circled her arms around his neck and gave him a big hug and a noisy kiss.

A murmur of soft laughter rose from the wedding guests as Marcus set her down beside him. Then with a flourish, the organist began playing the *Wedding March*.

Marcus took a few steps forward, his gaze locked on his bride. Sheridan smiled softly at him. The music swelled, and the guests stood to face Sheridan. She moved down the aisle, watching her groom, her beloved. Moments later she reached him, and Marcus took her hands in his. She let out a soft sigh, thinking only of the glorious miracle of their love.

"Dearly beloved, we are gathered today in the presence of God," Sonny Kelly began, his hands covering Sheridan's and Marcus's. For several moments he spoke of the divine institution of marriage, the responsibilities that Marcus and Sheridan would share, and God's loving guidance for their lives.

Then he paused, smiling. "You've asked to speak your vows to each other from your hearts — rather than repeating after me words from a prayerbook. So I give you this time to do so."

Marcus took Sheridan's hands in his and looked deeply into her eyes. "I pledge you my love, Sheridan O'Brian, now and forever. Our loving Father has brought us together. And with a heart overflowing with gladness, I pledge to cherish you, adore you, and honor you until the day I die." His eyes were filled with love as he slipped a plain gold ring on her finger. Sheridan thought she couldn't bear the sweet and tender joy that swept over her.

Sheridan took a deep breath. Her voice was soft and lilting as she began to speak.

"My darling," she whispered, feeling her eyes tear as she regarded Marcus. "My grandma'am used to tell me that when I was a wee babe, she prayed for that little boy somewhere in the world that God had already picked out for me. Now, here we stand, oceans away from my dear Ireland, where she prayed that sweet prayer. It took years, and thousands of miles traveling across continents and oceans, but in his perfect time, God led me here…to you."

In awe, she slowly shook her head, her gaze never leaving his. "Aye, it seems like some kind of miracle, Marcus. How blessed I am with such a gift of love!"

She let out a sigh and squeezed Marcus's fingers. "Ah, I'm goin' on now, aren't I?" There was soft laughter from their guests.

When she spoke again, her voice was low. "I will respect and honor you as God's anointed head of our family. I will stand by your side through the joys and sorrows of our days.

"And my beloved, always will I treasure the riches of our love for each other, for the love we have as a family."

Marcus's eyes filled with tears at her words, and Sheridan, touched, swallowed hard as she placed his ring on his finger. "My dearest," she finally whispered, her voice husky, "I pledge you my everlasting love."

After a moment, Sonny prompted, "And your gifts for the children?"

Marcus cleared his throat and smiled at his bride. They had carefully planned this ahead of time.

"Duncan," Marcus began, kneeling beside the boy. "Your mother and I want to give you this." He placed his pocket watch in the child's hand. "This was passed down to my father from his father, then given to me when I was a boy. Now I give it to you."

Duncan turned it over. "Wow," he breathed. "It says, 'Duncan Kelly Jade' on the back." He looked up, a wide smile spreading across his freckled face. For once, he was speechless.

Sheridan touched his shoulder. "It means you're part of our family, son. And you will be forever."

Then they turned to Evangelia, who daintily awaited her turn.

"Sweetie." Sheridan drew the little girl into her arms. "This is for you." And she fastened a small gold locket around Lia's neck. "It also has your initials inscribed on the back."

"Why didn't I get *my* new name on it?"

"Because it's too small for such a big name." Marcus gave her a hug. "But your initials — EKJ — stand for your new name."

Evangelia lifted her chin and interrupted in proud, bell-like tones, "Evangelia Kelly Jade, that's me."

Again, there was soft laughter from the guests.

Sheridan expected Sonny to continue on with the ceremony as planned. But instead, he looked conspiratorially at Marcus. "And the other gift you have for your bride?"

Sheridan glanced at Marcus, but his expression gave nothing away. He reached inside his coat pocket and withdrew an envelope.

"I've saved the best gift for last," he said simply as he unfolded the letter. Sheridan caught her breath as he began to read.

New York
September 7th, 1855

My sweet and dearest Sheridan,
I arrived just this morning in New York harbor. I hurried, of course, as quickly as I could to dear Aunt Fiona's, only to discover that she had sent you to San Francisco to begin a search that would lead you to Everlasting Diggins.
I am sending this letter in care of the Grizzlyclaw Gazette, *the place of business where Aunt Fiona said you had headed, hoping to meet with a detective hired by the kind editor. I hope that the editor will forward this on to you, wherever you may be in the mother lode.*

Dearest heart! As you can plainly see by this missive, your everlovin' twin brother is alive and well! I have had quite a time of it, to be sure, and I will tell you in person every detail of my adventures when at last we meet face to face.

A clipper ship is now anchored in the harbor, awaiting its departure for San Francisco two days hence. I am sending this letter with Godspeed, knowing how worried you must be. After settling some affairs here in New York, I plan to ride overland to California, reclaim Rainbow's End, and give you, my little sister, the biggest bear hug imaginable...."

Sheridan's eyes met Marcus's. When she could finally speak, her voice trembled with emotion. "Shamus is alive! And safe," she whispered. "My darling husband, you've made our wedding day perfect. Aye, perfect indeed."

Marcus drew Sheridan into his arms and kissed her. Beside them, Evangelia giggled and Duncan let out a small groan.

After a moment, Sonny cleared his throat. "Excuse me, but I believe I need to finish the ceremony."

But Sheridan and Marcus didn't seem to hear him; they just continued kissing. Finally, Sonny let out a deep sigh, "Ladies and gentlemen, may I present Mr. and Mrs. Marcus Jade and their children, Evangelia and Duncan Jade."

Triumphant music rose from the organ as Marcus and Sheridan, flanked by the children, stepped back down the aisle to the rear of the church. Their guests gathered around, everyone talking and laughing at once.

After a few minutes, Marcus drew Sheridan away from the joyful hubbub. Around them candles blazed, and strains of soft Christmas music rose from the organ. Even the soft glow from the stained-glass windows seemed to embrace the couple with light and love.

Sheridan looked up at her husband. "I love you, Marcus Jade." Her face reflected the wonder Marcus felt. "You've made my joy — my life — complete. Our wedding day...Shamus's letter...." She touched his cheek tenderly. "Aye, just feelin' your arms around me again."

Marcus kissed her lightly. "Something tells me we've got a lifetime of joy ahead, Mrs. Jade," he said, his heart overflowing as he beheld his bride.

"Aye," she murmured with a small smile. "I believe you're right, Mister Jade." Her arms slid around him, and he drew her close.

"My darling, Sheridan," Marcus whispered, his voice husky. "How I adore you."

And his lips met hers again.

Dear Reader:

While writing *Everlasting,* Marcus Jade became one of my favorite characters ever. I think it's because early in the story, he took on an unexpected dimension — that of a flawed, a very human, hero. This is especially true in his view of God. Though Marcus acknowledges God, he sees him as distant, impersonal, even unforgiving.

As Marcus's love for Sheridan grows, he is drawn to her child-like faith and radiant spirit — those qualities that reflect her Lord. Yet, when he hears Sheridan tell Duncan and Evangelia how deeply God cares for them, and how they can call Him Abba — or Papa — Marcus concludes: "Only children and saints have such a right."

There may be a bit of Marcus in us all. We may feel that we must earn God's favor. Nothing could be further from the truth. As Jackson Bent told Marcus after relating the story of the prodigal son, "I finally figured out that I didn't have to be perfect for God to love me."

Discovery of such mercy and compassion can draw us into the deepest love relationship there can be…that of sweet intimacy with Abba, our heavenly Father. He says to each of us, "I have loved you with an everlasting love; I have drawn you with loving-kindness." (Jeremiah 31:3)

We, his cherished children, come to him — just as we are, flaws and all.

And we are loved beyond measure.

Love,

Amanda MacLean

Write to Amanda MacLean
c/o Palisades
P.O.Box 1720
Sisters, Oregon 97759

PALISADES...PURE ROMANCE

Also by Amanda MacLean

Westward, Amanda MacLean
ISBN 0-88070-751-8
Running from a desperate fate in the South toward an unknown future in the West, plantation-born artist Juliana St. Clair finds herself torn between two men, one an undercover agent with a heart of gold, the other a man with evil intentions and a smooth facade. Witness Juliana's dangerous travels toward faith and love as she follows God's lead in this powerful historical novel.

Stonehaven, Amanda MacLean
ISBN 0-88070-757-7
Picking up in the years following *Westward, Stonehaven* follows Callie St. Clair back to the South where she has returned to reclaim her ancestral home. As she works to win back the plantation, the beautiful and dauntless Callie turns it into a station on the Underground Railroad. Covering her actions by playing the role of a Southern belle, Callie risks losing Hawk, the only man she has ever loved. Readers will find themselves quickly drawn into this fast-paced novel of treachery, intrigue, spiritual discovery, and unexpected love.

~ and ~
Promise Me the Dawn, a Palisades Premier Novel
(due early 1996)

NOTE TO DEALER: Customer should provide 6 coupons and you should retain the coupon from the free book (#7). We will send you a replacement copy of the Palisades novel you give away via Spring Arbor, consolidated freight. (In Canada, contact Beacon Distributing.)

PLEASE FILL OUT:
(ON PAGE FROM FREE BOOK ONLY)

FREE BOOK TITLE _____

ISBN _____

STORE NAME _____

ADDRESS _____

_____

SPRING ARBOR CUSTOMER ID# _____
(VERY IMPORTANT!)

BEACON DISTRIBUTING ACCOUNT # (CANADIANS ONLY) _____

STAPLE THE 6 COUPONS TOGETHER WITH #7 AND THE INFORMATION ABOVE ON TOP.

YOU MAY REDEEM THE COUPONS BY SENDING THEM TO:

PALISADES CUSTOMER SERVICE
QUESTAR PUBLISHERS, INC.
P.O. BOX 1720
SISTERS, OR 97759

CANADIANS SEND TO:
BEACON DISTRIBUTING
P.O. BOX 98
PARIS, ONTARIO
N3L 3E5

BUY SIX GET ONE **FREE**

PALISADES FREQUENT BUYER COUPON

Applies to any Palisades novel priced at $8.99 and below.

Dealer must retain coupon from free Palisades novel.

Consumer must pay any applicable sales tax.

AT PARTICIPATING DEALERS

PALISADES